French
Foreign Policy
since the
Second World War

Foreign Policy Studies

General Editors:
Geoffrey Goodwin
Herbert Tint

French
Foreign Policy
since the
Second World War

Herbert Tint

Weidenfeld and Nicolson Ltd
5 Winsley Street London W1

ISBN 0 297 99488 3
Printed in Israel

Contents

ACKNOWLEDGEMENTS   ix
ABBREVIATIONS   xi
INTRODUCTION   I

PART ONE
1   **The Need for Economic Aid**
    1944–51: From chaos to subsistence   12
    Aid in the 1950s : United States subsidies for
        French objectives abroad   22
    The ending of aid   25

2   **France, Germany and 'Europe'**

    The background   28
        (i)   Basic historical problems   28
        (ii) The situation in 1945   34
    1945–9: Keeping Germany divided and weak   39
    1949–54: The European solution   47
        (i)   The European Coal and Steel Community   47
        (ii) The European Defence Community   50
        (iii) The creation of EEC and Euratom   68
    1958–69: Franco-German relations under
        de Gaulle   75
        (i)   1958–63: The Adenauer era   76
        (ii) 1963–8: Disillusionment   86
        (iii) The end of the Gaullist era   98
    Franco-German relations since 1969   100

3   **France and the Soviet Union**

    The background   106
    General de Gaulle's Free French Movement and
        provisional government : relations with the

Soviet Union until 1946   112
1946–7: French attempts at an independent
  foreign policy   119
1947–53: The Cold War   121
1953–6: East-west thaw   128
1956–8: Renewed attempts at an independent
  French foreign policy   132
1958–63: De Gaulle's anti-Soviet phase   138
1963–8: A Paris-Moscow axis?   148
1968–9: Disillusionment   156
Franco-Soviet relations since 1969   160

4   French Policy Outside the Soviet and Atlantic Blocs

French culture as an instrument of foreign policy   164
  (i)   General principles   164
  (ii)   Geographical distribution of French cultural
    activities   169
    (a) The former empire   (b) *Francophonie*
    (c) Other areas
French economic and technical aid as an instrument of foreign policy   175
  (i)   General principles   175
  (ii)   Geographical distribution of French economic
    and technical aid   178
Decolonisation and its implications for French
  foreign policy   185
  (i)   The background   186
  (ii)   Colonial policy, 1944–58   187
  (iii) Decolonisation, 1958–62   195
Relations with the 'Third World' since 1962   200
  (i)   Relations with former French colonies in Africa   201
  (ii)   Relations with Mediterranean countries   203
  (iii) The problem of arms sales to South Africa   207
  (iv) Relations with countries in Asia   208
  (v)   Relations with countries in South America   211
French attitudes to the United Nations Organisation   212

PART TWO

5 The Diplomatic Service

Present Organisation   216
The Ministry of Foreign Affairs   216
  (i)   The secretary general   217
  (ii) The main Departments of the Quai D'Orsay   218
      (a) The Political Directorate   (b) The Direc-
      torate for Economic and Financial Affairs
      (c) The General Directorate for Cultural,
      Scientific and Technical Affairs   (d) The
      Directorate for Administrative Conventions
      and Social Affairs   (e) The Directorate for
      Personnel and General Administration
      (f) Other Departments

Representation abroad   225
  (i)   Embassies   226
  (ii) Consulates   228

Changes in Organisation   229
The historical background   229
Present problems   230

Personnel   231
Present methods of recruitment and training   231
Legacy of other methods of recruitment   234

Methods of Work   236

Appendix: Decision-Making in French Foreign Policy

The President of the Republic and the govern-
  ment   238
The constitutional position of Parliament   239
The foreign minister   239
The special position of the Foreign Affairs Com-
  mission of the National Assembly   241
The past as a possible guide to the future   243
BIBLIOGRAPHY   246
NOTES   253
INDEX   264

Acknowledgements

I should like to express my gratitude to the many members of the French Foreign Ministry who have given me much of their time during the preparation of this book, in particular to M. Victor A. Garès, press counsellor at the London Embassy, who arranged many of my interviews with French officials. It may be taken for granted that the views contained in this book are entirely my own, and that errors in the presentation of French policies must equally be mine.

The Nuffield Foundation and the London School of Economics and Political Science provided grants for research assistance and travel in connection with this book: I am grateful to both.

To Maureen Davison I owe a more general debt, but her help with the analysis of France's relations with the Third World was particularly valuable for this book.

Abbreviations

DDR	Deutsche Demokratische Republik
EAC	European Advisory Commission
ECA	Economic Cooperation Administration
ECSC	European Coal and Steel Community
EDC	European Defence Community
EEC	European Economic Community
EFTA	European Free Trade Area
ERP	European Recovery Program
FLN	Front de la Libération Nationale
GATT	General Agreement on Tariffs and Trade
IFOP	Institut Français d'Opinion Publique
IMF	International Monetary Fund
MLF	Multilateral Force
MRP	Mouvement Républicain Populaire
NATO	North Atlantic Treaty Organisation
OEEC	Organisation for European Economic Cooperation
PCF	Parti Communiste Français
RPF	Rassemblement du Peuple Français
SFIO	Section Française de l'Internationale Ouvrière
SPD	Sozialistische Partei Deutschlands
WEU	Western European Union

Introduction

The ways in which the foreign policy of a country may be studied are no doubt numerous. For the purpose of this analysis of the foreign policy of France since the Second World War, it has been assumed that one meaningful way is in terms of the preservation and extension of the country's influence abroad. If this method is deemed to require justification, the least that may be said is that countries use their contacts with foreign governments with these considerations as implicit data; it might indeed appear perverse to suggest that a country would willingly work for the diminution of its influence abroad.

That French governments – as will be shown – have throughout the period since the Second World War overtly striven to preserve and extend French influence abroad may be sufficient justification for using that twin aim as the basic structure for this analysis; it will also provide a criterion for the evaluation of their efforts. But for the purposes of this book these efforts will be evaluated primarily in terms of their success or failure from the French point of view, rather than from the dubious height of dispassionate objectivity. What is more, the analysis of the policies themselves will be conducted in accordance with the order of priorities with which they were invested by French governments and, in particular, in accordance with the positive policy goals of these governments.

This approach has significant consequences for the structure of this book. It means, for example, that there is no extended and consecutive analysis of French policy towards the United Kingdom because, after 1945, France only on rare occasions pursued positive policy objectives which involved London. Similarly, and on the same grounds, there seemed to be no good reason for giving extended and consecutive treatment to French relations with the United States, except during the immediate postwar years when France's main objective was to obtain massive aid from Washington. It may be taken for granted that French policy towards the United Kingdom and the United States receives a good deal of attention throughout this study, but it normally does so in a negative context, for example when the French try to cope with interference from London or Washington with their own positive policy objectives.

The degree to which a government can exert its influence abroad depends primarily upon its resources; a viable foreign policy therefore has to be defined in terms of the possibility of its implementation. All things being equal, there would be nothing viable about the foreign policy of a geographically and demographically small country with few economic and technological resources which sought to exert a determining influence upon a large country with a huge population and vast economic and technological resources. But, in addition to the limits which a country's resources impose upon its effective foreign policy options, there are many other factors which may diminish its freedom of meaningful choice. For example, if a country has a powerful neighbour it may well become obsessed with the problems of national security to the detriment of other theoretically possible objectives; or it might become so absorbed by its need of assistance from abroad that it loses the ability or even the desire to work out its own foreign policy goals. In 1945, France was among the nations which exhibited with the greatest clarity the most compelling constraints which can limit a country's options in foreign policy.

France's foreign policy, at least since 1870, has been severely circumscribed by the massive presence of Germany on her eastern border. Before 1870 France had dominated Europe by virtue of her geographical bulk, her large population relative to her neighbours, her strongly centralised administration, and her relative wealth; it is difficult to evaluate how far her intellectual prestige had flowed from her position of physical power. Understandably obsessed by Bismarck's unified empire, the French gradually came to realise that German hegemony in western Europe could only be challenged by a strong alliance system: the nineteenth century had seen a decline in France's demographic advantage over her German neighbour, and that decline continued into the twentieth century to a point when, in 1939, Hitler's Third Reich was able to draw its armies from a population nearly twice that of France. The only two European nations which, between 1870 and 1939, could redress the French balance against Germany were Britain and Russia, and it can therefore easily be understood why these countries figured prominently in French foreign policy designs whenever Germany presented an overt threat to France.

The effects of the second world war left Germany in a situation very different from that of the previous seventy years, but much French effort since 1945 has gone into trying to create international structures capable of containing future bursts of German energy. The decline in British power and the close involvement of the United States and the Soviet Union in European affairs have modified the Franco-German relationship quite as much as the defeat of Hitler. But the French certainly recognise that those disparities in power still exist which have, since 1870, made Germany the most immediately pressing foreign policy problem for them. There is abundant evidence that most French enthusiasm for some kind of European economic and, possibly, political integration originated in a desire for the containment of Germany. For that reason it seems justified to include our analysis of French efforts to create European institutions within the chapter dealing with French policy towards Germany.

But, although Germany even after Hitler's defeat seemed still to be France's most important external problem, the economic and political effects of the war prevented the French from playing any significant international role in trying to solve it. Already in the 1930s, a very serious economic constraint had been added to the demographic and geographic constraints on French foreign policy. An agriculturally rich country, her industries protected by forbidding tariffs since the seventeenth century, France had until the 1929 slump at least her prosperity to set against her many weaknesses in relation to Germany. Though the consequences of the United States' economic disaster hit France later than other industrial countries, the effects had still not been absorbed by the time war broke out in 1939. The social and political consequences of that fact in part explain the speed of the defeat in 1940. The German occupation, with its ruthless plundering of remaining French resources, ensured that France emerged from the second world war with a totally shattered economy.

For that reason alone, French foreign policy in 1945 could hardly even be described as attempting to preserve French influence abroad – let alone expand it – for, as General de Gaulle often used to remark, influence cannot be exercised when one is bankrupt. Indeed, France at that stage needed massive foreign aid merely to enable her population to survive. With a bread ration which was, even as late as two years after the final defeat of the Axis powers, at a lower level than at any time during the German occupation, plagued by high inflation which in the year 1946 alone caused prices to rise by 80 per cent, and a gross national product which in 1947 had managed to do no more than reach the level of 1910, international objectives – apart from requests for foreign aid – must have been an irrelevance for the French. It is for that reason that this study opens with a short chapter on the aid France requested and received from the United States after 1945. This aid was crucial to France internally, and the essential condition for any future French international role of any significance. It will be shown that the United States administration went to great lengths to appease French susceptibilities by ensuring that aid was given without any consequential demands that could be construed as interference with French independence. But this failed to prevent the French from developing the kind of resentment towards the United States that one has come to associate with countries at the receiving end of an aid relationship, and it helps to explain why, after aid had ceased to be an important factor in the French economy in the mid-1950s, French attitudes towards the United States tended above all to betray impatience and resentment over any sign of possible interference with French policy objectives. Indeed, it would not be an exaggeration to say that one of the main French policy objectives from the 1950s onwards has been emancipation from any positive relationship with the United States. It will be shown that, once French need for American aid had ceased, French governments only rarely exhibited a desire for positive collaboration with Washington, and then only when it looked as if there was a threat to their security or prosperity. Apart from the fact that gratitude is no part of the currency of international affairs, an obvious additional reason for this is that, in any major combined enterprise, France would almost certainly have less to contribute than the United States and therefore find herself in a subordinate role. The French withdrawal from the unified command structure of the North Atlantic Treaty Organisation is easily explicable in these terms.

Relations with Russia are second only to those with Germany in the French order of priorities. Today, France's links with the Soviet Union balance her relations with both Germany and the United States.

Since the creation of Bismarck's German empire, French policy towards Russia has been ambivalent. Before 1917 Moscow was abhorrent to Paris on ideological grounds, because the tsarist regime was the antithesis of what the politicians of the Third Republic said they wanted France to be like. The Third Republic was to bring justice and democracy to France, while Russia was seen as a reactionary tyranny. But the fear of Germany overcame French ideological objections, and an alliance with Russia was concluded in 1894. The reasoning behind the alliance was simple: once Germany knew that if she attacked France she would have to fight on two fronts – against the populous Russian nation on her eastern borders as well as against the French in the west – she would be much less likely to be truculent with Paris. The first world war showed this reasoning to have been defective.

After 1917 too Russia was abhorrent to the French on ideological grounds, but this time because the Communist regime in Moscow was tyrannical in a direction French politicians tended to dislike even more than tsarist reaction. Again, however, this abhorrence did not deter the French from probing the possibilities of an understanding with the Soviet Union when Germany became a threat to peace in the 1930s. What matters is not whether the French were sufficiently determined in their overtures to Moscow before the second world war, but the fact that it seemed natural for them to think of Russia as a desirable and useful counterweight to Germany, as a means of exerting pressure upon Germany.

In the greatly changed international system that resulted from the second world war, the place occupied by the Soviet Union in French foreign policy has not fundamentally altered. The main change is a consequence of the elevation of the United States and the Soviet Union to superpower status, and of the threat this poses to the independence of smaller powers. That in such a situation smaller powers like France, seeking to safeguard their independence, should attempt to play off one superpower against the other, is understandable and consecrated by ancient tradition. Since 1945, in their impatience with United States policies as they appeared to be affecting them, the French have often gone to great lengths to conciliate and indeed court the Soviet Union. It will be shown that this has not been a very effective way of influencing United States policy. But Russia's older role as a counterweight to Germany has remained the most important one for which French policy-makers again wanted to cast her after 1945. Whenever French efforts to contain Germany seemed to meet with too much resistance for the liking of the French – for example, either within the Franco-German system dreamed of by Adenauer and de Gaulle or in various versions of European integration – Paris tended to make approaches to Moscow that could be interpreted as attempts to persuade the Germans into greater compliance with French wishes. While it would be oversimple to suggest that French governments after 1945 never thought of the Soviet Union as anything other than a possible counterweight to Germany and the United States, it will be shown that this was nevertheless the most important positive policy objective Paris had set itself in Moscow during this period.

It will be shown further that French governments restricted their attempts to use the Soviet Union as a balancing factor against the United States and Germany to times when Paris was confident that Moscow was not on the verge of giving the Red Army orders to advance across the Elbe. For, at moments of such fear, Paris tended to view its American links with unwonted warmth and comradely helpfulness, and Germany as a vital ally.

The expectation of China's early accession to superpower status has to some extent modified the French attitude to Moscow, if only because Russia is likely to cease to be the only significant counterweight to the United States. From the point of view of fundamental French objectives – the kind of objective France can only effectively pursue once immediately pressing problems like the need for foreign aid and the long-term security of her borders have lost their urgency – the growing international importance of China takes the world another step in the direction Paris had wanted to go since it began to use Moscow against Washington. A relatively small country like France can today exert relatively little influence within a power bloc dominated by colossi like the United States or the Soviet Union; outside these power blocs, while the major countries belong to one or the other, the kind of success that can be achieved is unlikely to be a serious challenge to the superpowers. Recognising this, nationally ambitious French governments have, since 1945, looked on the existence of power blocs as at best a necessary evil, and have generally worked for their dissolution. French efforts in Moscow to create Franco-Soviet links outside the superpower system had part of their motivation in the same kind of thinking as has been behind French efforts in Peking in and after 1964: the loosening up of the international system. It will be shown that, under General de Gaulle, this aim was pursued all over the world.

Although French ambitions in foreign affairs, especially after 1958 under General de Gaulle, were so great that nothing less than a place among the most powerful nations could satisfy them, the slowness with which the superpower blocs were

7

withering away provided one of the reasons for the large-scale efforts to expand French influence outside the prestigious blocs. The Bandoeng Conference of 1955 had brought together a number of Afro-Asian countries that had remained aloof from both the eastern and western camps, and these countries were soon joined in their 'Third World' by the rapidly increasing numbers of nations newly emancipated from colonial rule. It was among these nations that the French were to attempt to win a position of influence.

At the time of Bandoeng, and in the years immediately afterwards, France had no hope of even gaining a hearing in the Third World. In the first place, Third World countries were obsessed with the problem of decolonisation: themselves almost entirely former colonial territories, they seemed primarily to be dedicated to the task of helping to independence countries still under colonial rule. In the mid-1950s the French record of decolonisation was poor. The Indo-Chinese states had succeeded in severing their links with France in 1954 only after the French had suffered a series of humiliating defeats in Vietnam. While the Bandoeng Conference was taking place, large and increasing numbers of French troops were doing their best to beat Algerian insurgents who were demanding independence for their country. And although Tunisia and Morocco were about to achieve their own independence with relatively little bloodshed, there remained the French colonies south of the Sahara for whom at that stage autonomy seemed remote. Above all, in 1956 there was the Franco-British attack on the Suez canal, an event hardly calculated to appeal to the Third World.

During these early years of the Third World, the persisting precariousness of the French economy would have been enough to prevent the French from playing a major role within it. Largely composed of relatively poor countries, the Third World, despite its anti-American diatribes, needed as much American assistance as it could obtain, and would have found France no substitute at all. In any case, the constant vilification to which the Third World subjected France at the United Nations and elsewhere would not have persuaded Paris governments to part with scarce resources in their favour.

After the return to power of General de Gaulle in 1958 both the economic and colonial situation changed drastically. Economically, France was beginning to reap the benefits of membership of the recently instituted Common Market, while in the field of decolonisation de Gaulle had, by 1962, done more than most Third World countries could have dared to expect. All the colonies south of the Sahara had been granted independence and, above all, so had Algeria. From that moment de Gaulle had the decolonising testimonials that could gain for him the attention and sympathy of the Third World. What was more, he now had the economic means with which to go some way to making their sympathy worth their while. It will be shown that, in the end, even the prosperity of the Fifth Republic was not enough to ensure for France a decisive influence within the Third World, despite de Gaulle's confident attempts to use the strength of the franc to threaten the American dollar on whose beneficence the subsistence of many Third World countries still depended.

No doubt, the curious political situation of the former sub-Saharan French colonies has something to do with the lack of enthusiasm for France shown by some of the Third World countries. It is indeed the case that the connection between Paris and the capitals of the former French black African territories is very close, and firmly cemented by a French aid programme of generous proportions. However, the causes of the continuing close links between Paris and the former colonies go far beyond considerations involving the actual territories themselves. French colonial and post-colonial policy has to be seen as a function of a much more fundamental and old-established datum of French foreign policy. For that reason, French policy towards the Third World countries – including former French colonies – will here be treated as a special aspect of that more fundamental datum. The fundamental datum in question is the belief of the French that they have a peculiarly important cultural mission to fulfil in the world, even though this mission is often expected to pay political and economic dividends. Without an awareness of this belief – more than half missionary – the zeal with which most French governments since 1945 have tried to assert themselves at the international level, even at times when they could barely feed their own countrymen, must remain an impenetrable mystery.

What has since 1945 made the domination of world affairs by the two superpowers particularly intolerable for the French is that it prevented them from effectively exerting their own influence in all but a very few geographical areas. The traditional French policy to conquer the cultural elites – not to speak of the markets – of the world through the massive and heavily subsidised export of the French language and culture was, after 1945, greatly compromised by the world's involvement in the cold war; it was also hindered by France's economic predicament. Nevertheless, the French continued even at that time to pour money into their efforts of cultural conquest. It will be shown that many Frenchmen have tended to see cultural penetration as a prelude to business, or at the very least as a prelude to some kind of political influence.

With increasing prosperity in the late 1950s and in the 1960s came not merely a vast expansion in French cultural programmes abroad, but also an adaptation of this policy to contemporary requirements in the form of foreign technical and economic aid. Here too it will be shown that the French themselves were quite explicit about the returns they expected from such aid. They were, and still remain, averse from according assistance where it is unlikely to pay political or economic dividends, and they concentrate their efforts where such dividends are likely to be highest. In effect, this means the former French colonies in sub-Saharan Africa. The economic advantages accorded to these countries through France's membership of the Common Market further reinforce her influence with them. French politicians and administrators may, and do, say that the independence of sub-Saharan countries can be demonstrated by the fact that they may at any time sever their connections with Paris, but this misses the point that the French have not put them economically into a position where they can do so without the certainty of destitution.

In the world as a whole, despite some very persistent cultural

INTRODUCTION

and economic courting, French influence has not so far reached
the eminence Paris governments have been working for. More
money than ever is being spent on propagating the French language throughout the world, even in countries like Britain and
Western Germany where one might have thought saturation
point had been reached long ago. Similar zeal is being shown
in the distribution of all kinds of French cultural material. But
the superpowers can hardly be won over to French thinking in
that manner, and the rest of the world needs economic and
technical aid more than French art exhibitions and language
lessons. And, however much French governments might have
fancied their chances at the height of their prosperity in the
mid-1960s, when General de Gaulle imagined he could dictate
economic policy even to the United States, optimism would
have been stretched to the point of lunacy if it were thought
that France alone might have the economic and technical resources to provide a credible alternative either to United States
or some kind of collective international aid to the underdeveloped countries that make up the Third World. Since these
countries are aware of this, their response to French overtures
tends to be guarded.

Meanwhile, as the power blocs unhurriedly demonstrate their
reluctance to disappear, and China still has to show that her
entry among the superpowers is imminent, French governments continue to search for a world role they consider to be
worthy of their country. Their resources, whether in nuclear
weapons or economic wealth, have so far failed to win them
effective influence anywhere outside black Africa, and their
international political stance has earned them little more than
sizeable, though precarious, export orders.

PART ONE

1

The Need for Economic Aid

1944–51: FROM CHAOS TO SUBSISTENCE

At the beginning of the third volume of his *Mémoires,* General de Gaulle described how, at the time of the liberation of France in 1944, the destruction of all communications systems had made even rudimentary forms of government impossible:

First of all, before a central authority can function normally, it must be able to obtain information, have its orders arrive at their destination, supervise their execution. But, for many weeks, Paris was without the means regularly to communicate with the provinces. Telegraph and telephone lines had been cut in innumerable places. Radio stations had been destroyed. There were no French planes suitable for communications work on the deeply-pitted airfields. The railways were to all intents and purposes at a halt. Of our stock of 12,000 engines only 2,800 remained. No train leaving Paris could reach Lyon, Marseille, Toulouse, Bordeaux, Nantes, Lille, Nancy. None was able to cross the Loire between Nevers and the Atlantic, the Seine between Mantes and the Channel, nor the Rhône between Lyon and the Mediterranean. As for the roads, 3,000 bridges were down; hardly 300,000 vehicles were roadworthy out of the former total of three million, but the dearth of petrol made a car journey an adventure in any case. Two months, at least, were needed before there was a regular flow of orders and reports, in the absence of which authority can be exercised only fitfully.[1]

This picture epitomised the state of France as a whole, and it necessarily affected the morale of the French. In April 1945, eight months after the liberation of Paris, at the moment when France was to have her first free postwar elections, 35 per cent of the French stated that food and transport were the most urgent internal problems, compared with 13 per cent who put the elections and the organisation of political parties first.[2]

At the end of that year 59 per cent said that they could heat only one room that winter, while 5 per cent could heat none at all.[3] Just before General de Gaulle's resignation in January 1946, another poll showed that there was no optimism about the economic future; only 29 per cent expressed hope.[4] In February 1946, 53 per cent said that the most important family problem was food, the nearest rival being clothing with a mere 18 per cent.[5] Bread cards, abolished in November 1945, had to be hastily reintroduced in January 1946. On 15 March 1946, Léon Blum, the veteran leader of the French Socialist Party (SFIO), set out for the United States as ambassador extraordinary. His objective was to obtain massive American help.

When, on 5 April 1945, Pierre Mendès-France had resigned as minister for economic affairs from the provisional government of General de Gaulle, it was because he had been refused the austerity programme that in his view could alone have prevented the need for large-scale foreign aid. De Gaulle had told him that the French had suffered enough. The consequence of what the departing minister called the 'policy of facility' led to acute inflation, which made exporting – even on the small scale that might then have been possible – a hopeless task. Thus it was not open to France to pay for the import of capital goods with exports, imports which were particularly badly needed to promote reconstruction and economic development. Moreover, the French reserves of some 2,600 million dollars provided inadequate cover for necessary imports. Lend-lease arrangements, which had yielded 3,200 million dollars, ended in August 1945, seven days after the surrender of Japan. And despite the carrying off into France of factories dismantled in Germany – a policy the French followed as ruthlessly as did the Russians – and the use in France of half a million German prisoners of war in the work of reconstruction (largely in the coal mines), little economic advantage and much political disadvantage came to France from those sources. Moreover, French efforts to delay German economic recovery prevented any serious contribution by Germany to French recovery for at least the remainder of the 1940s.

The political choices of the French at that time therefore made it particularly difficult for them to work out their economic salvation without large-scale foreign assistance. Most of that assistance was to come from the United States. Indeed, in his account of his visit to President Truman in August 1945, General de Gaulle stated laconically:

The President and Mr Byrnes underlined the American wish to help France to as speedy as possible a recovery, and even to increase her productive capacity; they stated that every request for equipment for the French mining industry would be given absolute priority by the United States.[6]

President Truman and Mr Byrnes [said that] the world as a whole needed, above all, economic recovery. At the moment all countries, including England and Russia, were asking for American aid. Now, France was certain to receive such aid, in the fullest measure possible.[7]

Long before the end of the war, plans had been discussed among members of the anti-German coalition for the economic future of the postwar world. Largely the work of United States experts, the plans tended to reflect American economic thinking. The foundation of this thinking was the liberal ideal of freedom of trade, with the premiss that large markets make for prosperity. At Bretton Woods, in the summer of 1944, organisations were created which were meant to help implement that ideal, though GATT (General Agreement on Tariffs and Trade) – one of the major means to achieving it – was not set up until 1947. The IMF (International Monetary Fund) was to fulfil the same function in the field of currency convertibility, and had at its disposal funds for short-term loans to tide member countries over rough patches in the exchange value of their currency. There was also the International Bank for Reconstruction and Development, whose aim was to find capital for the financing throughout the free world of schemes implied by its name. The aid provided for France by the IMF and the International Bank, together with that resulting from the negotiations between Blum and the US secretary of state, Byrnes, in the spring of 1946, constituted the first major postwar contribution of the United States towards French recovery.[8]

That loans from organisations like the IMF were not the right way of meeting the economic needs of France and the rest of Europe (Europe received 80 per cent of all drawings on the IMF in its first year of activity, 1947) soon became clear: short-term loans, which were all the IMF was meant to provide, were hardly a satisfactory way of rebuilding shattered economies of the size of that of France; and the long-term loans from the International Bank, contrary to the avowed world-wide function of the bank, went almost entirely to Europe in 1947 and 1948, where they were used mainly to help with balance of payments difficulties. The recognition that much more fundamental and solid assistance was required led to the formulation of the Marshall Plan.

What the French economy needed was straightforward gifts. On his return from Washington at the end of May 1946 Léon Blum told journalists that the first major gifts had already been received. War debts, including assistance given to the civilian population since the Normandy landings in 1944 and which had included some new industrial equipment, had been completely written off by the United States. Those debts had amounted to some 1,800 million dollars.[9] Then came the speech by the United States' secretary of state, General Marshall, who told his audience at Harvard on 5 June 1947 that, provided the countries of Europe were ready to help each other on the road to recovery, the United States would do all in her power to supply them with whatever they required towards that end, if necessary in the form of gifts. Having accepted the United States' offer, representatives from sixteen European countries, including France, met in Paris from 12 to 16 July 1947 to draw up their list of requirements. Their report was completed on 22 September 1947.

By then, however, it had become clear that France – along with Italy and Austria – would not be able to wait until Marshall Aid became available in the following year. Her economy was in desperate straits, causing her to cancel all non-essential dollar purchases and to use up her last foreign currency and gold reserves. The wheat harvest had been disastrous, amounting to less than half of the previous year's, and even poorer than that of 1945; coal production was also down on 1946. A public opinion poll of 1 October 1947 showed that 78 per cent of those asked recognised that the economic situation was worse than in the previous year,[10] and 35 per cent singled out food as the most affected item, while another 22 per cent put the cost of living as a whole first among their problems; 87 per cent thought that things would get worse still. The United States answered this immediate need by granting emergency interim aid amounting, for France, to 312 million dollars (Foreign Aid Act of 1947) for the period 17 December 1947 to 31 March 1948. 66 per cent of the official bread ration during that winter was provided free of charge by the United States to the French government through gifts of flour, as well as 60 per cent of the petrol ration and 20 per cent of the coal used. The agreement signed on 2 January 1948 between France and the United States left it in practice to the French government to invest the proceeds from the sale to the public of the American gifts, in accordance with the Paris government's own interpretation of the best interests of the French economy.[11]

The role of France in the negotiations for American aid was very much affected by the fact that, after 1944, 'within a period of five years the franc lost six-sevenths of its nominal value. Nothing like this had ever happened before in peacetime in the monetary history of a great industrial country. An "easy" economic policy *(politique de facilité)* had led to economic dependence. Of all the countries of Europe, France needed the largest amount of aid from the United States over the longest period.'[12] In the light of later developments it is ironical that it was the government of General de Gaulle which was responsible for a policy that was to lead to this degree of dependence on the United States, and which allowed French diplomacy so little scope in the negotiations for aid. Initially, France had only two bargaining points: first, American nostalgia for the country of Lafayette (but this feeling had been severely shaken by the apparent ease with which the French had slipped out of the war in 1940); and second, the danger of a Communist takeover in France if America did not provide material aid. However, once the United States began to see a Soviet military threat in Europe, France was presented with a third bargaining point that was going to be much more persuasive for much longer. As one American writer put it:

France had a geographical position in Europe that was of basic strategic importance both militarily and politically. In both senses, France was a natural channel for the exercise of American and British influence in western Europe. Unless France was sufficiently stable and strong, however, this position could not be used in any positive way. France could not act for or even with the United States and Great Britain if its weaknesses were open to pressure and exploitation by others. Conversely, and even if it had seemed desirable, France could not be eliminated as a force from the European picture. If left weak and unsupported, it could still act in a negative way on the basis of its geographical position, its recognised place in major power circles, and its nuisance value. Circumstances dictated that because France could not be done without, it had to be supported.[13]

It was a cool assessment, but it was matched by Frenchmen-in-the-street: 50 per cent thought that the Marshall Plan was primarily designed to provide the Americans with foreign markets, and only 18 per cent that it was the result of a sincere desire to aid Europe; another 15 per cent held that it epitomised the American desire to intervene in European affairs.[14]

However, although the French bargaining position was still weak in 1947–8, even the anticipated difficulties with the United States Congress over the level of aid asked for did not move the American Administration to exact more from the French than the promise of economic good behaviour: the objective of the Marshall Plan was that recipient countries should be able to stand on their own feet by 1952. And one only has to point to the amount of investment in the French nationalised industries for which American aid had been indirectly responsible to make nonsense of the favourite charge of the French Communist Party that France had become an American colony. In the three years 1948, 1949, 1950, United States aid was responsible for an average of just under 18 per cent per annum of all investments in France, most of which went into the nationalised industries. No sector was less likely to appeal to American administrators and politicians.

It is indeed important to recognise that French economic dependence on the United States did not bring with it political dependence in any significant way. The United States government refused to act upon even the moderate political suggestion at home that it should press for European unity, imprecise as that concept was in any case. Thus even Senator Fulbright was not listened to by the Administration when he said, apparently quite reasonably:

> I do not agree that we should as a matter of policy always leave the initiative to other nations. Furthermore, in requesting assistance from us, as virtually every country in western Europe has done, I think they have taken the initiative. Accordingly it does not seem to me that we shall be dictating to those countries or to any other country in any offensive sense if we suggest that under their present chaotic political and economic order they are not good risks either to repay loans or even to survive as democratic states. I am unable to see why the suggestion that they get together and form some kind of political and economic unity as part of the bargain is dictation or undue influence.[15]

This was the senator's reply to General Marshall's letter in which the American secretary of state had said that 'we should make it clear that it is not our purpose to impose upon the peoples of Europe any particular form of political or economic association. The future organisation of Europe must be determined by the peoples of Europe.'[16] However, even if the Administration itself exerted little direct pressure, there is no doubt that the attitude of the American Congress did, as it progressively demanded more evidence, before each annual vote for further US aid, that the European countries were helping each other towards recovery and prosperity. Knowing that the hand that fed them was committed to some vague idea of European unity, the representatives of European countries in receipt of American aid could not easily forget that cooperation was expected of them.

The absence of direct United States interference in the internal affairs of European countries is particularly well illustrated in the activities of OEEC (Organisation for European Economic Cooperation). With its headquarters in Paris, OEEC was set up in April 1948 to supervise the allocation of Marshall Aid to the sixteen countries that were to receive it. Its creation was to fulfil the double purpose of ridding Washington of the nuisance of having to face a constant queue of mendicant politicians, and to encourage the receiving countries in the pursuit of mutual cooperation of the closest kind. But, while the temptation was sometimes very great indeed for United States administrators and politicians to put pressure on European governments, this was usually resisted, and recipient countries were left in little doubt that 'it was a basic feature of American policy . . . [that] the concept of "friendly aid" . . . remained predominant in American thinking.'[17] OEEC countries alone ultimately decided the allocations of Marshall Aid within the framework of their organisation.

The Marshall Plan as such, as distinct from the interim aid that was to tide France, Italy, and Austria over the winter 1947-8, was voted by the United States Congress on 2 April 1948 (Foreign Assistance Act of 1948) and was to run until 1952. The European Recovery Program (ERP) was its main provision, and the Economic Cooperation Administration (ECA) in Washington was created to administer the funds. Bilateral agreements between the United States and recipient countries settled the details of how the aid was to be given and used. The French government, for its part, signed its agreement with the United States on 28 June 1948, and the French National Assembly ratified it on 9 July 1948.

Marshall Plan procedures were kept simple. Aid was to

consist mainly of raw materials, machinery, and technical assistance. The United States was to notify France of the value of its aid instalments, and the French government was expected to pay the equivalent of the aid in francs into a blocked account. The Americans and the French (in practice, the French) would then decide how to use the capital that had thus accrued, in accordance with what was held to be to France's best economic advantage. Finally, the French government was to be reimbursed, for its payments into the blocked account, from the proceeds of the sale of the goods it had received from the United States.[18]

With the creation of NATO in 1949 came the Mutual Defense Assistance Act. This provided two further sets of aid. On the one hand there was the same kind of aid as that already furnished through ERP, raw materials, plant, etc. but reserved for military purposes; on the other hand there were military supplies of all kinds. Administratively, the ECA also had responsibility for this new form of assistance, but it left questions relating to military supplies to the US Defense Department. The French government signed a new agreement covering this aid on 27 January 1950 and the French Parliament ratified it on 18 March 1950.

The already costly war waged by France in Indo-China, and for which the agreement of 18 March 1950 (catering solely for NATO needs) provided no help, was to elicit further assistance from the United States. On 23 December 1950 France, the United States, Cambodia, Laos and Vietnam completed negotiations which caused the United States to provide France with additional military productive capacity and weapons. It was agreed that the French military services would 'pay' the French treasury (i.e. use part of their budget allocation) for this form of American aid, but the government could use these 'payments' as it thought fit. However, the military equipment actually provided by the United States was free of charge. The net result, therefore, was that American gifts enabled the French to allocate their own funds to enterprises that were more economically useful than the war in Indo-China.

The outbreak of the Korean war in June 1950 led to a rethinking of the whole American assistance programme. France, like other European countries, had by then been brought to the point where its future prosperity seemed reasonably assured. The Korean war, although it created a political and economic crisis which threatened the entire achievement of Marshall Aid, nevertheless began the process of persuading American policy-makers that future aid should be concerned less with the internal economic soundness of recipient countries and more with the strengthening of their military potential for the defence of western interests as interpreted by the United States.

But the degree of recovery France had achieved by 1950 was still precarious. There had been eighteen months of relative financial stability; prices had moved little; in 1948 dairy products and petrol had been derationed. Public opinion polls showed that the French were becoming more optimistic: there were nearly as many people who thought that 1948 had been better than 1947 as there were who thought the reverse;[19] most of the polls until then had been entirely pessimistic. And by December 1948, 73 per cent thought that the Marshall Plan had already been of positive help to France, while 43 per cent actually wanted to give the United States something in return.[20] By April 1949, 46 per cent thought prices would fall – as against only 14 per cent in January – and only 13 per cent said prices would rise, compared with 52 per cent in January.[21] The euphoria did not outlast the Queuille government, which fell in October 1949, but things were getting better all the time. Whereas in 1948 France was the largest debtor towards other OEEC countries, by the end of 1949 she had become the largest creditor. On the other hand, her budget deficit in 1949 was still enormous; it amounted to 611,000 million francs, larger even than in 1948. American aid covered 49 per cent of that deficit. France clearly still had a long way to go before the effects of the First National Plan, drawn up in the immediate postwar period by Jean Monnet, and other forms of investment would enable her to pay her way. And it has been calculated that, in 1949, United States aid still covered nearly half the state's investments in France.[22]

The first international economic effect of the war in Korea was that it raised the cost of raw materials and transport. It did not seriously hit France until mid-1951, but was soon aggravated by speculation on the franc. Having to pay more for their imports and finding it hard to export, the French, at the end of 1951, had a balance of payments deficit of 1,105 million dollars. The United States helped with aid totalling 480 million dollars. But the increasing cost of rearmament, particularly after the outbreak of the Korean war, was such that it was no longer possible to believe in the optimistic forecasts of earlier years which had expected to see Europe back on its feet after the expiry of Marshall Aid in 1952. Already before June 1950 OEEC had warned that 'the level of government expenditures devoted to the reinforcement of defence might compromise the progress achieved in the last years if great care is not taken to combine economic policy as a whole with the normal implications of such expenditure.'[23] The Mutual Security Act, voted by Congress on 10 October 1951 and amended in June 1952, clarified a situation that had been only gradually understood since the formation of NATO. It was that once the industrial infrastructure of Europe had been reasonably well restored, American aid would in future be most needed for the rearmament of America's allies, a desideratum upon which Washington laid great emphasis. Thus, with the Mutual Security Act, the era of postwar American aid for European economic recovery had come to an end. From now on the United States were mainly interested in European rearmament.

AID IN THE 1950s: UNITED STATES SUBSIDIES FOR FRENCH OBJECTIVES ABROAD

There can have been few periods in French history during which the dictum *'on fait la politique de ses moyens'* was

less true than under the Fourth Republic. It will be seen
that time and again foreign policy desiderata were based on
the image of themselves which the French had proudly
created in previous centuries rather than on a realistic
evaluation of what kinds of policies they could actually
afford, economically and politically. They were fortunate
in that some of their objectives coincided with those of the
United States, as a result of which they received American
assistance that helped them to perpetuate at least a few of
their illusions. The pursuit of French foreign political
objectives with United States money and equipment became
particularly blatant after 1951, when France had regained
her economic breath at home. Thus French claims to political
leadership in Europe were enhanced by the fact that the
anti-Communism of French governments was most welcome
to the United States and elicited vast sums of American
money to bolster up the French economy, which otherwise
could hardly have served as a basis for any kind of serious
influence anywhere. Similarly, the French succeeded in
persuading the Americans, after a good deal of lengthy
argument, that their war against the nationalists in Indo-
China (1946–54) was really a war against Communism too;
this meant that American funds were made available to
them to pursue their policy objectives there as well. After
1954, the French attempted, this time less successfully, to
use the same method to help finance their war in Algeria.

If one looks in detail at United States assistance given to
France to enable her to pursue political aims she could not
otherwise have afforded, there is no arguing with the conclusion[24] that in the years 1951–4 the United States had paid
for over one-half of the cost of French rearmament; in 1954,
the last year of the war in Indo-China, the Americans had
made themselves responsible for as much as 60 per cent of
the cost of French rearmament, the particular contribution
earmarked for Indo-China amounting to 63,000 million
francs. In the final analysis, however, it does not matter
whether the aid was designated as defence or economic aid,
because what counted was that it enabled France to pay for

policies she wished to pursue, after the initial aim of reaching subsistence at home had been achieved. Thus if one discounts under what particular heads of expenditure American aid appeared, and if one merely registers its place in the French economy as a whole, two points are clear: first, in the years 1951–4 American aid took care, on average, of more than one-fifth of French budget expenditure; secondly, American aid did not merely help the French to balance their foreign trade but, during the years 1950, 1953, and 1954, it actually provided the French treasury with a surplus.[25] The recession in France following from the war in Korea, and which led not only to a drastic cutting of imports but to an even greater loss of exports, was in these ways much alleviated by American assistance. Thus the war in Indo-China could go on.

There were to be other economic crises, but until 1958 (and with the exception of the 1956 Suez affair) American aid could usually be counted upon as an ultimate remedy. For instance:

The year 1954 began precariously for [France]. There were no more loans to be had from abroad. On a number of occasions in 1952 and 1953 the treasury had scraped the bottom of all the barrels: very short-term loans from the International Bank for Reconstruction and Development, one of 23 million and another of 17 million dollars; it called in the holdings of French banks and deposited them with the Exchange Stabilisation Fund; it utilised the so-called 'special reserves' (89 million dollars), which were in fact purely and simply a gift from the United States to enable us to settle up with the European Payments Union when we had to. And the balance of payments position was scarcely more promising: economic activity had slowed down and protectionism was rife.[26]

In fact 1954 and 1955 eventually turned out to be relatively good years for the French economy, and this was largely due to American aid which enabled France to pay off debts and create reserves.

With the end of Marshall Aid in 1952, the Mutual Security Act of 1951–2 provided that future aid could only take the form of military assistance. The United States gave such assistance to the French economy in three main ways: first, by stationing United States' troops in France; secondly, by making off-shore purchases of two principal kinds: orders placed with the French government for food ultimately to be delivered to that government itself or that of another NATO country, but paid for by the United States, or orders placed by the United States directly with French firms, paid for by the United States, but where delivery could be taken by any NATO country (including the American Forces in Europe) according to need; thirdly, NATO infrastructure expenses on French soil. In the two years 1954–5 the French treasury received 1,190 million dollars from those sources. To this should be added an amount nearly as great covering a residue of Marshall Aid and aid for the war in Indo-China. During that period the French Treasury put aside nearly 1,500 million dollars, partly to repay loans and partly to increase its foreign currency reserves.

THE ENDING OF AID

The end of the Indo-Chinese war in 1954, the United States' refusal to finance France's increasingly costly conflict in Algeria, and Eisenhower's displeasure over Suez, all combined to make the French economic position in 1956 and 1957 very different from the immediately preceding years. Beginning in January 1956 with an unwonted and very large deficit with the European Payments Union (55.5 million dollars), 1956 and 1957 saw exports stagnate and import costs soar. Although at least one French economist[27] could see a silver lining (in the form of the growing import needs of a rapidly expanding economy) in an otherwise unrelievedly cloudy sky, the cost and consequences of the Suez fiasco and the war in Algeria, together with a crop failure and another run on the franc, made 1956 and 1957 the most catastrophic years for the French balance of payments since the three years after the liberation of France. The overall deficit amounted to 3,145 million dollars for these two years. In the past, such a situation would have been largely dealt with through American aid. But, given the United States' very negative reaction to Suez as well as their refusal to provide aid for the Algerian war, the French had to find new ways of financing their political choices. They did it in three ways, but here their continuing military links with the Americans were still of great help. First, they used the sum of about 1,000 million dollars paid by the United States for goods and services provided for their forces stationed in France, as well as a remaining small amount of American aid (now drastically reduced to 125 million dollars for the two years 1956–7). Secondly, they used up their reserves. Thirdly, they increased their foreign debt.

In a sense, at the beginning of 1958 life in France without American aid still seemed bleak:

> The prospects at the beginning of 1958 were grim. Apart from the gold holdings of the Bank of France (575.5 million dollars) the gold and currency reserves of the exchange stabilisation fund were approaching zero and, indeed, negative if one takes into account the debts contracted with the recognised intermediaries by way of the mobilisation of their reserves (*ratissage*). Few possibilities remained of getting further loans from either international organisations or other foreign sources. A serious balance of payments deficit was a distinct possibility.[28]

But although the deficit in 1957 was almost as great as that which, ten years earlier, had made the Marshall Plan a vital necessity, the basic economic situation of France had drastically improved. Aid of the kind furnished in 1948 and 1949, which had amounted to 820 and 1,070 million dollars respectively, was no longer necessary for survival, and had in fact diminished to a mere 60 million dollars in 1958. In 1947 French productive capacity had been derisory, investment from domestic sources necessarily small, exports negligible, and imports out of economic reach. By 1958 French productive capacity, especially in finished industrial goods, was considerable and increasing fast. What was more, the European Common Market had begun to function at the beginning of 1958, and France was able to draw on the facilities it provided for mutual economic assistance. Antoine Pinay's deflationary measures were also encouraging people to subscribe to loans which the state used, among other things, to increase its stock of gold. Finally, the return to power of General de Gaulle, after the revolution of 13 March 1958, further encouraged hopes of stability, and therefore confidence. De Gaulle's 20 per cent devaluation of the franc at the end of 1958 appeared to set the seal on France's economic independence. But it had taken fourteen years of sustained American aid to carry France to that point.

2

France, Germany and 'Europe'

(i) Basic historical problems : 'Henceforth the Germans must be considered to be the main enemy, indeed the only one from whom real harm could come to us.' Like Richelieu before him, Louvois who wrote these words in the 1680s clearly recognised the basic facts of life on the western part of the European continent. These basic facts were geographical and demographic. Anyone casting his eyes around the periphery of what might even then have been loosely called the French hexagon could look with satisfaction at the security afforded to him by the Atlantic, the Pyrenees, the Mediterranean and the Alps. But the frontier in the east presented him with a different picture: separating him from the vast multitude of some three hundred and sixty German states, it was very long and very ragged, and with a large part of it without natural defences.

Furthermore, France's growing domination in Europe had been built on the numerical superiority which Frenchmen enjoyed at that time over each of their neighbours. With a population of about twenty-two million, France had no need to fear even Prussia – probably the most ambitious German state – whose inhabitants were a scattered two and a half million. But if, as Louvois went on to say, the Germans 'gave themselves an emperor who was ready to get on his horse', the story would be very different. Then even the Austrians might be prepared to unite their efforts with those of the German states further north, bringing together a population that would exceed that of France by some ten million.

Since Louvois, certain geographical changes have from time to time made the frontiers more, or less, defensible. None of these changes, however, has altered the basic fact that

France's frontier with Germany is the longest land frontier she has with any single political unit.

Very much more adverse to France than frontier changes have been the demographic changes since the seventeenth century. By 1815, when Prussia was for the first time given a land frontier with France, that German state alone had a little over one-third of the population of France, which then stood at about thirty million. The very slow demographic growth of France in the last two centuries saw to it that by the time Hitler had collected Austria in 1938, a mere forty-two million Frenchmen were faced with seventy-six million Germans.

Given the mores of international society, it is not surprising that these geographical and demographic facts should have led Frenchmen who cared about the continued independence and territorial integrity of their country to view Germany with some apprehension. This apprehensive attitude expressed itself at the time of Louvois in a manner befitting the relative position of the two sides. The French simply annexed slices of territory in the east which they considered desirable for their defence, disdainfully ignoring German pamphleteers who called Louis XIV a French Attila by way of impotent retribution. By 1681 even Strasbourg had been secured. The French also did their best to keep the German states disunited, a policy in any case enthusiastically followed by these states themselves. Prussia and Austria, the two states able, and periodically willing, to take on the leadership of the German states, were throughout the eighteenth century encouraged by France to pursue their mutually exclusive interests, while the south German states were brought so much under French influence that it took a mixture of judicious marriages and brute force before Bismarck could finally triumph over their particularistic tendencies.

When Napoleon's critics reproach him for not having perceived the danger across the Rhine, what they mean is that by tidying up the German political map he had gratuitously increased the weight that was soon to smother France. This disdain for whatever danger Germany might have to offer has not, however, been an attitude shared by many Frenchmen since Louvois. Napoleon III's ministers did succumb to it in 1870, but they also succumbed to its disastrous consequences. Sedan and the Treaty of Frankfurt were for at least thirty years to be reminders of the folly of ignoring the growing strength of Prussia and her satellites. In fact it is no exaggeration to say that after 1870 the now unified German empire largely dominated the French political and intellectual horizon. Professor Renouvin's work on Franco-German relations during the period 1871–90,[1] has shown, with much documentary evidence, how even on many purely internal matters, such as what French bishops might be allowed to say from French pulpits during the *Kulturkampf,* the French felt constrained to adapt themselves to German exigencies. And it was the overpowering presence of Germany, now this side of the Rhine in Alsace and Lorraine, which provided the most prominent French intellectuals of the period with their major themes, most of which were concerned with political and moral regeneration in the face of the German threat. It was thus an attitude of fear, as well as one of hurt pride and, eventually, of defiance, which emerged from the total defeat of 1870.

It was also fear of Germany which made the French look for allies after 1870. It was a feeling Bismarck recognised so well as being appropriate to the French situation that he made it one of his main tasks to keep France isolated. In this he succeeded admirably until his retirement in 1890. By then, however, at least Russia had shown herself ready to do a deal with France. But, as distinct from those occasions in earlier centuries when France had used Russian ambitions in Europe for her own predatory ends (as in 1792 when she thus succeeded in defeating Prussia and Austria), Russian support after 1870 often seemed needed merely to keep France alive as an independent country. On several occasions, but particularly in 1875 and 1887, French governments felt constrained to plead with the Russians, as well as with the English, to intercede on their behalf with Bismarck lest his anger with Paris spill over into a preventive war.

Another reason for French impotence in Europe was the French colonial empire. From the time of the 1878 Berlin Congress, when Bismarck first sought to sublimate French revanchism through healthy exercise in Tunisia, a number of French politicians, army leaders and intellectuals allowed the energies of their countrymen to be consumed in the wilds of south-east Asia, and in Africa, where they came very close to making a new enemy of Great Britain without having lost the old one in Germany. It took the lucidity of Delcassé, and growing British apprehensions about Germany, to bring about the Franco-British entente of 1904, ten years after the Franco-Russian alliance.

French recognition that, alone, France was no match for Germany appears at every turn in the peace negotiations after the first world war, as well as in the opposition French politicians encountered at home whenever they were suspected of entrusting too much of the fate of France to the League of Nations. Not only France's desire, frustrated by her allies, to dismember Germany, but also the Locarno Treaty and the Little *Entente,* expressed that recognition. So did her slavish following of British policies in the late 1930s. But, then, few Frenchmen could allow themselves to forget that the first world war had cost them one and a half million dead. The attitude of apprehension was again vindicated in 1940, while that of defiance was clearly not present in sufficient strength.

However, the long German frontier and its demographic hinterland did not always elicit apprehension and hostility in the French after that famous statement by Louvois. The many French Protestants who had found refuge in Prussia in the seventeenth and eighteenth centuries had not merely been the instruments through which the armies of that German state were being transformed into the small but highly efficient fighting force which enabled Prussian rulers to satisfy their territorial hunger. They had also helped to make the German intelligentsia receptive to the universalist ideas of the Enlightenment in which they, like all minorities, had a vested interest. In France, the fact that Frederick the Great had shown himself an apt pupil of the *philosophes* marked the beginning of a long tradition among liberal intellectuals which led them to look to Germany with the same kind of longing that western Communists were later to reserve for Moscow. From Voltaire in the early eighteenth century to Renan in the late nineteenth century, via Madame de Staël during the Revolution, French intellectuals who objected to any of the many conservative tendencies that still prevailed in their own country saw in the German humanistic thinkers the prophets of tomorrow. In their blind hatred of reaction, they failed to notice that the Germany they were teaching their countrymen to revere bore little relation to the Germany that was rapidly transforming itself under Prussian leadership into a major threat to liberalism everywhere. They were still reassuringly quoting Goethe's homage to sour grapes ('Germans, it is in vain that you nurse hopes for the formation of a German nation. But this makes it all the easier for you to turn yourselves into true human beings'), when the Germans were already acclaiming their second generation of Romantic writers. This was a generation of traditionalists and authoritarians which, by 1811, in the words of Arnim 'refused to have any truck with Jews, Frenchmen and philistines', had for its slogan 'For God, King and Fatherland', and taught the supremacy of the state over the individual. The greatness of the misunderstanding of Germany under which most of the major French intellectuals laboured even in the second half of the nineteenth century was well brought out by Renan when, in 1870, France suddenly found herself crushed into submission by the putative liberals from across the Rhine. 'Germany has made the most important revolution in modern times: the Reformation. Moreover, during the last century, Germany has produced the most beautiful intellectual developments there have ever been'. Because they had taken these to be the basic verities about Germany, especially about the Protestant north, liberal French-

men had furthered the cause of German unification, a temptation which even Napoleon III had not entirely resisted. The
shock of 1870, and the behaviour of the Germans under Bismarck thereafter, brought many French liberals to their senses.
By then, however, they had completed their subversive work.

But the Treaty of Frankfurt did not turn all Frenchmen
into Germanophobes. On the one hand, French Socialists
canvassed ever more seriously the Socialist virtues of the
German working class, in a way that recalled only too clearly the earlier odes to the cultured German middle class so
fondly sung by French liberals. On the other hand, certain French politicians, for example Gambetta and Ferry,
were inclined to accept German hegemony in Europe in exchange for some share in the spoils. This was not because
these founder-statesmen of the Third Republic had any
particular admiration for the ethos that had set the Prussian
soldiery marching towards their conquests, but because they
thought that this was the attitude that would be most beneficial to France in her new, straitened circumstances. In this
they were the ancestors of men like Laval. By the turn of the
century, however, the successes of French diplomacy and
colonialism had changed servility towards Germany into
confident defiance. But the Socialist leader Jaurès was still
preaching brotherhood on the eve of the first world war. It
was to cost him his life.

After 1918 it took the idealism that fired at least some of
the supporters of the League of Nations to recreate, for a
while, the belief in the universal brotherhood of men. It is
probably in Giraudoux's *Bella* that the disagreements between Briand, who stood for this ideal, and Poincaré, who did
not, are most typically portrayed. We know that Hitler saw
to it that the idealism was short-lived, and its pacifist implications lethal for the nations that had again succumbed to it.

In fact, it was those Frenchmen who least believed in the
brotherhood of man who came nearest to reaching an understanding with the Germans in the 1930s and early 1940s.
Pathologically, or merely financially, afraid of the Russian
Communist threat in Europe in general and in France in

33

particular, various right-wing organisations in France saw Hitler's Germany as their best defence. Their sympathetic attitude to Germany stopped short neither of the desire to import German forms of 'strong' government so that France might be able to resist Communism more effectively, nor of collaborating with Hitler with the utmost dedication once the German armies had managed to overrun France yet again in 1940. Without them the Germans would have had a much tougher time during their occupation of France.

The primacy of ideology over national independence, which had expressed itself in the doctrines and activities of both the French Right and the French Left in the interwar years, had previously known only pale parallels, as for example in the attitudes of the émigrés during the Revolution. However, since 1944, the geographical and demographic factors have again provided the most important data around which French attitudes towards Germany have crystallised. At the very least it may be argued that they have been of no less importance than ideological pressures like Europeanism, many of which in any case have their origins in the considerations which had already exercised Louvois.

(ii) The situation in 1945: To a considerable extent, French policy towards Germany in the immediate postwar period was determined by such agreements as the Soviet Union, the United States and Great Britain had succeeded in reaching before the end of the war in May 1945. These agreements,[2] though concluded without the participation of French representatives, and frequently without the consideration of French interests, formed the framework within which French diplomacy had to operate.

It may be argued that the first step towards an allied policy on postwar Germany was taken when in 1941 Churchill and Roosevelt decided that there would be no negotiated settlement with Germany. It implied that they refused to deal with the Nazi government and, by extension, that they reserved the right to deal with the defeated enemy as they thought fit. In January 1943 this was followed by their declaration that they would demand unconditional surrender from Germany. In the summer of the same year the British war cabinet approved the Attlee report, which advocated that Germany should be occupied by the three big allied powers, and that each should have its own occupation zone. The terms of the report were to become established allied policy.

In October 1943 the first high-level allied talks were held in Moscow between the foreign ministers of the three powers. These prepared the ground for the Teheran Conference of the following month. They also led to the setting up of the three-power European Advisory Commission (EAC), which was given the dual task of preparing the terms of the German surrender and of suggesting the machinery for their implementation.

At Teheran the heads of the three allied governments agreed to the creation of three occupation zones in Germany. Stalin expressed the view that the French should not be given a zone, if only because their quick collapse in 1940 had made them unworthy of one. Roosevelt was no keener to elevate the French to a position of international importance. He detested General de Gaulle, who just before Teheran had enlarged his 'government' in Algiers (the French Committee for National Liberation) by the inclusion of members of the French resistance, and behaved increasingly as if he were the indisputable head of a legitimate French government. The American president also distrusted the French as a nation, to the point where he objected to having the American occupation zone in the south of Germany because he feared that an imminent revolution in France would threaten American supply lines. The EAC reached agreement on the delimitation of the zones in June 1944, and their decisions were only slightly modified later.

In September 1944 Churchill and Roosevelt met at Quebec. They agreed in principle on the acceptance of the Morgenthau Plan, which provided for the dismemberment and deindustrialisation of Germany. Although this kind of policy was soon abandoned in favour of something less overtly vindictive, the agreement between the two statesmen (also reached at Quebec) that it was too early to provide for a French occupation zone lasted rather longer. On the other hand, at the October conference between Churchill and Stalin, the latter told the British prime minister that he was in favour of partitioning Germany and of providing a special status for the Ruhr and the Saar. It is a moot point (see chapter 3) whether Stalin, who had previously expressed himself against this kind of dismemberment, was here influenced by the fact that General de Gaulle's government was being recognised by the three allies on 23 October, the day after Churchill had sent his report of the meeting to the United States president. Certainly, Stalin knew that de Gaulle was violently opposed to any kind of German unity and advocated detaching certain areas (particularly the Ruhr and Saar) from the Reich, preferably to bring them under French control. When de Gaulle set out on his journey to Moscow in November 1944 there cannot have been any doubt in his mind, any more than in that of Stalin, that a *rapprochement* between the two could be to their mutual advantage in their dealings with Britain and the United States.

Considerably irked by the major allies' habit of making decisions even about Germany without French participation, General de Gaulle, a week before his government received official recognition from the allies, demanded representation for his country on EAC. This was granted on 11 November 1944, and René Massigli took his seat on the commission two weeks later. At the time, Georges Bidault, de Gaulle's foreign minister, spoke of the Rhine as a French river. But the demand for a French occupation zone was still at that stage turned down by both Roosevelt and Stalin. It was not until after de Gaulle's Moscow visit at the end of 1944 that the United States president agreed in principle to granting the French such a zone. This was on 19 January 1945, after he had refused a request from de Gaulle that he be allowed to talk to the three major allied leaders before their projected meeting at Yalta: de Gaulle had 'warned' that the French government could not allow itself to be bound by decisions affecting Germany which it had not helped to make.

Meanwhile the French had made other demands in EAC. They wanted to take part in the signing of the surrender document and claimed that the French text should be considered as 'authentic' as the English and Russian texts; they reiterated their demand for zones of occupation in Western Germany and in Berlin; they wanted to share responsibility with the other allies in the Control Authority; they agitated for the separation of the Ruhr from the rest of Germany, for the elimination from German soil of all war industries or near war industries; and they expressed their wish to occupy the Rhineland. At the end of December, faced with unexpectedly heavy German military pressure in eastern France and de Gaulle's declaration that his country would have fifty divisions by the end of 1945, the United States State-War-Navy Coordinating Committee advised the president that it would be 'in the best interests of the United States that France resume her traditional position as a principal power capable of playing a part in the occupation of Germany and in maintaining peace in Europe'.[3] During the same month the arming of eight French divisions, long held up by the United States, was carried out with unwonted speed.

At Yalta, in February 1945, the main pressure for French participation in the occupation of Germany came from Churchill. This was no doubt largely because Roosevelt had suggested that United States troops would return home within two years, a fact that also reinforced the British belief that France should participate in the control machinery in Germany: Britain was hardly in a position to face the Soviet Union alone in Europe. De Gaulle, during his Moscow visit at the end of the previous year, had in fact received no Russian support for his claims in Germany, and at Yalta the Soviet Union was no more anxious to satisfy French demands than was Roosevelt. And when, as a result of Churchill's persistent efforts, Roosevelt had succeeded in persuading the Russians that, as a favour and not as a right, the French should have their zone, Stalin still objected to their having a seat on the Control Commission. But even there Churchill got his way before the conference was over.

In April 1945, a month before the end of the war in Europe, the French reminded the major allies of their claim to a zone by insisting that only their own troops should be used within the area allocated to them. They asked that their zone should contain a sector of Berlin, as well as the provinces of Hesse-Cassel, Hesse-Nassau, Baden, Württemberg, the Saar, the Rhine province and the Palatinate. Their claim was substantially met at the beginning of May 1945. But the Russians, who had withheld their consent until agreement had been reached with Britain and the United States on Berlin, had succeeded in having the French sector in the German capital carved out of the previously agreed British and American portions, as in Western Germany. The Russians' lack of enthusiasm for the Paris government was again shown when they tried to prevent the French from signing the armistice in Berlin, and when they refused to allow them to sit on the Reparations Commission set up at Yalta..

The Potsdam Conference (16 July–2 August), attended by the leaders of the Soviet Union, the United States and Britain, was mainly concerned with the problem of Germany. The delimitation of occupation zones, reparations procedures, denazification, war crimes, population transfers, all were discussed there. Yet despite France's obvious interest in these subjects, she had not been invited to the conference. Though she protested at this, she nevertheless accepted most of the decisions made at Potsdam. But in a note of 2 August 1945 the French government stated its refusal to allow a central administration to be set up in Germany. Moreover, the United States' and British objection to having the Rhineland and Ruhr separated from the rest of Germany was as disagreeable for France as was, for the Soviet Union, the same countries' failure to recognise the Oder-Neisse line as a definitive border. A further attempt by de Gaulle, before he gave up the leadership of his country in January 1946, to keep Germany divided and weak, was made during his visit to President Truman in August 1945. He argued that a visibly harmless Germany would have the effect of drawing the satellite states of the Soviet Union away from her, for it was chiefly their fear of Germany which kept them tied to the Russians. Then the Soviet Union would be too busy dealing with these states for her to be able to embark on an adventurous policy abroad, as the Americans were increasingly fearing that she might. However impressed President Truman might have been by these arguments, within a year his secretary of state, Byrnes, was making his famous speech in Stuttgart (6 September 1946) in which he was openly courting the Germans, no doubt to win their support against the Soviet Union.

1945–9: KEEPING GERMANY DIVIDED AND WEAK

At least for the first four years after the war, French governments tended to deal with the problem of Germany in terms of traditional reflexes rather than pragmatically. Their refusal to treat Germany as a single unit, in accordance with the Potsdam decisions, was, as has been seen, not the first sign of their atavistic urge to see the country of the defeated enemy divided up, nor was it the last. French governments, as a matter of routine until 1948, more fitfully thereafter, adhered to this approach in their dealings with the other members of the Control Commission, as well as in the policies they attempted to put into practice in their own occupation zone.

French arguments against a central administration in Germany were of three kinds. First, they alleged that Germany had in the past managed to remain peaceful only when there was no central administration to set her on the road to authoritarianism and imperialism.[4] Secondly, there was the material argument, according to which a united Germany would again soon be industrially so formidable as to constitute once more an international threat either through its industrial power alone or through the renewed use of that power for military purposes.[5] Thirdly, it was plausibly supposed that a divided Germany was less of a threat to France from the military point of view.[6] In addition, there was the less widely stated fear that a centralised administration might seek to perpetuate the West German boundaries which the French badly wanted to change.[7]

In practice, these considerations led the French to object to the clauses of the Potsdam agreement that called for the uniform treatment of the population throughout Germany, the creation of administrative departments (for example for economic affairs) under the aegis of the Control Council and responsible for the whole of Germany, and the promotion of a balanced economy through the encouragement of interzonal cooperation. To get their way, the French were determined to use their place, and the right of veto that went with it, on the Allied Control Council in Berlin which was to implement the Potsdam agreement. In fact, they did this so effectively, and thereby managed to cut off their zone from the rest of Germany so well, that they provided the Russians with an unnecessary precedent for their own iron curtain policy in eastern Germany.

An important reason for retaining close and sole control over their zone was that the French wanted it to be harnessed to French economic requirements. In a speech in Baden-Baden (5 October 1945), General de Gaulle went so far as to speak of integrating the zone into the French economy.[8] This would certainly have been one way of guaranteeing the delivery of material reparations from Germany as compensation for the damage that country had done to France. There were, however, limits beyond which the French could not go, not least because they required the cooperation of the other occupying powers if French aims for the rest of Germany were to have any hope of success. But, more particularly, the rigorous economic policy for their zone,[9] which had kept imports to a very low level during the first years of the occupation, could not be continued indefinitely. For, apart from wanting to exact reparations from the Germans through the suppression of demand in their zone, the French also wanted to win over the population.[10] And to the degree to which the Anglo-American zones did better by their Germans than the French, to that degree also was the success of that French aim likely to depend upon improvements in the standards of living in their own zone.

Probably the greatest economic benefit of the occupation was to come to the French through their control over the Saar. Since one of France's most pressing needs was for coal, the Saar mines were particularly important to her. With her own coal deposits traditionally quite unable to supply all her needs, and imports from the Ruhr dependent on British cooperation (upon which total reliance could not always be placed), complete control over the Saar became a major policy objective in the immediate postwar period. As will be seen, for reasons that had at least as much to do with Anglo-American interests as with their good will towards France, Britain and the United States were at length to agree that the French should have a permanent right to occupy the Saar, that they should take over the ownership of the coal mines there, that the territory should be part of the French customs and currency area, and that it should be removed from the jurisdiction of the Control Council. The fact that the Russians, who were still demanding that Germany be treated as one unit, rejected the French claim was as welcome to the British and Americans as it was unwelcome to the French Communist Party. The latter was still anxious to participate in the government of France – which required that specifically French aims be pursued – while the former were anxious to enrol France on their side in the apparently imminent break with Russia.

Although the Russians had made their opposition to French aims clear on several occasions, particularly at the meeting of allied foreign ministers in Paris in July 1946, the French took with them to the Moscow Conference of the same powers in April 1947 a comprehensive plan for Germany which incorporated most of the demands they had so far made.[11] While they were prepared to accept central coordination in Germany for relatively minor activities such as transport, trade and postal communications, they insisted that for all matters with overt political implications the largest unit should be the Land. The Land was to have charge of its educational system, and it was to have its own budget and civil service. The Rhineland, the French still maintained, should be internationalised, the Ruhr placed under international control with its coal output boosted (for obvious reasons), and its other industries restricted (for other obvious reasons). For the Saar, the French put forward the policy previously stated and already accepted in principle by the British and Americans. Opposition on most points came mainly from the Russians, though the United States and Britain had no wish to have the Soviet Union participating in an international Rhineland or Ruhr, and, if only for that reason, opposed the French on that aspect of their policy. The French therefore gained little support for their overall German policy at the Moscow Conference and though they continued to hold to it and put it forward until the end of 1947, they recognised that they would have to modify it. But Russian intransigence over the Saar finally convinced them that their immediate interests would be best served if they accepted the Anglo-American offer on that territory. The acceptance of that offer marked the end of France's first postwar attempt to play an independent part in international politics, though the rapidly deteriorating relations between Washington and Moscow would soon have compelled a choice in any case.

However, until 1949 the policies overtly advocated by the French in relation to Germany underwent no marked change. What changed was the expectation of their fulfilment and the conditions which had seemed to make their fulfilment imperative.[12] There can be little doubt that the main cause of the gradual revolution in French thinking about Germany was the growing seriousness of east-west differences, and the French decision to support the west. That decision brought France benefits which made a tough policy towards Germany unnecessary and, perhaps, self-defeating. For example, it has already been seen that France had her way over the Saar because this territory was presented to her as a kind of prize by the British and Americans for finally siding with them in their differences with the Soviet Union. In October 1947, 87 per cent of the Saar population actually voted for economic union with France, which was consummated on 14 November 1947 when the French National Assembly gave Georges Bidault a majority for the introduction of the French franc into the territory. East-west differences also indirectly helped to alleviate France's need for German reparations through the role these differences played in the introduction of the European Recovery Program, though to what degree the Marshall Plan was a direct consequence of these differences is much disputed.* But the conflict

* See above, pp. 15–20.

certainly was responsible for the creation of the North Atlantic Treaty Organisation (NATO),* which not only tried to protect western interests in Europe militarily against possible aggression by the Soviet Union, but also – at least indirectly – helped to allay French fears about a military resurgence of Germany. For the creation of NATO implied the continuation of a United States presence in Europe, which was also a guarantee against a German military threat to France.

If, to these politically persuasive considerations, one adds the increasing American and British pressure to alter French foreign policy so that it could accept the union of all three western occupation zones in Germany, French acquiescence, by 1949, to the establishment of a central German government for all the three western zones is largely explained. But French acquiescence came slowly. The Frankfurt Charter of January 1948 – drawn up by the British and American military governors and the German minister-presidents of their respective zones – had foreshadowed the formation of a West German government in at least the Anglo-American zones, and had elicited French protests. But the charter had only been the culmination of a series of Anglo-American measures to limit their economic and political commitments in Germany while at the same time providing an incentive to the Germans to throw in their lot with the western powers in the cold war against the Soviet Union. The simultaneous process of streamlining commitments in Germany and wooing the Germans may be said to have begun with the creation of the Bizone, that is the amalgamation of the British and American zones in Western Germany, after the failure of the Paris foreign ministers meeting in July 1946. At that time the French, still astride the east-west fence, had explained their refusal to join as an attempt to prevent the complete collapse of four power control.[13] The excuse cut no ice with the powers responsible for the Bizone, and though the United States were not prepared at that stage to press too hard for a change in French policy – they went so far as actually to subsidise the French zone – they, together with the British,

* See below, p. 124.

43

were overtly ready to act independently of France to attain their aims in Germany. For example, they announced that, despite well-known French opposition, they would raise steel production in the Ruhr as part of their policy to make the Bizone economically self-sufficient by 1949. They were also turning over the control of the Ruhr mines to the Germans, though not the distribution of the coal. Both these steps showed the French that total refusal to cooperate economically with the Bizone would shortly give them no voice of any consequence in the industrially most significant area of Germany, and on which many of their future expectations depended. With these considerations in mind, the French gradually convinced themselves that the union of their zone with the Bizone would not be the disaster for their aims in Germany that they had alleged. Within a year of the Marshall Plan coming into force they were finally to accept the creation of the German Federal Republic, which was to be formed from the merged western occupation zones, including their own.

It was not, however, in those terms that the case for a change in France's German policy was presented to the National Assembly. Georges Bidault, in a debate on 13 February 1948,[14] stated that the Soviet Union's refusal to join in the ERP made the solution of the German problem within the wartime four-power alliance unlikely. He said that, as a consequence, only a 'European' answer was feasible, in the sense that only a United Europe could provide a guarantee against future aggression. However, Bidault's speech still included the demand for the permanent occupation of the Rhine provinces, and for other traditional safeguards such as the continued control of industries with a war potential.

Ten days after Bidault's National Assembly speech, at the London Conference attended by Britain, the United States, France and the Benelux countries, the French agreed to the association of Western Germany with the ERP. However, they could not yet bring themselves to accept the establishment of an economic trizone, although, paradoxically, they agreed that political union, to which they had objected still more, ought to precede economic union.[15] No doubt the Russian

44

blockade of Berlin, imposed at the end of March 1948, acted as a spur to further French collaboration with Britain and the United States. At any rate, by April, and despite opposition from the French administration in Germany, practical cooperation between the Bizone and the French zone was being anxiously discussed by the countries concerned. At the second session of the London Conference, which began two months later, the French government finally gave its consent to the integration of the whole of Western Germany into the western European economy at least within the confines of ERP, and to the establishment of a West German government under a system that would be democratic and federal, with a Lower House of Parliament elected by universal suffrage.[16] It was, however, agreed that the allied occupation forces would remain in Germany, and that the distribution of Ruhr coal, coke, and steel would remain under international control. Thus, although for over three years the French had been dragging their feet – thereby delaying interzonal cooperation and the setting up of any kind of German state uniting the occupation zones – Bidault in 1948 finally felt constrained to adopt the German policy of his Anglo-American allies in the light of the new international situation and France's inability to stand on her own. But public opinion in France as yet refused to follow, and within a month of the London Conference Bidault was disavowed by the National Assembly and found himself out of office. As a result, it took another fifteen months before the French zone was fully merged with the Bizone.

During the National Assembly debate on the decisions taken at the London Conference in June, it was obvious that the bankruptcy of France's German policy since 1944 was recognised by many speakers. Paul Reynaud acidly wondered how much longer the government was going to countenance the likelihood of isolating France from her remaining allies, the Slav group of nations having already been successfully alienated.[17] Nevertheless, the 'European' solution to the German problem, put forward by André Philip, failed to move the majority of the Assembly, which, on 17 June, went on to vote narrowly in favour of a policy that provided for a renewed French attempt to gain international control over the Ruhr, continuing reparations deliveries, prolonged occupation, and the refusal to see a central government in Germany. Even so, by mid-November 1948, largely because the French saw the need for a currency reform in all the three zones in Western Germany, the economic unity of the three zones was accepted by the Paris government.*

Determined opposition to changes in French policy towards Germany came not only from old-established prejudices among members of the National Assembly and Frenchmen-in-the-street. It came very effectively also from the French military authorities in Germany. Since General de Lattre de Tassigny's early reign in the French zone immediately after French troops had entered German territory in March 1945, the army seemed to resent interference with its own plans for the zone. British and American military commanders often felt moved to protest at the apparent differences between the avowed policies of Paris governments and what actually happened in the French-occupied areas; indeed, the politicians in France were themselves quite well aware of the wilfulness of their occupation authorities. André Philip spoke of the creation of satrapies in Germany.[18] The London Conference of November 1948, at which precise measures for the implementation of the new German policies were to be discussed, was preceded by a typical Anglo-American ploy to put pressure on Paris, both to bring about a speedier conversion of the French government to these new policies and to give Paris courage in its dealings with the French occupation authorities: on the eve of the conference the bizonal commanders issued law no. 75 which left the determination of the ownership of the German coal and steel industries to the future German government. It was for the French to decide whether they wanted to make a constructive contribution to the setting up of that government in the near future.

In September 1949 the German Federal Republic finally

* Full acceptance was signified on 18 November 1948 when France negotiated a commercial agreement with the three zones.

came into being, as a result of the fusion of the three western zones and the approval earlier that year of the constitution for the republic by the three western military governors on the anniversary of Germany's surrender. Thus, by 1949, French safeguards against renewed German aggression depended on Anglo-American guarantees and the integration of West Germany within a wider economic and, soon, military complex. The hope of containing the former enemy by mere force had gone, except among those for whom the world had stood still since 1944.

1949–54: THE EUROPEAN SOLUTION

(i) The European Coal and Steel Community: It has been alleged that the French invented the European Coal and Steel Community (ECSC) as a device to keep Germany permanently disunited.[19] The supposed reasoning was that the creation of the ECSC entailed the incorporation of the Ruhr within it, and that the Soviet Union would never allow German reunification while the bulk of German industry remained firmly associated with the west. Such cynical calculations, if they were in fact made, were overshadowed by two more commonly expressed motives. The first was that everything should be done to unite Europe – in some sense of that phrase – so that the old continent could again play a major political role in world affairs; ECSC would have an obvious part to play in such a union. The second was that in the absence of permanent military control over Germany, the integration of Germany within a larger European framework would offer a meaningful guarantee against renewed German aggression; the close integration of the Ruhr coal and steel industries with those of France and other west European countries was thought to make an excellent beginning.

Robert Schuman, on whom Jean Monnet had prevailed to launch ECSC, admitted from the start that the drive to bring it about was essentially political and not, for instance, economic.[20] British participation in the scheme, which the French had sought within a somewhat wider economic framework in April 1949, was refused by the Labour government. But the political motivation of Robert Schuman and his supporters in the drive towards European integration was not only strong enough to triumph over British aloofness; it also, in the opinion of those who worked with him,[21] could not be adequately accounted for by the fact that fellow Christian Democrats happened to be in power in Western Germany and Italy. It was generally accepted that Schuman would have tried to implement the plan irrespective of the political complexion of the governmental parties in the countries concerned.

Support within France for this policy came mainly from the Socialist Party (SFIO) and the Christian Democratic Party (MRP). But General de Gaulle and his followers in the anti-Communist *Rassemblement du Peuple Français* were at the end of the 1940s so impressed by the Soviet threat to Europe that they wanted a far more radical policy for a tighter and wider European union than even Schuman was advocating. The latter's refusal at that time to countenance German rearmament – in which he was at one with Monnet – made an ironical contrast, in the light of later Gaullist policy, with the bald statement by the Gaullist General Billotte that German rearmament was an obvious necessity, and General de Gaulle's own rhetorical question 'In the name of what could one prevent the West Germans from defending themselves?'[22] It may be noted that, by 1952, this Gaullist doctrine had been replaced by the much vaguer Europe-of-Nations concept, whose insistence on the maintenance of the sovereignty of nations squared much better with General de Gaulle's characteristic brand of nationalism. The change of policy coincided with de Gaulle's conclusion that the Soviet threat to western Europe had diminished. The 'European' convictions of the SFIO and MRP parties, however, remained largely unaffected by these new Gaullist considerations.

ECSC, then, in the eyes of its founders, was mainly to fulfil a political function. It was thus in line with earlier attempts to promote the political union of Europe – like the

European Movement created by the Hague Congress in May 1948 – and with the thinking behind the Council of Europe, founded later in 1948. But neither Bidault, who was prime minister at the time, nor the French Parliament, seemed initially particularly impressed by the ECSC project. Bidault, for one, was more interested in safeguarding his country's future through the strengthening of the ties with the United States, and Parliament took eighteen months to ratify the ECSC treaty, allowing itself to be diverted by the early debate on the European Defence Community (EDC) which coincided with that on the Schuman plan. Even so, given its far-reaching consequences, the time interval between the publication of the ECSC project and its implementation was relatively short. It was on 9 May 1950 that Schuman first told the French Council of Ministers of the project, announcing it later that day publicly at a press conference. The treaty,[23] which was to run for fifty years and which set up a High Authority (Haute Autorité) to control the coal and steel production of member states (France, West Germany, Italy, the Benelux countries), was signed on 18 April 1951, and the High Authority finally began to operate in Luxembourg in August 1952 under Jean Monnet.

Both within and outside the French Parliament – apart from expected Communist hostility – the main criticism of the ECSC had turned on the loss of sovereignty it entailed for France while Germany had as yet none to lose.[24] On the other hand, such popularity as it managed to achieve was largely based on the idealistic desire for some kind of United Europe which, in the determined absence of Great Britain, was then optimistically to be built on the foundation of Franco-German reconciliation. In fact, the change in the French concept of 'Europe' – from a union with a Franco-British foundation to one with a Franco-German foundation – was almost entirely due to Britain's increasing aloofness. In July 1946, even General de Gaulle, in a speech at Bar-le-Duc, had been looking forward to a powerful 'Europe' of which Britain would be a part,[25] but by 1950 he had begun to talk about Franco-German collaboration as the basis for a 'modern' Europe, in connection with which he was already harking back to the work of Charlemagne.[26] That the assumption of an enduring coal shortage, upon which some advocates of the ECSC treaty had built their case, turned within a decade into a preoccupation about what could be done with an actual surplus, only worried those whose prime concern was economic. Even if the surplus had been persuasively predicted, it would have left the majority of ECSC supporters, whose motives were political, quite unmoved.

(ii) The European Defence Community: Although the Communist takeover in Czechoslovakia in 1948 and the Berlin blockade of 1948–9 had provided the first occasions for serious, if more or less discreet, thinking among some of the western allies about the desirability of German rearmament, the lifting of the blockade in May 1949, like the creation of NATO a month earlier, had seemed to make the issue less urgent. Especially for the French, the most idealistic talk about European union had fallen very far short of the advocacy of German rearmament in any kind of context. Even during the National Assembly debates on NATO at the end of July 1949, the French government was to state categorically that German membership of the Atlantic Alliance was inconceivable: Germany was disarmed and was to stay that way.[27] The Petersberg agreements, signed by the western allies and the German Federal Republic in November 1949, contained an undertaking by Chancellor Adenauer to keep his country disarmed.

It was not until the outbreak of the war in Korea in June 1950 that the United States began openly to press for German rearmament. Churchill, it is true, had already spoken of the incorporation of German units within a European army in the House of Commons three months before the North Koreans invaded the South, but western governments had been most reticent to express such opinions in the open, if only for fear of French reactions. As late as the

end of July 1950 the French high commissioner was instructed to oppose the creation of a West German para-
military motorised police force,[28] which had been asked
for by Konrad Adenauer, the West German chancellor, as
some kind of answer to the East German government's
recently formed armed police units. Although the United
States at that time joined the French in their rejection of
Adenauer's request, it was barely a month later, at a meeting
of the foreign ministers of Britain, France and the United
States, as well as at the NATO ministerial council in
New York that immediately followed it, that the Americans
put forward their plan for the raising of twelve German divisions with a tactical air force. Robert Schuman, who
represented France, expressed astonishment at this apparent change of heart, and not least because the United
States had a measure of apparent British backing for their
proposal: even on arrival at New York Ernest Bevin, the
British foreign secretary, had still declared that German
rearmament was undesirable.[29] By the time of the NATO
ministerial council meeting, where the matter was discussed,
everyone's views had seemingly evolved enough for there
to be unanimous criticism of French objections to German
rearmament. Schuman did, however, obtain a respite, for
the final communiqué suggested that the implications of
German participation in European defence were to be further examined, and recognised that in West Germany itself
there was some reluctance to rearm. The French had therefore at least gained time.

It was at this stage that the French prime minister, René
Pleven, put forward an alternative plan for a German contribution to European defence. There was no doubt by that time
that the United States was determined to have some kind of
German rearmament and, as the British defence minister had
allegedly said to Jules Moch, his French colleague at the
New York meetings in September, future American aid
to Europe seemed to depend on the United States getting
their way on this.[30] Moreover, since the British foreign
minister, Ernest Bevin, had manifestly made up his mind

to keep in line with the Americans, and had thus abandoned his opposition to the rearming of West Germany, the French position had become untenably weak. Nor was this a good time for the French to put up a show of independence, because news of their armies in Indo-China was decidedly gloomy and indicated the need for further American assistance in that area. In these circumstances the French conceded the American demand, at the same time trying to limit its effect.

Pleven proposed a plan for German rearmament whose main features were the absence of undue haste and the absorption of the eventually constituted German military units within the framework of a European army, where their lack of autonomy would render them harmless to their allied neighbours. The French prime minister motivated his request that the process of German rearmament should not be rushed by the need to persuade his countrymen that it was indeed necessary, for the French were as hostile to it inside Parliament as outside.[31]

The Pleven Plan was interesting in that it initially tried to extend the ethos of the ECSC into the military sphere. When the prime minister presented the project to Parliament in October 1950, it was the European aspect he stressed. He said that 'the French government had hoped the implementation of the Coal and Steel Plan would accustom people to the idea of a European community before the most delicate question of a common defence system was raised. World events, however, allow no such respite. . . . The nations of Europe need to know that their collective security is assured, [and] the French government proposes to solve this question in the European spirit'.[32]

The Pleven plan amounted to the creation of a European Defence Community which would be headed by a European minister responsible to a European Assembly. The army of this community would be composed of units from member countries, each unit too small to warrant its having its own general staff; some thirteen thousand men for each national unit was later agreed. It would be the function of the European minister to obtain from member countries the units and equipment required. The prime minister added that no one, not even the Germans, wanted to run the risk of creating a purely national German army, and that his plan for an EDC made the best of a bad job.

The National Assembly was not impressed by Pleven's plan, except in so far as it could be construed as playing for time until, somehow, it would be found that the Germans did not have to be rearmed after all. Although it actually provided the prime minister with a face-saving majority at the end of the debate, the Assembly in fact only approved the government's declaration ' . . . [that] it would not permit the creation of a German army and high command'.[33] A public opinion poll taken in October 1950 seemed to confirm the country's hostility to the rearming of the Federal Republic: just over 50 per cent opposed German participation in a European army, about 29 per cent were for it, and 21 per cent abstained from expressing an opinion.[34]

That the Pleven Plan did not die there and then was due to German objections to what looked like its only viable alternative. At the beginning of 1951 France, Britain and the United States began talks with the West German government to explore the possibility of German participation in NATO; these talks had been proposed at the NATO meeting of deputy foreign ministers in London in September 1950 as a means of overcoming French fears (and those of others) about German rearmament without the delays which the Pleven Plan would entail. But, as the German government observed time and again, 'the German Federal government would sign no agreement that left a number of essential questions open: non-discrimination, which was connected with the formation of effective nationally homogeneous fighting units, German participation in the Supreme Command, and the raising of German contingents by German authorities. . . .'[35] Since at least the French violently objected to the rearming of Germany under purely German control, the possibility of solving the problem of Bonn's contribution to western defence through straight German membership of NATO failed. The parallel discussions, held in

Paris, to give substance to Pleven's plan for a European army within NATO, seemed, therefore, to provide a more hopeful solution. Since all member countries were expected to sink their national forces within a common army under a supranational commander, the Germans would not be discriminated against when that demand was made of them too.

Although talks about the Pleven Plan began in Paris in February 1951, only Belgium, Italy and Luxembourg joined the French and West Germans in their attempts to solve the problem of German rearmament within NATO on European lines. The Dutch did not take the plan seriously until October, while the British made it clear from the start that they were no more interested in a European army than they had previously been in the ECSC. On the other hand, General Eisenhower, then supreme commander of NATO forces, rallied to the Pleven Plan in the summer of 1951, and was followed by the American Administration in the middle of September. Thus, the French government seemed to have won its point that the only tolerable form of German rearmament was that which entailed the rigorous control of all German forces by at least the rest of the European powers of the ECSC.

However, by early 1952 the putative participants in the European army had watered down the supranational element to the degree where most of the important decisions had to be taken by a Council of Ministers of all the member countries who had, moreover, to be unanimous. This was one of the reasons which prompted the French National Assembly to express its dislike of the scheme, since by implication the Germans would have a veto as well. Members of the National Assembly also thought that the danger arising from German rearmament was too great so long as the national units could be as large as thirteen thousand men, particularly since the British and United States governments had given no guarantees of their continuing presence on the European continent.[36]

The qualms of the National Assembly did not, however, prevent the French government from joining the other two western occupying powers, in May 1952, in granting the

West Germans sovereignty over their country, although the actual implementation of that principle was to depend on the coming into force of the EDC treaty. Moreover, at the behest of the Socialists, the French government held up the signature of the contractual agreement restoring German sovereignty until the United States and Britain had provided France with a guarantee of assistance if the Germans broke their part of the agreement.

But until the ratification of the EDC treaty, German rearmament necessarily remained merely a topic for abstract debate. And as the debate went on, opposition to the ratification of the treaty grew in France. This was due to a number of reasons, many of which could ultimately be traced back to inherent French distrust of Germany. But an immediate major reason for a hardening in the French position was the increasing political importance of the nationalist supporters of General de Gaulle, for the internal political situation in France had compelled the Centre parties, around which most governments of the 1950s were formed, to seek support from the Right. At the same time, Georges Bidault had replaced Robert Schuman at the Quai d'Orsay and the new foreign minister had little of his predecessor's idealism about Europe. Moreover, although Bidault seemed to place his hopes for national military survival in the Atlantic alliance – which was not a doctrine uncritically shared by all Gaullists – the Gaullists were not slow to support his line that 'il faut faire l'Europe sans défaire la France'.[37] The nationalist element in Bidault's outlook found a rather more specific echo in Gaullist objections to the loss of control by the French government over at least that part of the armed forces that was to belong to the European army; for one thing, quite apart from the dishonour that was alleged to follow from a nation giving up responsibility for its army, it was thought intolerable that a 'victorious' nation like France should be treated in the same way as a defeated Germany, and that Britain should be allowed to remain aloof.[38]

The opponents of EDC were greatly helped by world events. Stalin died in March 1953, the Korean war ended in July

1953, and the argument was apparently given substance that a period of *détente* was imminent which would certainly be disturbed by German rearmament, a prospect that was a constant subject for Russian complaints. Besides, to the degree to which there was a *détente,* to that degree also was there less need for German rearmament. The sense of military urgency had therefore gone, and EDC looked like becoming largely an ideological and political issue. But for the United States, which bore the main burden of European security, a significant German contribution to NATO strength remained an important objective. In the face of growing French hostility to EDC, the United States secretary of state, Dulles, made his notorious remark at the end of 1953 that his country would have to engage in an 'agonising reappraisal' of its policy in Europe if EDC were not speedily brought into being. It was not, however, that kind of hectoring which was likely to convince a nationalist Frenchman of the error of his ways. What was more, the possibility that a deal could be done with the Soviet Union that would end the war in Indo-China was, by the beginning of 1954, a powerful reason for not alienating the Russians by rearming the Germans, although the counter-argument was to be heard that EDC could be used as a means of exerting pressure on the Russians to be more helpful over Indo-China. If the Russians failed to respond to either approach, the French could always use the prospect of their ratifying EDC as an inducement to the United States to provide more assistance in Indo-China. Many Frenchmen believed that all these calculations came out in favour of first testing Soviet intentions before again seriously contemplating German rearmament, especially since they felt quite certain that the United States – despite Dulles's blunt speaking – would not pull their troops out of Europe whether Paris ratified EDC or not.[39]

The fact that EDC also involved a loss of national sovereignty became a major argument against the project in 1954. The argument had, of course, been heard from the beginning – as it had been during the ECSC debates – but it was given more point by the painful reverses in Indo-China during 1954. The

Geneva talks (May/June 1954), which ended the war in Indo-China, poignantly reminded the French of their military humiliations which had led to these talks, at just the time when they were also being asked to give up responsibility altogether for a large part of their armies. The prospect, especially in those circumstances, was unbearable for many army leaders in particular, and Marshall Juin showed his disgust so openly that he fell out with his government over it.[40] Nor did one have to be an incorrigible Gaullist to feel that way: the Jacobin tradition within the French Socialist Party saw to it that the party was evenly split on the issue, although its 'European' inclinations were well known.[41]

However, as a result of continued and increasing pressure from her allies, France was forced to decide on EDC in 1954. Pierre Mendès-France, in his investiture speech for the premiership on 18 June 1954, called the EDC problem 'un des plus graves cas de conscience qui ait jamais troublé le pays'. His account[42] of the reaction of France's NATO partners to French delays over the ratification of the EDC treaty accurately described their exasperation, but seemed to have little effect on the National Assembly to which it was given:

> They are exasperated, as they kept telling me, by the way French policy has been conducted over the last few years. They have been saying that when they proposed German rearmament we preferred a European army, but that when they accepted the European army we wanted additional protocols inserted which, when also granted to us, made us go on to demand a number of preliminary guarantees. They said that now these conditions have been met we are asking for yet more and that, if still more is granted to us, some other French head of government would come to another conference in six months' time and ask for something else.

It is difficult to be certain whether it was distrust of Germany or the refusal to abandon control over French forces which was uppermost in the minds of the parliamentarians when, on 30 August 1954, they finally rejected EDC by 319 votes to 264. The fact that opponents of EDC were soon to join most of its supporters in acquiescing to the restoration of German sovereignty argues, at least, that distrust had become less paranoid. Moreover, the speed with which German rearmament was agreed after EDC had been rejected may be taken as a sign that it had been the supranational element which had been the supreme objection, since the NATO framework within which German contingents were soon to take their place retained the national identity of the constituent forces, without increasing the safeguards against future German misbehaviour over those already contained in the EDC project. On the other hand, there is no reason for assuming *a priori* that the considerations that had prevailed among parliamentarians when they rejected EDC were identical with those which later allowed them to accept German rearmament within NATO. The feeling that France's allies, who might still be needed, could not be permanently frustrated must have played an important part in their final acceptance of the NATO solution, particularly since there was a growing fear that the western allies might rearm Germany even without French cooperation. It is even conceivable that the EDC debate finally awoke some French politicians to the realisation that Germany was unlikely to remain disarmed forever, and that the chance must be taken to control German military growth while that was still possible. Then there was the fact that Mendès-France linked the second issue to a vote of confidence, after having refused to do this in the case of EDC; some members of the French Parliament may have been swayed by this, too. However, the opposition of the French Communist Party to German rearmament throughout the EDC debate can be accounted for in the simplest terms: it reflected Soviet opposition. As for public opinion, expressed in public opinion polls,[43] it may be said that it is unlikely to have played a significant part in the parliamentary vote, since the European-minded third of the samples which supported EDC was matched by another third that disliked it, while an equal number was undecided. All sections of the country were too evenly divided for any one part to be able successfully to influence the decision of the others.

The international consequences of the French rejection of EDC were shortlived. The Germans, having been told by their chancellor, Adenauer, that only their enemies in France opposed EDC, were naturally taken aback by the size of the opposition. The United States secretary of state, Dulles, growled that Mendès-France had betrayed him. But neither the Germans nor the Americans had long to wait before the French government repaired most of the damage. And the argument of some of the opponents of EDC, that its rejection would cause the Soviet Union to adopt a more flexible position both on disarmament and on the reunification of Germany, was quickly disproved by events.

If the rapidity with which the problem of German rearmament was solved after the French rejection of EDC suggests that it was fear of the loss of sovereignty rather than fear of Germany which had been responsible for French hostility to the European army in 1954, there is no logical reason to conclude from this, as did Raymond Aron,[44] that the negative vote of the National Assembly finally signified the French abandonment of the idea of a federal Europe. The army – particularly in France, and particularly after its fate in 1940 – occupies a special place in the range of values of a nation, and cannot therefore be taken as a fair index to the nation's feelings on other matters. The fact that within two years after the rejection of EDC the Common Market had been largely negotiated shows the unwisdom of drawing general conclusions from one particularly highly charged sample. Jules Moch, a former Socialist defence minister hostile to the EDC project, also assumed that it was the supranationality of EDC rather than the wish to avoid German rearmament that finally defeated EDC:

The anti-EDC majority was an accidental and ephemeral coalition. If the vote had taken place on the question of German rearmament rather than on EDC the majority would have become a minority. It would have lost most of its sixty-seven Gaullists, a large number of the sixteen dissident Gaullists, and members of the 'classical' Right who were opposed to EDC not because it would rearm the Germans but 'denationalise' our army. Among these one hundred and eleven deputies one would easily have found the twenty-eight votes that would have transformed the [anti-EDC] majority into a minority.[45]

If this analysis is correct, French attitudes to Germany had changed a great deal since 1945. No doubt, France's economic renascence and her comforting links with the NATO powers had helped to give her enough confidence for a saner assessment of the danger the Federal Republic presented to her in the 1950s.

Within two days of the anti-EDC vote in the French National Assembly, the British government invited the United States and the six countries that were to have formed the EDC to a conference in London; the Canadians, at their own request, were also to come. Churchill, prime minister at the time, and his foreign secretary, Eden, were plainly looking for a way of salvaging something from the EDC debacle. In mid-September Eden arrived in Paris, after a series of discussions with the other governments that were about to be represented at the London Conference from 28 September. The talks between Eden and Mendès-France showed that the French had not entirely shed their dislike of German rearmament. In this dislike they were joined, as Eden had discovered, by the Benelux countries. Also, the Soviet Union kept up a barrage of messages and warnings to Paris, which ranged from promises of instant help against Germany, via assurances that it was really Germany that was France's enemy, to the threat that the Franco-Russian treaty of 1944 might not stand the strains of a French endorsement of German rearmament. But it took Mendès-France less than twenty-four hours to accept Eden's plan for the German Federal Republic's entry into NATO. Three major factors had led to that acceptance. First, the prospect of British and United States participation in the plan was thought to make the French less vulnerable to German pressures than they would have been inside EDC. Second, such loss of sovereignty as was entailed was allegedly shared by all. Third, it was generally taken for granted that Germany would at that stage have been rearmed by the Americans even without French consent. In the circumstances, Mendès-France had probably obtained the best possible terms.

The Eden Plan consisted in a renewal of the 1952 Bonn agreement – conditionally restoring German sovereignty – whose implementation was to have coincided with the coming into force of EDC. The restoration of German sovereignty was now to be part of a package deal involving German (and Italian) membership of NATO within the suitably amended 1948 Brussels pact.* Initially directed also against a future threat from Germany, the Brussels Pact was now to include West Germany, which was to contribute forces similar in size to those earlier expected from her for EDC. A central agency was to excercise control over all the allied armed forces on the continent, including those of Germany. The provision for control made for the equality of status of all allied forces, but it also ensured that British as well as French forces overseas – in Algeria for example – would remain under the command of their national governments. The provision for control also constituted a compromise acceptable to the Germans, whose demand for parity of status for their forces was thus not too obviously flouted. In addition the Eden Plan precluded Germany's acquisition of certain kinds of arms, especially of nuclear weapons. Two further points in favour of France's acceptance of the Eden Plan were, first, the United States' explicit assurance that they would retain a sizeable stake in the defence of Europe, and, second, the British promise to keep at least four divisions and parts of the Royal Air Force on the continent of Europe, except in cases of the gravest emergency in other parts of the world.

A new element was introduced into Franco-German relations when the French accepted the part of the Eden proposals which suggested that German reunification was one of the fundamental objectives of the western allies. Even though the French added that the Germans should undertake to

---

* See below, p. 124.

bring about reunification, or a revision of borders, only by peaceful means, the theoretical acceptance of the principle of German reunification indicated a clear break with the insistent French postwar demand that Germany must remain divided and weak, a break which the creation of the Federal Republic had made less clearly. West Germany's acceptance of these terms was to lead the western allies to treat the Bonn government as the true representative of the whole of Germany, East as well as West.

With all these points agreed in principle at the London Conference, the participating countries decided to meet again in Paris on 20 October 1954, to draw up precise plans for their implementation. Before then, however, there was a debate in the National Assembly on the results of the London meeting. Lasting from 7 to 12 October, the debate was instructive not least for the light it shed on foreign policy decision-making. For reasons which had little to do with the merits of the case as a foreign policy issue, the SFIO and the MRP adopted attitudes to the London agreements which, theoretically, should have been surprising. The SFIO had been split over EDC because at least half of its deputies seemed conscience-stricken about rearming Germany or about the loss of French sovereignty it entailed. But the party was anxious to regain its unity, and on balance it preferred to do this by uniting behind Mendès-France and the Atlantic alliance rather than by opposing both. Even if it is true, that, 'pour garder la solidarité atlantique, M. Moch se déclare . . . prêt à commettre même quelque chose qu'il considère comme une erreur', the main motive for the SFIO's vote in favour of the Eden proposals was its desire to regain party unity,[46] otherwise the call for Atlantic solidarity would at that stage have been just as ineffective as it had been during the EDC vote in August. On the other hand, it was the MRP's dislike of Mendès-France which seemed to dictate the way it voted on the issue of German rearmament. Because Mendès-France had been thought lukewarm on EDC they had not minded voting for it – which accorded with their European outlook. But because he was actively advocating the acceptance of the Eden proposals they refused to support them in spite of their European outlook. The reason for their dislike of the prime minister is also illuminating, because it too had nothing to do with the merits of any political issue. According to the well authenticated story,[47] the MRP had been upset because their leader, Bidault, had been prevented from obtaining the credit for making peace in Indo-China; the Laniel government to which he belonged had fallen before he could do so. Mendès-France, following him, was to succeed where Bidault had failed, and for this the MRP seemed unable to forgive him. No doubt too much should not be made of the role of single issues in the determination of policy, but there is little doubt that in this case these personal issues loomed larger than actual foreign policy considerations.

Mendès-France finally obtained his confidence vote on the London agreements after a five-day debate that ended on 12 October 1954. Most of the 113 votes against the prime minister came from the Communists – they had 101 seats – with some Gaullists providing the remainder. The MRP made up most of the large number of abstentions (152). Apart from the argument, used by the MRP in particular, that the London agreements provided for too little European integration, the most striking element of the debate was the constantly recurring theme that renewed talks with the Soviet Union were desirable so that German rearmament might at least be kept within narrow limits. Nevertheless, on the day following the Assembly's vote for him, the prime minister was received by General de Gaulle, a fact widely interpreted as signifying the general's endorsement of the London agreements.

A week later the Paris Conference began. Its first discussions involved only the three western occupying powers and the German Federal Republic, who had to settle the problems resulting from the ending of the occupation statute. These powers were then joined by the other countries EDC had been meant to bring together. They modified the Brussels Treaty, admitting to it Federal Germany and Italy, and institutionalised its arrangements in the new Western European Union (WEU). There was then a meeting of the fourteen

NATO countries, whose main purpose was to authorise the admission of the Federal Republic into the organisation within the WEU framework, leaving it to the NATO commander to integrate WEU forces as far as was compatible with military efficiency. In fact, when the countries taking part in the Paris meetings signed their agreements on 23 October 1954, they did little more than endorse the implications of the London Conference.[48] The most important consequence of the Paris agreements was that Germany could be rearmed but that, unlike the forces of her major former enemies, her entire army would be under international control.

A significant concession made by the French to Chancellor Adenauer, to induce him to accept the frankly unequal status for the German army within NATO, concerned the Saar. At La Celle-St Cloud, on the eve of the Paris meetings, as well as in the margin of the meetings themselves, Mendès-France and Adenauer had engaged in the toughest bargaining to determine to what degree, if any, the French could maintain their control over the Saar. The German chancellor records that he had secured enough political support at home to enable him to refuse his signature to the Paris agreements if the Saar were not at some stage to be given the opportunity of opting for a return to Germany.[49] It was after midnight, early on the day the Paris agreements were to be signed, that the two heads of government finally reached a compromise which gave the Germans substantially what they wanted. Article VIIc of the jointly elaborated project for a European status for the Saar provided Adenauer with the basis for his success. The article said that there was to be a referendum in the Saar on the future status of the territory – pending a peace conference – and that this should be followed within three months by elections for the local legislature. Adenauer hoped that this was 'the great chance for the return of the Saar to Germany',[50] for he anticipated that the Saar would first reject the new European status proposed by the French and then confirm, in the legislative elections, its attachment to Germany. France would not, he thought, feel able to ignore Saar feeling expressed with such force, especially since he expected Anglo-American pressure to be exercised in accordance with the principle of the self-determination of peoples. The German chancellor therefore signed the Paris agreements along with the rest of the members of the new alliance. Adenauer's calculations were vindicated when the political union of the Saar with the Federal Republic was finally completed on 1 January 1957.

There was intense diplomatic and internal political activity in France between the signature of the Paris agreements and the ratification debate in the National Assembly, for it was not at all a foregone conclusion that Parliament would feel any happier about the Paris agreements than it had done about EDC. In the diplomatic sphere, the Soviet Union showed that it was particularly anxious to impress upon the French the undesirability of rearming Germany, in the hope that the National Assembly could be induced to give the same verdict on this occasion as it had done on EDC. In answer to another Soviet initiative, Mendès-France firmly declared at the United Nations* that he would accept no proposal for a European conference before the Paris agreements were ratified, though he would consider a four-power conference in the spring of 1955. Early in December 1954 the Soviet Union increased its pressure by stating that the Paris agreements were contrary to the spirit of the Franco-Soviet treaty, and a week later actually went so far as to declare that French ratification of the agreements would mean the end of the Franco-Soviet treaty.

At the same time, inside France, the MRP kept up its anti-Mendès-France vendetta by stressing the alleged dangers of German rearmament within the provisions of the Paris agreements: the same spirit was shortly to cause it to vote against the first parts of the 1955 budget. At the same time the PCF (Parti Communiste Français) systematically voted against everything proposed by the government, though for reasons of foreign policy principles which assumed that what is bad for the Soviet Union is bad policy. On the other hand, the 'European'

* See below, p. 259 (note 49).

65

members of the SFIO and Radical Parties, though disappointed by Mendès-France's failure over EDC, seemed prepared to back him at this stage, while the anti-EDC Socialists and Gaullists also appeared satisfied with the Paris agreements. But when it finally came to the ratification vote just before Christmas 1954, the National Assembly decided to reject the Paris agreements by 280 votes to 259. Nearly all the MRP had either voted against the government or abstained, thereby joining the PCF and some Socialists and Gaullists.

The rejection by the National Assembly of the Paris agreements aroused a degree of consternation inside France and abroad that had not been reached even after the failure of EDC;[51] the failure of EDC had, after all, been openly predicted by many shrewd observers. Moreover, the adverse National Assembly vote not merely seriously called into question the authority of Mendès-France but it also threatened to undermine whatever confidence France's allies had left in her as a worthwhile partner. It was because the French prime minister was aware of both these facts that he at once sought ways to reverse Parliament's decision. In less than a week he had found a procedural device which allowed deputies to revise their earlier vote. After some deep heartsearching, that is what they did. Though a large number of MRP members voted against Mendès-France even when given their second opportunity, their leader, Robert Schuman, this time voted for the government. The fact that the prime minister had tied the second vote to one of confidence is less likely to explain the government's majority of 287 against 256 than fear of the reaction of France's allies to yet another rejection.[52]

The Paris agreements finally came into force on 5 May 1955, setting up the WEU and admitting Germany and Italy into NATO. Two days later, the Soviet Union ostentatiously denounced the Franco-Soviet treaty by way of reprisal, though its practical value to France had been miminal since its signature. A week later the Soviet bloc created the Warsaw Pact as a reply to WEU. However, despite this show of displeasure, at the end of May the USSR accepted a French proposal for a four-power conference. It was to be held in

Geneva in the latter half of July. The French vote on WEU had thus succeeded in promoting West German integration into Europe without, after all, causing a serious break in relations with the Russians.

The so-called thaw in the Soviet Union and its satellites that had followed the death of Stalin, particularly after the 20th Congress of the Russian Communist Party in February 1956, also had its implications for Franco-German relations. In particular, it promoted greater clarity in France's public attitude towards German reunification than was contained in the London agreements. Although since the end of the war re-unification had been one of the avowed aims of all the occupying powers, including the Soviet Union, the French had always been at best only reluctant supporters of it. After all, it had never been a secret that a divided Germany was likely to present the French with fewer problems than a unified one. But since all Germany's conquerors had soon after the war begun to vie with each other for German support on their side of the east-west cold war, they all used the emotive bait of reunification to woo the former enemy. How much either the Russians or the western allies were interested in German reunification as a valid and desirable aim in its own right is difficult to discover in all the propaganda on the subject from both sides. What is certain is that neither side was prepared to concede unification unless it could be sure of controlling the whole of Germany after it had been granted.[53] But the 'thaw' in Russia coincided with what looked like a new Soviet approach to reunification. Khrushchev showed little interest in it, preferring to consolidate the East German regime's place within the Soviet bloc, and giving priority to east-west relations as a whole rather than to the then obviously pointless wooing of the Federal Republic. However, as Soviet policy on German reunification became more negative, French policy on it became more positive. This was almost certainly because the French knew that Germany could never become united without Russian consent, and that they therefore ran no real risk in advocating reunification at that stage. The political dividends for the French, in terms of German good will, which might be derived from the championing of reunification therefore involved no compensating risk.

(iii) The creation of EEC and Euratom: In mid-November 1954, Jean Monnet announced that he wanted to leave ECSC to devote himself entirely to the cause of European integration. EDC had recently been rejected by the French Parliament, and the prospects for a United Europe looked bleak. The Council of Europe seemed to have become an ineffectual talking shop, ECSC stood out as an isolated experiment without likely emulators, and the plans for WEU scarcely had more than military significance; in any case, the Paris agreements had appalled him, if only because they gave Germany an army. It was economic and political integration that Monnet wanted to promote. In May 1955 the foreign ministers of the Benelux countries, who were anxious to retain Monnet for ECSC, suggested to their three colleagues in the organisation that they should seek further ways towards European integration in the economic sphere and through cooperation in non-military atomic research. The Benelux suggestion actually led Monnet to offer to remain at ECSC headquarters, but the French government at that time no longer wanted him there. This was because the Gaullists in the Paris cabinet disliked Monnet too much not to take this opportunity to get rid of him, even though they actually went a long way with the Benelux suggestions that Monnet himself had largely inspired, and despite the fact that René Mayer, with whom they wanted to replace him, was an admirer of Monnet. At the beginning of June 1955, representatives of the ECSC countries met at Messina, officially to choose the new head for ECSC.

The Messina Conference turned out to be the starting point of the European Economic Community or Common Market. But, as with ECSC, it must be noted that although the EEC project had obvious economic significance, it was its political implications that most exercised the men who proposed it. Most of these men had been inspired by Monnet, and it was they who drafted the plans and schemed for the implementation of the plans by the politicians. As Monnet put it: 'L'unité de l'Europe n'est pas seulement, n'est même pas d'abord, une question économique. Elle est la condition même de notre sécurité et de notre liberté individuelle'.[54] Given Monnet's reaction to the Paris agreements, there can be no doubt that he was thinking at least as much of Germany as of the Soviet Union when he spoke of security. This was also true of men like Pierre Uri, one of Monnet's collabora- tors, who saw himself as the originator of the Common Mar- ket.[55] It is interesting that at this stage of the planning for the Common Market the 'technocrats' around Monnet thought themselves as unaffected by the attitudes and theories of politicians as they allegedly had been at the time of the Coal and Steel Community project. What was more, they con- sidered that the orthodox civil servants were as unimagina- tive and ineffectual as the politicans when it came to promoting new ideas. Uri blamed the failure of EDC on the fact that rou- tine civil servants had handled the problems associated with it.[56]

The Messina Conference, apart from confirming René Mayer as successor to Monnet at ECSC, was presented by Pierre Uri with specific plans for the creation of an eco- nomic union for the countries participating in ECSC, as well as for an organisation within which these countries could cooperate in the atomic field. The delegates agreed that France, which had taken the political initiative in launching ECSC, should not be called upon to do so again in this case. They finally entrusted the Belgian Paul-Henri Spaak with that task. And since the Germans were reluctant to treat the Euratom project for atomic cooperation as a separate problem, it was decided to propose EEC and Euratom simultaneously to the governments of western Europe. In October, Jean Monnet announced that he was about to launch his Action Committee for a United Europe, and for this he soon had the open sup- port of the German Socialist opposition as well as that of the leader of the French Socialist Party, Guy Mollet. For what it was worth, at the WEU meeting in Paris at the end of 1955, the United States secretary of state Dulles also gave his sup- port for the new steps towards European integration.

At the crucial time in the early part of 1956, when they had to make up their minds about EEC and Euratom, the general elections of January 1956 provided the French with a pro-European parliamentary majority, and Guy Mollet became prime minister. The fact that Mendès-France, who was for a few months a member of that government, was against the new steps towards a united Europe did Mollet and his pro-Europeans no more harm than the few Gaullists the elections had left in prominent positions. As the 'European' debate became more intense, reaching its climax with the National Assembly debate in January 1957, it was interesting to see in which terms the different political and economic interest groups defended their several positions.

Broadly speaking, there were six points which tended to re-cur, singly or in various combinations, among the active supporters of EEC and Euratom, though some of these points were mutually exclusive and were not necessarily made by the same people. These were (1) that the newly proposed organisations provided additional ways of integrating Germany into Europe; (2) that integration was not merely justifiable in terms of future security but also as an end in itself; (3) that France needed larger markets for her expanding industries and that a European Common Market provided the right outlets and incentives for greater expansion and prosperity; (4) that greater European integration was capable of producing a powerful political unit that could enable Europe to talk to the Soviet Union and the United States on equal terms; (5) that France ought to seek the leadership of such a united Europe; (6) that the basic debate about whether Europe should become a supranational entity or simply some kind of confederation of sovereign states need not delay the implementation of the plans for EEC and Euratom.

In February 1955 Adenauer had been correctly informed by his Foreign Ministry that, in France, 'if one disregards the Communists and a tiny nationalist group, there is quite clearly general agreement that the free European nations must work closely together. But while some wish immediately to establish a supranational government within the framework of a single state or a federal state, others wish to bring about that collaboration without the loss of national sovereignty'.[57] The failure of EDC and the ineffectiveness of the Council of Europe were, in the same document, explained in terms of that split in French opinion. The stability of French public opinion about European union as a general concept, and of the majority wish for it, was shown in *Sondages*,[58] which early in 1955 reported that 64 per cent were in favour of such a union as compared with 61 per cent in 1947. On the other hand, *Sondages* noted that during the period from the final EDC debate to the signing of the treaty of Rome in 1957 which instituted EEC, there was no great desire in France for a supranational Europe; in the absence of Great Britain from such a union, and given the continued distrust of Germany, the Frenchman-in-the-street preferred to make do with economic cooperation.

Sondages did however also bring out that the desire for European union increased with educational attainment. This may explain why Parliament had a somewhat higher number of supporters for European union than the national average. Here the rational grounds for union were of greater significance than the emotional arguments against it. For example, MRP politicians, when they were not convinced Europeans on idealistic grounds like Robert Schuman, supported the EEC project for very practical reasons. Much of their political support came from rural areas, which stood to gain considerably from an agricultural Common Market, while their Catholic trade union (CFTC) expected concrete economic benefits from EEC. The economic argument – particularly how EEC would stimulate economic growth in Europe and thus enable the old continent to stand up to increasing competition from the Soviet and United States economies – was frequently used by other parties too. Certainly the SFIO leaders used it, and it helped them to get their members' firm support for EEC.

The British refusal to join was widely deplored by most EEC supporters, although their interpretation of that refusal varied widely. Socialist speakers during the crucial

National Assembly debates in January 1957[59] reassuringly cited Britain's membership of WEU as a sign of her growing interest in Europe. But Britain's aloofness was used by some as a reason for condemning the entire project. For example, as a member of the Radical minority that was against EEC, Mendès-France used the absence of British interest in the Messina decisions to make some of the points even pro-EEC politicians took seriously. Britain, he said, would be needed in the proposed community as a counterweight to Germany at both the political and the economic levels. French commitments in Algeria, as Edgard Pisani was to state in support of Mendès-France in the Senate, were crippling France's diplomatic standing and economic potential, as a result of which the German Federal Republic would be able to exercise undue influence in the proposed organisations. Against this, Maurice Faure maintained that Britain retained an insular mentality, and the opportunity of making Europe into a viable economic unit, capable of competing with the United States and the Soviet Union, should not be lost on that account. Moreover, far from being an impossible challenge for France in her current difficulties, the Common Market would help her to emerge from these difficulties more quickly. The alternative suggestion, to create a European free trade area, which was said to be acceptable to the British, was rejected by Faure and most supporters of EEC as inadequate; they wanted common economic planning as a minimum aim, and thought they could cope with the Federal Republic.

The Gaullists, for their part, were no longer a cohesive parliamentary force after the 1956 elections. And on 'Europe' they were split, some quite intransigent in their nationalism, others hoping that the benefits to France could not only be economic but also political, in the sense that France would emerge as the leader of a European coalition of nation states, particularly if she had German support. Already in 1950, de Gaulle had said in a press conference that the vision of what Germany and France might achieve together could be very dazzling indeed: 'it would mean that, in a modern context, i.e. economic, social, strategic, cultural, Charlemagne's design would be brought to fruition.'[60] As Bjøl rightly put it,[61] de Gaulle had for a long time looked upon the creation of 'Europe' as an extension of the interests of France. Although he was always rather imprecise in the accounts he gave of the limits of 'Europe', Germany and France were for him, at least after 1950, always the centre of such a grouping of nations.

Euratom, being negotiated at the same time as EEC, provided arguments that often had a bearing on attitudes being adopted towards the Common Market too.[62] The Communist Party condemned both, on the Gaullist grounds that they involved a major abdication of French sovereignty. More specifically, and predictably, the PCF alleged that Euratom would furnish the new Wehrmacht with atomic weapons, while EEC would bring about large-scale imports of Volkswagen which would spell ruin for the French car industry. But there were others for whom Euratom was almost more important than EEC. Thus Guy Mollet, his disgust still fresh at President Eisenhower's interference with Franco-British action in the Suez Canal area in 1956, wanted to speed up the French atomic weapons programme that had been approved by the Mendès-France administration in 1954. Euratom was, for Mollet, a way of encouraging Europe's independence in the nuclear field, a necessary step in the creation of 'Europe', and a major hope for future European energy supplies, the need for which was stressed by the closure of the Suez Canal in 1956. How often, he asked rhetorically in the National Assembly debate in January 1957, 'when faced by the United States – either too impulsive or too slow in recognising a dangerous situation – or the Soviet Union, giving cause for disquiet and sometimes still threatening, how often in such circumstances have we wished for the existence of a united Europe that was a world power, not neutral but independent'.[63] That the Suez adventure had made the French more anxious to bring about a united Europe was emphasised by Alain Savary, the *rapporteur* of the National Assembly's Foreign Affairs Committee for EEC, in the ratification debate in July 1957. 'It is beyond doubt that the Suez affair has made the creation of Europe more urgent and necessary for public opinion', he said.[64] It was clear, however, that without a European nuclear industry, military independence from the United States was a fantasy. For many Gaullists who had reservations about EEC, Euratom – which they tended to see as a potentially militarily useful organisation – was the sweetening of the pill.[65]

The National Assembly had two votes on the Messina projects. The first, at the end of the debate in January 1957, produced a majority for the projects of 332 against 207. The second, in July, after the ratification debate on the final version of the EEC and Euratom treaty (signed in Rome on 25 March 1957), provided a majority of 342 against 239. The lower majority at the second vote is largely explained by a change of mind among the Gaullists, who were worried by the supranational implications of 'Monnet's Europe'.

The main provisions of the Rome treaty, with its 248 articles and several appendices, included the elimination between member countries of customs dues and quotas, the creation of a common tariff structure in relation to third parties, the free circulation between member countries of persons, services, and capital, a common agricultural policy, and the coordination of economic policies. Despite Gaullist restiveness, the supranational character of EEC and Euratom was in fact less pronounced than that of ECSC. Nor did Mendès-France's fear of a bureaucratically controlled Europe turn out to be justified. Although there was to be a European Commission in Brussels to provide the administration for EEC, and certain powers of initiation and decision had been given to that Commission, it was the representatives of the member countries who were to be in real control. Moreover, each country had in practice a veto on all decisions. The fact that the powers of the Brussels Commission were eventually to be increased, and that on certain important issues national vetoes were at some stage to be capable of being overridden by qualified majority votes, was in 1956 too remote to provide widely persuasive arguments for those who claimed to discern the seeds of a supranational dictatorship in the new organisation.

FRANCE, GERMANY AND 'EUROPE'

For the French the Common Market did not have an easy start. Even before the treaty was finally signed, the demands of the Algerian war and the aftermath of Suez had brought such pressures on the franc that the Paris government had felt compelled to suspend its convertibility. By the beginning of 1958 France's gold and foreign currency reserves had practically disappeared, despite the imposition of import restrictions. It was therefore not a good time for France to have to face the competitive demands of the Common Market.

The political upheavals in the spring and summer of 1958 worsened France's situation, to the point where her very survival as an organised society was called into question. The army and settler revolt in Algeria, which had begun on 13 May 1958, inflicted such damage on the fabric of the French state that it not merely brought down the country's legally appointed government and the legally established political institutions of the Fourth Republic, but it also made it quite impossible for several years to predict what kind of state would eventually emerge when relative stability returned.

It was left to General de Gaulle, whom the army and the Algerian settlers recalled to power in 1958, to lead the French back into some kind of order in his Fifth Republic. That he maintained France's place in EEC was an early indication that he had no intention of allowing his country to return to its inward-looking, protectionist past, and that his postwar visions of a 'European' future for Franch had not been abandoned.

1958–69: FRANCO-GERMAN RELATIONS UNDER DE GAULLE

Under General de Gaulle's presidency of the Fifth Republic there were three distinct periods in Franco-German relations. First, the Adenauer era, which lasted until the German Chancellor's retirement in 1963. Second, the Erhard and early Kiesinger period, which may be said to have ended with the crisis of the franc in 1968. Third, the brief months from the end of 1968 to de Gaulle's resignation in 1969. When these three periods are examined it will become clear that their differences are largely determined by changes in the way the Federal Republic saw its role in Europe, rather than by French designs.

(i) 1958–63: The Adenauer era: Adenauer welcomed General de Gaulle's accession to power. The Fourth Republic had increasingly filled him with dismay because its weaknesses had prevented it from being an effective promoter of European union. But the German chancellor had no illusions about de Gaulle's internationalist fervour. He hoped, however, that the general would accept some form of European integration, at least for reasons of French national self-interest. He applauded the inclusion of 'Europeans' like Mollet, Pinay, and Pflimlin in de Gaulle's first government, and even more the appointment of Couve de Murville as foreign minister. Maurice Couve de Murville had been French ambassador in Bonn until he went to the Quai d'Orsay as minister, and Adenauer thought highly of him:

> [He] had been an excellent Ambassador who was well acquainted with conditions in the Federal Republic and had sought to promote close Franco-German collaboration. . . . He had participated in the conclusion of the European treaties with understanding, energy, and success. . . . [He] was a friend of Germany.[66]

Furthermore, Adenauer quotes with great approval Couve de Murville's early policy statement (25 June 1958), according to which three factors would continue to dominate French foreign policy: France's geographical position as a part of western Europe; her membership of the Atlantic community; and her responsibilities in Africa.[67] The German chancellor clearly hoped for much from the first of these three factors, especially since Pinay had assured him that de Gaulle accepted the treaty of Rome despite his preference for pragmatically evolved institutions over drawing-board bureaucracies like the Brussels Commission.

From September 1958 to September 1963 Franco-German relations were a function of the understanding Adenauer and de Gaulle succeeded in establishing between themselves.

Until Adenauer's first visit to Colombey-les-deux-Eglises on 14 September 1958, the two men had never met. The German chancellor made the journey with mixed feelings. He felt that de Gaulle's general outlook would be very different from his.[68] On the other hand, there was some evidence that de Gaulle had for some time had a favourable view of him;[69] for one thing Adenauer was not enamoured of the British, and not a little distrustful of the durability of United States protection. It therefore seemed as if there was a basis for cooperation between the two. Furthermore, Adenauer, as a man from the Rhineland, had opted for the love rather than the hate relationship with France, one or the other extreme apparently forcing itself upon Germans living in close proximity to the French. The Federal Republic under Adenauer consequently presented de Gaulle with interesting possibilities. Increasingly strong industrially and economically, the Bonn Republic was nevertheless still an easy and vulnerable target in international politics. What de Gaulle could offer was a kind of protection against some of the consequences of the Federal Republic's international weaknesses, in the hope that he would gain in return a measure of influence over Bonn policies. Unlikely though this bargain looked to many observers even in 1958, it became the working hypothesis of Gaullist thinking about Franco-German affairs. During the Adenauer era it often looked as if it might indeed work.

The Soviet Union in particular made much use of Bonn for all kinds of diplomatic target practice, and it was for that reason that de Gaulle soon tried to assume the role of Bonn's protector against the east. In talks between him and Adenauer at Bad Kreuznach in November 1958 – de Gaulle was returning the chancellor's visit – the Federal Republic's problems with the east received a great deal of attention. West Berlin, Adenauer and de Gaulle concluded, was to remain firmly outside the control of the German Democratic Republic. Moreover, it was pledged that France would not recognise the Pankow government, a Gaullist concession to that curious Bonn neurosis which led to the somewhat hysterical assumption that if anyone gave diplomatic recognition to the German Democratic Republic the world would come to an end. It soon also emerged that France was to protect Federal German interests in her own dealings with the Soviet Union. In practice, this meant principally that the Paris government undertook to encourage Moscow to agree to German reunification. It was not lost on anyone that French arguments in Moscow on reunification, even if seriously put forward, could only be persuasive if West Germany could be shown to be absolutely harmless to her eastern neighbours. Bonn's involvement with NATO was no recommendation at all, but it was just possible that its links with France might eventually do the trick. If it were under benign French influence, the Federal Republic could be acceptable to the east. Similar arguments, based on meekness, effectively dissuaded the Federal Republic from contemplating the acquisition of nuclear arms in contravention of the 1954 treaty, at least while its desire for reunification remained. After all, no Russian government was likely to accept German reunification as well as German atomic weapons. And what Frenchman could? Finally, de Gaulle tried to allay latent German fears that the French might do a deal with the Soviet Union at Germany's expense.

The lack of realism about these Gaullist objectives did not perhaps become widely apparent until after Adenauer's departure from active politics in 1963. But there is no evidence to suggest that Adenauer himself saw France as a valid replacement of the United States in the defence of German interests. Echoes of the joint Adenauer-de Gaulle communiqué issued after the first Colombey meetings in 1958, according to which cooperation between France and the Federal Republic would strengthen the Atlantic alliance, can be found in many utterances by the German chancellor during the succeeding five years. Perhaps Professor Grosser[70] was right in thinking that there was a tacit agreement between Adenauer and de Gaulle according to which Adenauer would help the French president in the assertion of European claims vis-à-vis the United States within NATO, while de Gaulle would support Adenauer's case with the Soviet Union. But it is difficult to believe that the German chancellor could ever have supposed that the French were able alone to protect his country against a possible onslaught from the east, or that he would in any case have wanted that kind of dependence for the Federal Republic.

Moreover there was one important part of German policy in eastern Europe which de Gaulle explicitly and publicly disavowed. This related to the Oder-Neisse line. Since the war, it had been the firm policy of the western allies and, later, of the Federal Republic, that the eastern frontiers of Germany could not be settled before the final peace conference. Because the question was of obvious importance at least to Poland, which had come out of the war with frontiers that were deep inside prewar Germany, the Soviet Union and her allies had long pressed for German recognition of the present *de facto* border along the Oder-Neisse line. Of all the members of the Atlantic alliance, only General de Gaulle had seen fit to break the western habit of refusing such recognition before an agreed peace treaty had been signed. At his press conference of 25 March 1959 he linked the German acceptance of the Oder-Neisse line with the possibility of German reunification. He said:

> The reunification of the two parts of Germany into a single Germany that would be entirely free seems to us the aim and objective, the obvious destiny of the German people, so long as it does not call into doubt its present frontiers in the north, south, east and west.[71]

Although the statement was made slightly more palatable for the Germans by the reference to reunification, de Gaulle's recognition of the Oder-Neisse line can be traced back to his talks with Stalin in 1944.[72] If Adenauer consoled himself with the thought that the French president thus paid the minimum price for being persona grata with Communist leaders, and thereby made reunification a little more likely, he did not admit it in public. He was, like John Foster Dulles, completely inflexible when it came to dealing with the eastern bloc.

Nevertheless, the understanding between the German chancellor and de Gaulle was very real. The solidity of the foundation of that understanding may be judged from Adenauer's account of how de Gaulle assessed the place of Germany and

France in Europe. To begin with de Gaulle had noted that:

> The French people has no illusions about the benevolence and good will of other people towards it. This is particularly true so far as the Soviet Union is concerned, although it has not written off the Soviet Union completely. Nor has it any illusions about the United States's good will, competence and skilfulness. The Americans will remain Americans. I am not bothering to speak about England, which is a secondary problem and remains an island.[73]

Not only did Adenauer entirely share de Gaulle's scepticism about the good will of other countries, but he also agreed that, in reply, France and Germany must form the basis of a Europe that could stand on its own feet: Adenauer had said as much to de Gaulle in his own analysis of the world situation early in the talks at Colombey in September 1958.[74] And it seems that Adenauer accepted France's moral leadership in such an *entente*.

In concrete politics, Franco-German relations between 1958 and 1963 worked out almost entirely to de Gaulle's satisfaction. It would not even be an exaggeration to say that the president of the Fifth Republic treated his German counterpart somewhat shabbily from the very beginning. If one looks at something as basic to the Franco-German *entente* as its attitude to the United States within the Atlantic alliance, it must have been quite a shock to the German chancellor to discover that de Gaulle, without even a courteous warning to Bonn, had suggested that NATO should be ruled by a triumvirate that was to include France with the United States and Britain, but which excluded the Federal Republic. De Gaulle had addressed this proposal to President Eisenhower within less than two weeks of his Colombey meetings with Adenauer, and all the emotional Carolingian rhetoric that had gone with it. According to André Fontaine,[75] Adenauer sent de Gaulle a letter pointing out the inconsistency between greater French NATO involvement and the Franco-German agreements reached only a few days before; but Adenauer in his Memoirs mentions neither the de Gaulle proposals to Eisenhower nor any kind of reaction on his part. It may, nevertheless, be taken for granted that the inconsistency had not escaped him and that it cannot have increased his confidence in de Gaulle's avowed German policy.

Understandably, many differences arose between France and the Federal Republic about what their relations with the United States ought to be. Adenauer, in his Memoirs, recorded repeated exchanges with the French on the question of United States influence in Europe. De Gaulle had made it clear that he resented European dependence on the Americans and that he wished to minimise it. Although that was also Adenauer's attitude, the manner in which the two men wanted to change the situation was rather different. The French, like the Germans, were keen to retain United States nuclear protection and the presence of American soldiers in Europe, but de Gaulle was becoming increasingly ambiguous about the degree of integration he was prepared to accept within NATO. That worried the Germans, because they took far more seriously than the French the apparent American linking of integration with a continued United States presence in Europe. While still, until 1962, preoccupied with the Algerian problem, de Gaulle sought to reassure Adenauer about his intentions by explaining that the only kind of integration to which he objected was that which completely destroyed the national character of the armed forces within a supranational command.[76] But it was obvious that de Gaulle had already taken the measure of the United States' attitude to Europe, and was trying to infuse some courage into Adenauer. He reasoned that the United States needed Europe as much as Europe needed the United States, and that consequently Washington would put up with a great deal of harrying from the Europeans without taking the final step of leaving them to stew in the Soviet pot. But Adenauer felt constrained to end a lengthy discussion with de Gaulle's prime minister, Debré, in October 1960 by underlining 'once again that every Frenchman, Dutchman, Belgian, Italian, and German knows that, without the United States, he would be lost against an opponent as thoroughly equipped with nuclear weapons as the Soviet Union'.[77] More firmly, after taking note of de Gaulle's Grenoble speeches, which coincided with the end of his talks with Debré, Adenauer pointed out that 'according to the wording of the reports, these speeches were not compatible with NATO and the relations between the EEC countries. I . . . stated most earnestly that the Federal Republic would not follow France along that road'.[78]

The lack of success of this aspect of French policy remained apparent throughout the years of Franco-German euphoria under Adenauer: the Federal Republic, though far from wishing to increase them, just did not see how it could risk any weakening of her links with the United States, however much she might have liked to have 'Europeanised' these links. De Gaulle's argument that the United States might, when it came to the crunch, not be a reliable defender of the European continent – because their intercontinental missiles made the defence of Europe an unnecessary burden for them – also failed to tempt Adenauer away from the Americans. This was not just because he recognised the contradiction between that thesis and the one also advanced by de Gaulle that the United States needed Europe, but also because the implication that Europe would in the end have to rely mainly on Franco-German defence resources, with the emphasis on the eventual French nuclear deterrent, 'frightened' Adenauer (he says) when this was first seriously mooted during his visit to Paris in December 1959.[79] Economic reasons alone, he felt, would prevent Europe from being able to face the kind of armaments programme that would be required for an adequate European defence system. Adenauer continued to hope that United States involvement in Europe would also be seen in Washington as being in the best interests of the United States, and that the Europeans might therefore have a good deal of leverage when they sought to increase European influence in defence decisions. There is no evidence that Adenauer ever seriously accepted the view that the French could provide adequate protection for his country against the Soviet Union.

De Gaulle also used America's increasing involvement in south-east Asia, and in other parts of the world, to persuade Adenauer of the growing uncertainty of American interest in Europe. At their meeting in Paris in February 1961, soon after the Kennedy administration had taken over in Washington, the French president suggested to the German chancellor that even with the best intentions towards Europe which the United States could muster, Kennedy might just not be capable of meeting his commitments in Europe as well as in the rest of the world. Europe, de Gaulle concluded, should at least be prepared for that eventuality. Somewhat tactlessly, Adenauer reminded de Gaulle that France was still very preoccupied with Algeria, and concluded that the Federal Republic as well as the French might therefore usefully pray that Kennedy could indeed carry out his promises in Europe.[80] Adenauer underlined the same points in his talks with the American president in April 1961 and, for what it was thought to be worth, received the assurances he sought.

In the face of continuing anti-American pressure from de Gaulle when he was in Bonn for discussions in May 1961, Adenauer reported on his meetings with Kennedy, and expressed the view that the United States was a dependable ally. In his Memoirs[81] the chancellor noted that the French president was lamenting the impending meetings between Kennedy and Khrushchev. When Adenauer pointed out that French actions in NATO were not increasing the solidarity of the alliance either, and were in fact giving comfort to the Russians, de Gaulle apparently failed to see the point. On the other hand, de Gaulle's argument that the integration of national forces within NATO in peacetime was a deplorable violation of national dignity, and weakened patriotic fibres, failed to convince Adenauer. Unlike de Gaulle, Adenauer firmly believed that only a strong and manifestly united NATO could be a satisfactory deterrent to the Soviet Union. But this did not prevent the German chancellor from putting up before President Kennedy the strongest case for greater European participation in NATO decision-making.

With the different emphases on relations with the United States and NATO that have been noted, the French and German heads of government also used their May 1961 meetings in Bonn to assess the possibilities for an extension of European political collaboration. They were agreed that such collaboration would, among other things, strengthen Europe's position within NATO. Although what they would want to do with their increased political weight in their dealings with the United States was likely to be different in the end, Adenauer and de Gaulle decided that they would encourage further political collaboration among the EEC countries, even at the risk of arousing the suspicion among some EEC members that the Germans and French were preparing to rule the organisation.

At this stage, the possible inclusion within EEC of Great Britain and other EFTA countries (European Free Trade Area, set up in 1958 as an answer to EEC and consisting of Britain, Sweden, Denmark, Norway, Austria, Switzerland and Portugal) became a major issue. As French and German pressure within EEC towards greater political collaboration increased, so the simultaneous request for admission by the British again highlighted the differences between the Federal Republic and France over the European role of the United States. Harold Macmillan, the British prime minister, had declared in the House of Commons at the end of July 1961 that his country would apply for EEC membership, a step in which he had been encouraged by President Kennedy. Adenauer and de Gaulle had no difficulty in agreeing that British entry would provide a considerable challenge to their own growing domination of EEC. But, although the Bonn and Paris governments were also agreed that the United States was trying to use eventual British membership of EEC to increase their own influence in Europe, Adenauer's greater need of United States support in Europe made him more reluctant than de Gaulle openly to condemn the British application on these grounds. Nor did Adenauer imitate de Gaulle in publicly condemning the Anglo-American agreement made at Nassau at the end of 1962, which appeared to make Britain's dependence on the American nuclear deterrent even firmer than before. However flabby the chancellor thought Kennedy to be in his dealings with the Soviet Union – even after the Cuban missile crisis in 1962 – he was not prepared to risk a display of open hostility towards Washington. Thus, after de Gaulle had finally rejected the Macmillan application at his 14 January 1963 press conference – using the

Nassau agreements as 'proof' that Britain was not 'European' – Adenauer 'emphasised that on no account should the American link be abandoned, but that the United States must be made to feel its responsibilities'.[82] There can be no doubt about the intensity with which both Adenauer and de Gaulle resented the Anglo-American *entente*. But, equally, there can be no doubt that Adenauer knew that he had more to lose than the French by sulking about it.

During the period of EEC negotiations with Britain, de Gaulle had used the ending of the Algerian war in 1962, the mild British and American reactions to the building of the Berlin wall, and Adenauer's disappointment over Kennedy's failure to deal more severely with the Russians over the Cuban missile crisis, to encourage the German chancellor into ever closer collaboration with him. The highest point in the Franco-German *entente* came with the signature on 22 January 1963 of the treaty of friendship between the two countries. The treaty was to promote ever more intimate consultations and cooperation in the fields of foreign policy, defence, education, and youth exchanges. Having been accepted by the Federal Parliament on 16 May – with a Socialist-inspired preamble insisting on its non-exclusive character – and the French National Assembly on 14 June, it came into force on 2 July 1963. Nothing could have highlighted Franco-German designs more than the rapid implementation of this treaty so soon after the decisive rejection of Britain's application for EEC membership.

The populations of France and Germany had been prepared for the official consecration of their relationship by two state visits, those of Adenauer to France and of de Gaulle to the Federal Republic. If Adenauer's visit was a reasonably cordial affair, that of de Gaulle was a triumph. 'De Gaulle came to Germany as President of France and leaves it Emperor of Europe', said *Der Spiegel*.[83] That was early in September 1962, three months after the German chancellor had been to France. By the time the general had reached Hamburg he had pulled out all the stops. At the German War College in this old Hanseatic town he even brought himself to eulogise the Wehr-macht:

But to what can and should the solidarity of our armies amount in that Franco-German union that all the circumstances call for? The fact is that neither the French nor the Germans have ever accomplished anything great, nationally or internationally, without the close involvement on either side of the army. Given our nature, as well as the common danger, the closest cooperation between our armies . . . is thus essential to the union of our two countries.[84]

The speech showed a remarkable readiness to forgive and forget.

But eight months after the signature of the Franco-German treaty Adenauer visited de Gaulle at Rambouillet. The chancellor was about to resign, and this was a farewell visit. In October 1963 Dr Ludwig Erhard succeeded Adenauer. The euphoric era was over.

(ii) 1963-8: Disillusionment: In 1961 Adenauer had replaced von Brentano with Gerhard Schröder at the German Foreign Ministry. Given what was known about Schröder, a more 'Atlantic' outlook in German policy could have been expected to follow that change. But the forceful influence that Adenauer exercised over the cabinet prevented Schröder from initiating new policies. With the accession to the chancellorship of Erhard, however, the French orientation of the Federal Republic's foreign policy changed sharply. This does not seem simply to have been because of the rather weaker leadership Adenauer's successor imposed upon his ministers, which allowed the foreign minister more scope, but also because the chancellor himself largely shared Schröder's preferences. Confronted with the new situation, de Gaulle used the one weapon which, at that stage, was certain to make an impact on the Federal government: he took a new interest in the countries of eastern Europe, including the German Democratic Republic (DDR). Having repeated his recognition of the Oder-Neisse frontier in 1959, the general was already a relatively acceptable western politician in the Communist countries. At the end of 1963 he went so far as to name Pankow, the DDR's seat of government, among the capitals of the totalitarian bloc, knowing perfectly well that

such a gesture touched a very sensitive area in the nervous system of the Federal Republic.[85]

On the whole, however, de Gaulle's displeasure, and his flirtations with the east, did not deflect the Erhard government from its Atlantic policy. This may have been in part because Adenauer's successor suspected that de Gaulle would never, in any case, allow the Federal Republic to get in the way of policies he wanted to pursue. For example, despite the provisions of the Franco-German treaty of 1963, no consultation with the Federal Republic took place before so internationally significant a step as the French recognition of the Communist government in Peking in 1964. Erhard may also have been encouraged to take a less French-orientated line by pressure from the Social Democratic (SPD) opposition. It will be recalled that the strength of that pressure had been enough in the Bundestag debate on the Franco-German treaty, that is even under Adenauer, for the Social Democrats to succeed in having a preamble included in the treaty which stated the Federal Republic's determination to continue to uphold its connections with the Atlantic powers and its EEC partners. Thus the Bundestag had voted for a text which freed the Federal Republic from any necessary association with Gaullist foreign policy designs, and it had done so without prior consultation with the French government. General de Gaulle had considered both the procedure and the preamble an insult.

Under Erhard, German policy on NATO increasingly diverged from that of France, particularly because de Gaulle was by then openly proposing to withdraw France completely from the integrated command structure of the organisation. Erhard appeared to feel the need for NATO in direct proportion to de Gaulle's coolness towards it.

For France, the withdrawal from NATO marked the final stage in the long history of bickering with the United States about the French role in the running of the organisation. De Gaulle had taken the first step towards the break in March 1959, soon after Eisenhower had refused his request for a Franco-British-American triumvirate to direct NATO, when he removed the French Mediterranean fleet from NATO control. The American project, in 1960, for a multilateral naval force (MLF), had impressed neither de Gaulle nor Adenauer. Multi-nationally manned ships, even when armed with nuclear weapons, provided no kind of answer to the Paris-Bonn demand for greater responsibility in NATO decision-making, especially when it was obvious that the actual use of the MLF's nuclear weapons could only be sanctioned in Washington. In June 1963 de Gaulle also withdrew his North Atlantic fleet from the NATO command. Then Adenauer retired and, with Erhard, Bonn's differences with Paris over NATO became spectacular. Where, under Adenauer, the only major quarrel with Paris had been over the continuing need and likelihood of American involvement in Europe, under Erhard the Federal Republic actually agreed to take part in the MLF scheme which President Kennedy had seen fit to revive. De Gaulle's disgust at this was no doubt accompanied by his horror at having the Germans thus associated, however remotely, with the use of atomic weapons. Although President Johnson finally decided to drop the MLF project, the creation within NATO in 1966

* Since the 1960s, especially since her withdrawal from NATO, France's defence policy has relied almost entirely on the so-called *force de frappe*, the French-developed nuclear strike force. The force is the culmination of plans begun in 1954, and confirmed by Guy Mollet in 1957. The implementation of the plans encountered many difficulties. Denied help from the United States and Britain, and hardly expecting any at that time from the Soviet Union, the French found it as difficult to develop a nuclear bomb as to find the means of conveying it to a target. In 1960 they exploded their first atomic device in the Sahara. By 1971 they were still without a hydrogen bomb that was manageable enough for delivery to a target, and it was expected that it would not be before 1975 that a rather unsophisticated hydrogen bomb would be ready for the French strategic forces. Economy measures introduced after the riots of spring 1968 had led to the slowing down of the nuclear programme, and by 1970 only three nuclear submarines were more or less operational; two more were planned. But these submarines were to be the successors to the 62 Mirage planes that had been the first nuclear bomb carriers of the *force de frappe* in the mid-sixties. Delay in putting the submarines into service meant that France had to go on relying on their Mirage-based deterrent. But the credibility of that deterrent depended on the fact that the planes had such a short range that they had to

of a nuclear committee – ostensibly for the participation of major member countries in atomic decision-making – could hardly satisfy de Gaulle either. He knew that the ultimate decisions would still be taken in Washington, and refused to have France join the committee. But Bonn did join, and the French president disliked both this new show of independence and this additional German access to the atomic trigger. On 1 July 1966 de Gaulle withdrew all French forces from the NATO command.*

The general's claim that France, despite her NATO policy, still remained ardently attached to the Atlantic alliance, came strangely from a soldier who must have known that nothing effective could be expected from a force that would delay serious cooperation with its allies until it was confronted with a real crisis. Certainly no German government in the 1960s could have played that kind of game with NATO. But because of the understandable and touching German desire to maintain friendly relations with France, and to encourage de Gaulle to take a continuing interest in the defence of the Federal Re-

---

be refuelled by tanker aircraft made in the United States, and over enemy territory at that (if the Soviet Union were the target).

Nor was there much to reassure those who relied on help from France for their defence in what was known of French strategic thinking. That Paris, at least until 1968, did not like the American-inspired NATO strategy of a graduated response to aggression was perhaps understandable, because this entailed the possibility that hostile forces could have made their way into France before NATO Headquarters had decided that the enemy had come to stay. On the other hand, France's aim to use nuclear forces against an enemy from the moment of overt aggression merely meant that France might be annihilated in a preventive nuclear attack. It was, after all, unlikely that an aggressor would not have taken into account the French intention to use their limited nuclear capability on the half-a-dozen cities on which it was targeted, and he would therefore have accepted that risk from the start in favour of the profits to be derived from massive nuclear aggression. An alternative view, that the French intended to use their nuclear weapon only as a detonator to guarantee United States intervention at their side against an aggressor, is unconvincing, since it is quite unclear why the Americans should be readier to help the French if they go to war without prior American agreement than after having obtained it. And if the French had been prepared to await American agreement, it is not easy to see why the French were quite so unhappy with their fate inside NATO.

public, Bonn made bilateral agreements with Paris which ensured that French troops in Germany, hitherto under NATO command, would remain there.

Within EEC the Erhard administration also developed views and policies which went against those advocated by France. In 1965 this led to a major and prolonged crisis in the organisation. But General de Gaulle had not waited until then before lamenting the fact that 'treaties [i.e. the Franco-German treaty] are like young girls and roses: they do not last very long.'[86] At any rate, in the spring of 1965 the French president demanded of EEC that the agricultural provisions of the Rome treaty, beneficial mainly to France, be implemented, as agreed since 1962, irrespective of certain other provisions to which France objected. The German Federal government demonstrated the degree to which it had emancipated itself from Paris by actually taking the initiative in opposing this French claim while France was herself failing to heed another provision of the treaty that was important to her EEC partners. The Federal government, supported by the remaining non-French members of the community, wanted the early introduction of qualified majority voting on a number of matters within EEC, as envisaged by the Rome treaty, and which would have made for further political integration. Knowing de Gaulle's reluctance to relinquish even the degree of national sovereignty which such a procedure would entail, the Brussels Commission and the non-French countries of the Common Market, with the Federal Republic in the forefront, tried to wrest from the French an agreement on qualified majority voting, in return for which they offered to agree on the generous terms on agriculture the French were seeking. But de Gaulle's aversion from such quasi-supranational proposals was so great that he seemed prepared to sacrifice the benefits of the agricultural Common Market rather than accept these proposals.[87] Moreover, the French president detested at least as much the increased powers requested by the Brussels Commission, which would have resulted from the financing of the agricultural Common Market as the Commission wanted to work it. The Commission had proposed that it should itself prepare budgets which were to be voted upon by the European Parliament, and which would dispose of funds obtained from duties paid on imported industrial goods from non-EEC countries. These funds were at least in part to be used to subsidise EEC agriculture, mostly French, to modernise it and ensure for EEC farmers a decent standard of living. In this major quarrel, the basically European orientation of the Federal Republic (and of the other non-French EEC members) again clashed with the essentially nationalist Gaullist outlook. The quarrel raged from July 1965 to May 1966 and, while it lasted, the French practically boycotted EEC. But in the end, despite all the bold talk by the other five, de Gaulle won the substance of all his points. He had done it by calling the bluff of his Common Market partners, particularly Germany's, for whom the survival of EEC, even in its old form, was preferable to its possible death at de Gaulle's hands. However, that de Gaulle himself could hardly have politically survived in France if he had actually taken his country out of the Common Market was soon to dawn on even the most obtuse.

The 1965-6 crisis foreshadowed what, at the end of the 1960s, looked like a decisive change in the Franco-German relationship. During the crisis, the greater economic strength of the Federal Republic had begun to give it enough confidence to enable it to triumph over its international political inferiority complex. No doubt bolstered up by United States encouragement, the Bonn administration had flexed its diplomatic muscles and found, to its obvious gratification, that they were stronger than at any rate the French had hoped. Moreover, the aftermath of the 1965-6 EEC crisis had made it obvious to most observers that in the last analysis French threats to leave EEC were likely to be empty. The French administration's hands were shown to be less free than de Gaulle would have liked. Even if he had been prepared, *in extremis*, to wreck the Common Market, neither French industrial nor agricultural interests would have been inclined to follow him. The low Gaullist vote at the presidential elections at the end of 1965 was a warning – and very obviously taken as such by the president – that at least French farming interests were ready to oppose his wrecking tactics with all the considerable power at their disposal. In that situation the role in EEC of the Federal Republic became increasingly commensurate with its status as the strongest economic power in the community, whose attitudes would ultimately be crucial within the Common Market to the success of French industry as well as of French agriculture. The increasing strength of the German economy, and the relative weakening of that of France, were bound to create a state of affairs which could make it difficult for the Federal Republic not to exercise a greater degree of influence in EEC than before. And that could only be done at the expense of France.

General de Gaulle did not, of course, shout from the Elysée roof tops that the leadership of France was being challenged within EEC, nor that his hands were now tied so that his periodic threats to leave the organisation no longer had to be taken seriously. Over the renewed application for British entry into EEC in 1967, for instance, he again threatened to take his country out of the community if there were continued pressure by his partners for Britain's admission. And, as in 1963, after a good deal of angry protesting, France's partners allowed de Gaulle to get away with it. After all, it was the tenth anniversary of the organisation, the heads of government of the Common Market countries were meeting in Rome to celebrate it, and the Kennedy tariff talks with the United States in Geneva had gone well for EEC: it was clearly no time for a family showdown. Thus, when even after the EEC Commission had pronounced in favour of opening negotiations with Britain, de Gaulle at his press conference of 27 November 1967[88] firmly repeated his opposition to British entry, his EEC partners were relatively mild in their reactions. The German foreign minister, Willy Brandt, had taken the lead in toning down the anger of other non-French members of the Brussels organisation. Himself an enthusiastic believer in the expansion of the Common Market, he felt that nothing was to be gained from attempts to coerce France into accepting British membership. The reasons for Brandt's circumspection were probably not only that he wished to do nothing that could jeopardise the future of EEC, or that mystical postwar Bonn feeling that Franco-German friendship had to remain a basic datum. He was almost certainly also motivated by the fact that his own attempts to conciliate eastern European countries, including the Soviet Union, needed at least French good will.

Indeed, it is likely that the Germans were at that time worried about the possibility of a French deal with Russia, perhaps at Germany's expense. There was much evidence during the summer of 1967 that the Federal government was nervous about the hectic pace of French contacts with the Soviet Union: when de Gaulle went to Bonn for the routine talks regularly provided for in the Franco-German treaty of 1963, the Federal government made its concern quite clear.[89] And on what kinds of issues had de Gaulle spoken to the Soviet leaders when they twice came to see him during the crisis of the June war in the middle east? As it was, the Bonn government had been unable to understand how de Gaulle had managed to align himself with the Soviet Union over the Six Day War. In fact, there is no doubt that since Adenauer's resignation in 1963 the Federal government's collective heart had been made to flutter quite often by de Gaulle's attempts to obtain a *rapprochement* with the Soviet Union. It was hardly a secret that Dr Erhard, in his talks in Paris in February 1966, had been much exercised by the imminent visit to the Soviet Union of the French president.[90] Even in 1967, in its reaction to de Gaulle's renewed veto on Britain's entry into EEC, the Kiesinger administration had shown itself unwilling to brave the general and whatever he might concoct with the Soviet Union.

But in 1968 the situation changed rapidly and drastically. To begin with, France's EEC partners had not really taken de Gaulle's No to Britain as a final answer. Even the Germans, with their particular difficulties, had merely decided to treat the French with some diffidence, not to abandon the idea of an enlarged Common Market. On 4 January 1968 the Federal foreign minister told the newspaper *Die Welt* that he was in favour of bringing about British entry by stages, and eight days later he publicly appealed to the French to allow Britain into EEC. The Benelux countries issued their own statement a few days afterwards, in which they reaffirmed their desire for the enlargement of the Common Market.

It was at this stage that de Gaulle's susceptibilities began to be somewhat bruised. Already irritated at the continuing pressure from his five partners, he reacted sharply when they and Britain attempted to use WEU as a new weapon against him. Since the French administration had refused to allow EEC even to open negotiations with Britain, WEU – consisting of all the EEC countries as well as Britain – seemed to those who wanted to enlarge the Common Market an excellent forum in which to discuss the contribution Britain could make to Europe's future and, in general, to work out common policies on a number of issues of mutual interest. It took a year before de Gaulle's patience broke to the point of inciting him to withdraw French collaboration from WEU. 'WEU was created in 1954', declared the French government in February 1969, 'as a reply to the military preoccupations of the time. But, since the end of last year, an offensive is under way which seeks to bring about regular discussions among the seven of questions relating to politics, defence, technology, and international economics. This offensive clearly aims to outflank the Common Market'.[91] The French reaction had come after even the German foreign minister had finally thrown caution to the proverbial winds and berated de Gaulle over his 'rigidity'. Although the exact words spoken by the German foreign minister have been much disputed – he had been addressing a provincial congress of his SPD party in February 1968 – he left no doubt during the remainder of 1968 that he was no longer prepared to choose his vocabulary with the same care as before.

It was not only over British entry into EEC that Franco-German attitudes clashed at this time. De Gaulle's desire to embarrass the United States economy and discredit the international status of the American dollar, though initially backed for strictly non-Gaullist economic reasons by Bonn and the rest of EEC, eventually came up against the usual German reluctance to have a showdown with the Americans. In 1967, the theoretical discussions that had been carried on for some time among the ten richest states (generally known as 'the

Ten'),[92] about the desirability of increasing the world's monetary reserves, had acquired new urgency. The needs of the industrialised countries to export their goods were being seriously thwarted by the lack of international liquidity. One of the most glaring consequences of this was the enormous adverse payments balance of the United States. De Gaulle gleefully seized the opportunity to try to teach the Americans an economic lesson, and he expected at least the rest of EEC to follow him. To begin with, he had the satisfaction of seeing all the Common Market countries agreeing upon a policy that was inspired by European-centred considerations entirely to the taste of the French president, except that these considerations had nothing to do with a desire for French leadership. For example, at their meeting in Brussels early in July 1967, EEC finance ministers had worked out a common position which their United States colleague seemed quite unable to shake when he met them and the other members of the Ten in London soon afterwards. Among other points, the EEC countries demanded, and obtained, a right of veto in decisions on special drawing rights, the device by which international liquidity might be increased. It was this kind of display of EEC unity which inspired de Gaulle, at his press conference on 27 November 1967, to speak with great optimism of the ever closer collaboration between the Six that was 'to balance the immense power of the United States'.[93] But this optimism, genuine or not, was soon shown to have been unfounded.

From the beginning of 1968, de Gaulle's increasingly hard line towards the United States' economic difficulties lost him much support in EEC. The Germans certainly did not share his view that the Americans should use orthodox methods to correct their balance of payments difficulties: deflation and restrictions on imports into the United States were the last things German industry wanted. Nor was it easy to see what France herself had to gain from such measures, especially since her trade balance with the United States was in deficit. The truth is probably psychological: the Americans tended to invest a good deal of money in several European countries, including France, and de Gaulle was unhappy about increasing

American ownership of French industries. Nor was it a secret that the general was delighted to be in a position to embarrass the United States, which had for so long preached orthodox economics to Europe, and from which he himself had suffered many slights in the past. The flow of gold from the United States through French, or allegedly French inspired, selling of dollars, was a typical phenomenon of the time. The differences of opinion between France and her EEC partners, led by the Federal Republic, about how to deal with the United States, were exhibited very clearly during their Rome meetings late in February 1968. But what must have been far more displeasing to de Gaulle was the communiqué issued on 7 February at the end of the visit to the United States of Jean Rey, the secretary general of the newly combined ECSC and EEC Commission in Brussels. Far from using the Independent-Europe-Superpower verbiage, the communiqué serenely spoke of Europe as 'an equal partner of the United States in the building of a peaceful, prosperous and just world'.[94] De Gaulle's 1967 ardour for EEC, already cooling because of his partners' refusal to follow his anti-American line, needed little more than Jean Rey's current utterances to send him back to his suspicions of Brussels 'technocrats'. Indeed, at about the same time, Jean Rey publicly stated that no country had the right to consider that its views were always necessarily right; in the context, he was clearly talking about France and de Gaulle's continuing veto on British entry into EEC. He was publicly backed by Willy Brandt, at the time Bonn's foreign minister.

The weeks that followed increasingly underlined the continuing divergence of French and German attitudes. Both among the Six at Brussels (25 March 1968) and among the Ten at Stockholm (29–30 March) the French continued with their hard line while the Germans and the EEC Commission – as well as most of France's other partners – wanted a policy that would be of help to the United States. The French even used the particularly serious economic situation of the Americans at that time to argue against the early institution of the special drawing rights – to increase world liquidity – upon which the Ten had finally agreed at their Rio de Janeiro conference in

September 1967. Then came May 1968, when the entire massive, obstinate, infuriating or impressive (according to taste) Gaullist machinery was brought to a stop. Street riots and strikes paralysed France, and the French international Gaullist persona, so carefully and astutely built up over a decade, disintegrated overnight, to be followed by the French economy.

With de Gaulle suddenly and incredibly at bay, Bonn decided to take the plunge. For the first time since the second world war, a Federal German government proceeded to demonstrate that it had not only the ability but also the will to follow policies in which it believed, irrespective of French (or, at that time, any other country's) displeasure, and to follow these policies through. On 20 November 1968 the Ten met in Bonn, under the chairmanship of the Federal economics minister. For some weeks there had been frantic buying of German currency, on the assumption not only that it was the hardest currency at a time when the dollar as well as sterling and the French franc were at their weakest, but also that it might actually be revalued. In Bonn, the French, British, and Americans combined to ask the Federal government to revalue the German mark, so that pressure would be taken off their own currencies. The French, in particular, had had to contend with so much speculation on the franc since May that they had already lost a large part of their reserves. But, insistent and persistent as the pleas to the Germans were, Bonn refused to yield. The most the Bonn government was ready to concede was a Federal levy on exports and a reduction in the cost of imports. Its reluctance to do more was, of course, understandable. Many international economists thought that at least the dollar and the French franc were overvalued (sterling had in fact been devalued in November 1967), and it seemed more equitable to the Germans that the French, for a start, should devalue rather than that they themselves should revalue. Admittedly, Bonn's attitude hardly demonstrated that degree of solidarity with Paris for which General de Gaulle claimed to have been working. But then it was difficult to see what the general had lately done for Bonn.

For the president of France it had been enough of a gruelling experience to have again to account to foreign bankers and politicians for the way the French economy was going, this being a necessary consequence of having to make use of foreign loans to repair the economic damage of 1968. But actually to be pressed to devalue his currency, the symbol of the stability of his regime, was intolerable for him. Yet, during and after the Bonn meeting, this is exactly what happened, although the pressure to devalue came at least as much from French as from foreign sources. However, what hurt most was perhaps the statement by the German finance minister at the end of the Bonn meeting that 'the manner in which devaluation is to be handled is left to the French government'.[95] Had Franco-German relations really come to that? Not only had no single French official so far made the slightest public mention even of the possibility of devaluation, but here was a senior German minister who seemed actually to be suggesting that, while the French might be permitted to settle minor matters, the major economic decisions affecting her were now taken in Bonn.

The denouement was all Gaullist drama. While everybody was talking about devaluation of the franc as a certainty, with only the percentage in dispute, de Gaulle decided on 24 November not to devalue at all. The decision was almost certainly taken on political and not economic grounds. The loss of face devaluation entailed would have been catastrophic for him. Ambivalently, British and American ministers congratulated him on his decision: devaluation of the franc might have hurt the dollar and sterling too, but to see the general in currency trouble, after all he had done to embarrass them during recent years, cannot have been the most tragic of experiences for them.

(iii) The end of the Gaullist era: De Gaulle never recovered from May 1968 and its national and international consequences. By the end of April 1969 he was out of office for good. During the months between the crucial Bonn meeting and his resignation, relations with the Federal Republic remained at routine level. Nevertheless, when Michel Debré, as French foreign minister, went to Bonn in March 1969 to pre-

pare the regular Bonn-Paris summit meeting, he was thought to have left the Federal government in no uncertainty about de Gaulle's resentment at its behaviour during the currency crisis.[96] The general himself, at the actual summit meeting in Paris on 13 March 1969, perhaps remembering the inevitable fate of young girls and roses, complained little. But his statement later in March, that the talks had been entirely satisfactory,[97] merely underlined the fact that the real differences between the two countries had not been faced. Neither on currency reform nor on British membership of EEC, two of the major problems of the day, did the two governments see eye to eye. The fact that the German foreign minister still tried to keep his temper with the French, and recommended caution in dealing with de Gaulle, could not have hidden from the public, let alone from the politically literate, that Franco-German relations at that stage were based neither on a community of view, nor, of course, as during the Adenauer period, on Gaullist prestige. Indeed, had it not been for the tremendous emotive power behind the Federal Republic's policy of reconciliation with France, the economic strength of Bonn might well, by 1969, have prompted and enabled her to claim the hegemony in EEC that de Gaulle had manifestly though vainly been seeking for a decade.

Whether de Gaulle's German policy had been a success or not must obviously depend on the criteria one uses. His grand idea of Franco-German collaboration to create a European power structure under French leadership had clearly failed. Even with Adenauer it could not have fully succeeded, since Adenauer was seen to have had too acute a recognition of his need of the United States to go the whole Gaullist hog. De Gaulle might be thought to have been more positively successful in the encouragement he gave to Franco-German collaboration and the consequent ending of the myth that the Germans were 'natural' enemies. It would, however, not be in keeping with his priorities if one concluded that the success of the latter atoned in his eyes for the failure of the former. Indeed, in 1968, when the first five years of the Franco-German treaty were being celebrated, political commentators tended to point out that the only visibly successful consequence of the treaty had been the *Office Franco-Allemand pour la Jeunesse*. One million, eight hundred thousand exchanges of young people had been arranged between the two countries through the *Office* since it had come into being in 1963.[98]

FRANCO-GERMAN RELATIONS SINCE 1969

When Georges Pompidou took over the presidency from General de Gaulle in 1969, his diplomatic inheritance was scarcely more impressive than his economic one. In fact, since the French economic crisis in 1968, fears that EEC might be increasingly dominated by the Federal Republic became very real in France. It had even been rumoured towards the end of de Gaulle's presidency that he was at last considering allowing British entry into EEC as a counterweight to Bonn's new strength.[99] It was symptomatic of this attitude that *Le Monde* reported[100] how resentment at United States investments in France had been replaced in French business circles by resentment at the 'insolent health' of the Germans. It was pointed out that the combined turnover of the ten biggest German firms was then as great as that of the twenty-five biggest French firms put together. Similarly, contrasting the two countries in terms of the agriculture to industry ratio, the report reminded its readers that only 10.6 per cent of the active population of the Federal Republic was engaged in agriculture, as against 16.6 per cent of the French. By way of consolation, the author added that the Netherlands and Italy had had a higher rate of industrial growth during the previous decade than West Germany, although the rate of the latter was still higher than the French. Obviously, were German reunification to become a reality, the gap between the two countries would become even more serious for France.

The apparently widening economic disparities between France and West Germany have had much influence on French morale and, consequently, on attitudes towards West Germany. One of the most glaring illustrations of these disparities at the end of the 1960s and in the early 1970s was the contrast between the prosperity of the German province of Baden and the very much more slowly developing areas of Alsace just across the Rhine. The fact that Baden progressed twice as fast meant, among other things, that the higher wages there attracted many thousands of French workers. They crossed the border each working day to take advantage of the results of the faster growth rate, and returned home to their families in Alsace in the evenings. The same was happening in the Moselle area, where a report published by the local Chamber of Commerce in April 1970 provided the striking information that, in Metz alone, thirteen firms employing 3,655 men had lost 887 because they preferred to work across the border.[101] It may be imagined that, were this kind of situation to continue or even to deteriorate for the French, it would no longer be fanciful to ask the question already put by Frenchmen in 1969,[102] whether the Germans were now to achieve by economic means what they had been unable previously to achieve militarily.

It can, however, hardly be said that Willy Brandt's coalition government – which had taken over in Bonn after the October 1969 elections – made any attempts to profit from its economic strength in its relations with France. On the contrary, where his predecessors had refused to revalue the mark and thus help France (and other countries), Brandt not only did just that soon after taking office, but also revalued by as much as 9 per cent, which was greater than the French had dared hope. It is true that President Pompidou, heedless of Gaullist wrath, had devalued the franc in the summer by 12.5 per cent. As a result, foreign money began to flow back into France, though slowly, and French exporters took full advantage of the revaluation gift with which the Germans had presented them. And new ways of collaboration between the two countries were invented as the Brandt government gave proof of its good will. For example, a Franco-German training and tactical support aircraft was to be produced, to be in service after 1975, which was to make the Germans less dependent on the United States and was to bring the French useful outlets for their, at that time, hard-pressed aircraft industry.

Nor in EEC did the Brandt government press its advantage unduly. On the contrary, it finally brought about the agricultural Common Market for which the French had been clamouring for many years. Unpopular among German farming interests, whose high production costs made the French formidable competitors, German governments had fought shy of implementing that part of the drive towards a united Europe. At the height of the franc crisis, in October 1968, the German economics minister, Karl Schiller, had even gone to the length of suggesting that cheap French agricultural products – the result of French farm surpluses – were a vice, and that the French should not rely on others to save them from their own sins. But, as the Germans well knew, for the French government it was not just politically and economically impossible to depress or subsidise French agriculture any further; it had also been taken for granted since the beginnings of EEC that in return for French acceptance of free market conditions for industrial products – which greatly benefited the Germans – the Germans would accept the same conditions for agricultural products to benefit the French. The Brandt government finally accepted that principle at the Hague Conference of the heads of governments of EEC countries at the end of 1969, though as part of a package deal which allowed also for the resumption of talks on British membership.

The relative flexibility shown by President Pompidou at the Hague was also evident in his dealings with the United States and NATO. This meant that fewer occasions for friction arose between Bonn and Paris over their respective views on the role of the United States in Europe, and that Federal German governments were no longer called upon to make agonising choices between friendship with the French and the military need for the Americans, as had often been the case under de Gaulle's presidency. On the other hand, substantial differences of view remained, particularly on how much integration there ought to be of the forces of the Atlantic alliance countries for maximum efficiency. President Pompidou gave no evidence of being prepared to go back on de Gaulle's withdrawal of French forces from NATO command. But the Bonn government, for its part, was as nervous as ever of any sign of a lessening of the United States commitment to Europe.

There is no doubt that the fitful thaw in east-west relations throughout the 1960s made Franco-German disagreements about NATO at least to some extent an academic matter. The thaw was primarily the result of the recognition that, if war came, international suicide would come too; it was not the result of a sudden international accession to a higher morality. Both the French and West German governments tried to exploit the new situation for their own ends, the French beginning to court the Soviet Union in earnest in 1964 and the Germans after the Socialist Willy Brandt became foreign minister in the coalition government in December 1966. The French wanted to use the Soviet Union as a diplomatic tool with which to encourage the Germans towards greater cooperation with Paris, and as a counterweight to United States influence in Europe. At the same time they hoped to be able to persuade the Russians to release their hold on the Soviet satellite countries in eastern Europe, so that the French could enrol these countries in the crusade for a more independent European Europe. Bonn, on the other hand, needed Soviet support for what it knew to be the difficult cause of reunification, as well as for a better deal for Berlin and its relations with the German Democratic Republic and the other Communist satellite countries. The Federal Republic could also derive much economic benefit from improved relations with the east.

On the whole, there was no overt cause for conflict between Paris and Bonn on their eastern policies. It has been seen that both felt they had much to gain from an easing of tension and an increase in collaboration with the east. But both countries were very sensitive about the worst that either could do to the other in its dealings with the east. The Federal Republic, as has been shown repeatedly, often had nightmares about a Franco-Soviet deal behind Germany's back and at Germany's expense. The French, for their part, became increasingly touchy about Bonn's negotiations with the east, as the Federal Republic's growing economic strength seemed to encourage her to take a more independent line. At their worst moments the French not only feared a new Rapallo, but in particular they contemplated with little relish the prospect of German reunification that such an understanding with the Soviet Union might, remotely, be able to bring about. Already towards the end of de Gaulle's presidency open irritation at the German government's diplomatic activities in eastern Europe was sometimes manifest. De Gaulle himself was said to have made Bonn responsible for a good deal of the motivation that had sent Warsaw pact troops into Czechoslovakia in August 1968: the Federal Republic had allegedly been too imprudent in its haste to conciliate the east.[103]

When President Pompidou first went to Bonn in September 1969, for the regular meeting with the Federal government provided for in the Franco-German treaty, Chancellor Kiesinger and he stated that they intended to work for 'exemplary cooperation' *(coopération exemplaire)*. It was said that this referred mainly to their dealings with the east. Nothing in the public utterances of either the Bonn or Paris governments suggested that there was any real disagreement about what line to follow, and this impression was further encouraged after the Paris meetings between the two governments at the beginning of 1970. By that time Willy Brandt had taken over as chancellor from Dr. Kiesinger, and it was well known that he would redouble German efforts in the east.

But by the early summer of 1970, Chancellor Brandt's haste to get his pacts with Poland and the Soviet Union finally signed, and to reach concrete agreements also with the DDR, began to elicit some unhappy comments in Paris. It was suggested, officially and in the press of both countries, that Brandt might be giving away too much in all that precipitation, though no one was heard in Paris openly to admit that the fear was at least as much that in return the Germans might also gain too much for French comfort. German negotiators and policymakers were asked with some insistence to safeguard the rights of the western allies in Germany – in Berlin in particular – and the French even called upon the British and Americans to back them up in this.[104] In early July 1970, during

Pompidou's talks in Bonn, French nervousness about the German negotiations in Moscow received much public attention, even though the final communiqué repeated the standard formula that the Federal Republic had the full backing of France in her attempts to 'normalise' her relations with the east.[105]

Since the basic data of the Franco-German relationship are in the foreseeable future likely to remain what they have been in the past, the future, however surprising, is likely to be best understood when set against the background of that past.

3

France and the Soviet Union

If the Soviet regime were not, on the whole, run by pragmatic men, the possibilities of friendly relations between France and the Soviet Union would not be great. No country had done more than France to make life as difficult as possible for the rulers of Russia after their successful revolution at the end of the first world war. The French had tried, by all the means available to them, to have the revolutionaries put down. To that end they promoted civil war in Russia, sent troops (their own and other peoples', for example the Czechs'), blockaded the country, tried to isolate it internationally, and finally toyed with the idea of coming to an agreement with Hitler's Third Reich to bring about the ultimate downfall of the Soviet regime.

More than any other nation, the French had laboured to prevent the Russian leaders from taking their place in the interwar councils of nations. When the Soviet Union was finally admitted to the League of Nations in 1934 she was indeed well supported by Barthou, the French foreign minister. But by then the French had become apprehensive about Hitler's intentions and hoped that the Soviet Union would be a useful addition to world pressure for continuing disarmament. In any case, such French hopes did not last long, and had never really been shared by the large majority of Frenchmen who would have no dealings with as ideologically repulsive a regime as that of Communist Russia. At the crucial Munich Conference in 1938 no Russian representative was present, for the simple reason that no one had thought fit to invite one to attend. The point about the French in the 1930s was precisely that they were unable to make up their minds about which enemy they detested more: Germany or Soviet Russia.

It has to be recognised that French loathing of the Communist revolution, and of its ultimate triumph, had several understandable reasons. For a start, the revolutionaries at once wanted to take Russia out of the war against the central powers, at a time when, in 1917, the French had to contend with mutinies among their own troops and were particularly hard pressed by the enemy. Frenchmen tended to feel that the Russians were leaving them in the lurch. There were, however, less patriotic reasons for loathing the Communists in Russia. Many of these reasons had to do with the revolutionaries' avowed aim to abolish private property, and with the fact that the large Socialist movement in France could be expected to derive great strength from a successful revolution in Russia.[1] Indeed, the first postwar elections in France were fought largely on the issues presented by Communism. In the event the French Socialists lost the elections, and then went on to split up into a Communist section and a Democratic Socialist section.

Still more immediately materialistic a reason for disapproving of the Soviet regime was its repudiation of the debts of tsarist Russia. Since the late 1880s, when the French replaced the Germans as the largest investors in Russia, some twelve thousand million francs (pre-1914 value) had been lent by French investors to the Russians. The complete loss of this money by a fair cross section of the French middle classes necessarily coloured their reactions to the Soviet regime.

There was a perhaps even more serious reason for French hostility to the Soviet Union, which should be examined in some detail. It concerns Russo-German relations and was responsible for French readiness, even on the eve of the second world war, to believe any rumour according to which the Soviet Union was about to do a deal with Germany. That the *prima facie* hostility between a Nazi and a Communist Government was not enough to prevent such a deal was demonstrated by the Ribbentrop-Molotov pact of 1939. The separate peace the Russian Communists had made with the Germans in March 1918 had been only the beginning of a whole series of arrangements which the two countries made for each other's benefit during the interwar years, and without worrying unduly about Russia's former western allies. Both countries knew that together they could rule central and eastern Europe as they thought fit, particularly since the western allies had demonstrated their inability, in 1918 and 1919, to intervene successfully in Russia when they were united in their detestation of the Revolution. Since then the United States and Britain had decided to leave the new regime alone, and the French showed that they too had learned that intervention at the distances involved was very hazardous.

The fact that both Germany and Russia had come out of the first world war as internationally ostracised countries did much to bring them together. In 1922, at Rapallo, they waived their reparations claims against each other. When the French marched their troops into the Ruhr in 1923 to exact reparations from the Germans, the Russian government issued a message 'to the world', declaring the French expedition 'illegal and criminal'. In Moscow thousands of workers demonstrated against 'French imperialism', and *Izvestia* ² expressed the fear that the complete domination of Germany by France would make the Russian border with Poland more dangerous than before because Poland was France's ally. The Russian government showed its solidarity by sending money and cereals to the Germans who were striking in protest at the French invasion, even though the German government was wary of Communism in its own country and was not conspicuously happy about Russian intervention in its affairs.

In 1926, the Locarno treaty between France, Britain, Italy and Germany, which settled Germany's frontiers in the west (but not in the east with Poland and Czechoslovakia, where the Germans refused to commit themselves, thus bringing about the bilateral agreements between these countries and France) was seen by the Russians as a German betrayal of the Rapallo spirit. But it was only a temporary setback, if setback it was at all. In April 1926, only six months after Locarno, the Germans signed a treaty with the Soviet Union in which they pledged themselves to remain neutral in case of an east-west conflict, and not to participate in anti-Soviet policies. About the same time, though on too small a scale for Russian needs because of her own difficulties, Germany made loans to the Soviet Union when richer countries refused. German industry benefited from French reluctance to trade with the Soviet Union, although the French were, paradoxically, anxious to import Russian oil. For Stalin, at the end of the 1920s, France was 'the most aggressive and militaristic of all the most aggressive and militaristic countries in the world'.[3]

In the 1930s, faced with reviving German nationalism and with Nazism, both the Soviet Union and France had carefully to reexamine their attitudes to each other and to Germany. The Russians knew that the French were basically hostile to them (except perhaps for a sizable number of the 20 to 25 per cent of the electorate which regularly voted for the Left), as well as that Hitler's Nazis were aggressively anti-Communist and coveted the Ukraine. The French, on the other hand, had to weigh up how far the designs of their 'natural enemy' across the Rhine could make it desirable for them to come to an arrangement with the detested Soviets in the interest of national survival.

Already in 1931 the Soviet Union asked the French to sign a non-aggression pact with them. The French, disappointed by the failure of Briand's conciliatory policies towards Germany, agreed. The pact was initialled at the Quai d'Orsay in August 1931. But it took well over a year before the French finally signed it. In the meantime, France had taken a number of initiatives which underlined for the Russians that Paris would not be an unambiguously reliable partner. For example, within a month of initialling the pact, the French had tried to come to an agreement with the Germans without any prior consultation with the Soviet Union. In any case, a very large number of Frenchmen, not necessarily of the Right, were quite openly voicing the view that the slightest hope of an accommodation with Germany was better than a binding agreement with the Soviet Union. Even so, in May 1935, the French brought themselves to sign a mutual assistance treaty with the Soviet Union, applicable to Europe only. But Stalin's suggestion that this should be followed up with military agreements was coolly received in Paris.

In these circumstances it is not surprising that the Soviet Union tried to find its own answers. This is not to say, of course, that the good faith of the Soviet Union under Stalin could be taken for granted more easily than that of France under her various anti-Bolshevik middle-class governments. Also, there were influential Russians – Voroshilov, for example – who positively preferred an understanding with Germany to links with France. But the geographical and demographic position of Germany in Europe is such that, when she is bent on trouble, only the spectre of a war on two fronts may deter her. However, once the good faith of either partner in an east-west alliance against Germany is in doubt, the only safe course is for the other country to seek an accommodation with the possible enemy. During the remainder of the 1930s this is precisely what happened, although both France and the Soviet Union on a number of occasions went through the motions of trying to reach an agreement with each other. Indeed, when Franco-Soviet talks did not actually proceed in see-saw fashion, so that when they were off they were replaced by German-Soviet talks, negotiations were carried on in parallel between, on the one hand, Germany and the Soviet Union and, on the other, France and the Soviet Union.

The increasing involvement of Britain in Europe complicated matters still further. In the second half of the 1930s no French government made any significant international move without British approval, and Britain was as ambivalent about the Soviet Union as was France. What was more, British governments seldom exhibited the Germanophobia of their French counterparts, so that British influence in fact worked against closer French collaboration with the Soviet Union. Moreover, neither France nor Britain thought much of the Red army. For its part, in 1935 *Pravda*[4] printed an article by Marshal Tukhashevsky in which he pronounced the French army incapable of offering serious opposition to Germany.

Finally, French links with Poland and the states of the little *entente* made relations with the Soviet Union even more complex. These countries, Poland in particular, tended to be as suspicious of the Soviet Union as of Germany. When it was clear that Hitler would lead Europe into another war, at least Poland preferred to face the Germans alone rather than allow the Russians into their country.[5]

On 23 August 1939 the German foreign minister, von Ribbentrop, arrived in a swastika-bedecked Moscow to sign a non-aggression pact with the Soviet Union.[6] France and Britain were left to try and stop Hitler alone.

It cannot be said that the Russians behaved generously to the French in their defeat in 1940. The new French ambassador presented his credentials in Moscow on the day Paris, imminently to be taken by the Germans, was declared an open city. (The French had withdrawn his predecessor from Moscow when, as a result of the Russian attack on Finland in the autumn of 1939, the League of Nations had made the righteous gesture of expelling the aggressor from its midst.) It was on the day Paris was captured that Molotov, the Soviet foreign minister, first received the new ambassador. Two days later Molotov sent congratulations to Hitler. The French ambassador's official presentation to the Soviet president was arranged for the day the Franco-German armistice was signed. Although some of these coincidences may have been no more than coincidences, the disdain of the Russians was unmistakable. To make it clearer still, they downgraded their diplomatic representation to the French by sending only a *chargé d'affaires*.

As the French government in the unoccupied zone, at Vichy, warmed to Hitler's New Order, a grotesque, if brief, new period opened in Franco-Soviet relations.[7] It may be said to have started with the appointment of Gaston Bergery as ambassador to Moscow in April 1941. Bergery brought with him a message from Marshal Pétain's government, which enjoined the Soviet Union to help in the building of the New Order. France, the message affirmed, would accept no one's hegemony within that Order, which was directed against no one. It appears that the Russians made no immediate reply. On the following day the French were told, improbably, that the Soviet Union could not be part of a European system that was dominated by a power in which workers and peasants did not have the same position as in Russia. Some ten weeks later, when the Germans invaded the Soviet Union, Bergery was recalled, and Vichy severed diplomatic relations with Moscow on the pretext that Soviet agents were subverting France.

Within a month, French volunteer legions began to train for the Russian front, to promote the New Order still more vigorously. It is true that they wore German uniform, and that they were not actually sponsored by the Vichy government. But the first contingent left Versailles in September 1941, with the best wishes of Marshal Pétain.[8] Then, a month after the first anniversary of the German attack on Russia – which had brought Hitler the message from Laval that he hoped for a German victory so that the world would be safe from Bolshevism – Vichy created its own *Légion tricolore* which was to fight against the Soviet Union in French uniform. Finally, there came into being a French Waffen SS, the Charlemagne division, which wore German uniform, swore an oath of allegiance to Hitler, and received the same enthusiastic support from the Vichy government as the rest of the New Order's anti-Soviet campaign had done.

GENERAL DE GAULLE'S FREE FRENCH MOVEMENT AND
PROVISIONAL GOVERNMENT: RELATIONS WITH THE
SOVIET UNION UNTIL 1946

After Hitler's attack on the Soviet Union, General de Gaulle declared his solidarity with the Russians. When the break came between Vichy and Moscow, de Gaulle asked that Moscow should establish direct relations with him. Three months later, in September 1941, the Soviet Union recognised de Gaulle as the head of all the Free French.[9] But although it also spoke of its desire to restore French independence and greatness, the Soviet declaration was as silent on the question of restoring all their former territories to the French as the British had been when they had given recognition to the general in June 1940. Moreover, Stalin showed little tact in appointing as representative to de Gaulle his former envoy to Pétain. Ignoring the implicit slight, de Gaulle wanted to send some of his troops to the

Caucasus to fight by the side of the Russians. But the British, who needed them in Libya, dissuaded de Gaulle from doing that, and he sent a squadron of planes instead, the Normandie squadron.[10]

In 1942 came the first clear-cut attempt by the Russians to use de Gaulle against the Anglo-American allies. Moscow promised him the total restoration to France of her prewar empire, provided he could persuade Britain and the United States to open a second front in Europe in the near future. There was soon to be no doubt about de Gaulle's readiness to use differences between the Soviet Union and its two main allies for his own ends. But his influence with the British and the Americans was minimal, and it is unlikely that the Russians were unaware of this. Yet, somehow, they concluded that he might at that time be a useful ally against the English-speaking countries. Indeed, in 1942, relations between the Soviet Union and de Gaulle became so close – largely because of his perennial troubles with Britain – that a Russian periodical thought it could plausibly print a story according to which the Free French leader was moving his headquarters from London to Moscow.[11] At the end of September 1942, at de Gaulle's request, the Soviet Union issued a statement which recognised de Gaulle's movement as 'solely qualified to organise the citizens and territories of France for the war'. For de Gaulle this meant that the Russians recognised him as the person to control France at the liberation.[12]

Soviet support, according to de Gaulle's representative in Moscow,[13] was crucial in keeping him at the head of his movement when the British and Americans tried to replace him with General Giraud in 1942 and 1943, after their occupation of Algeria and Morocco. In fact, Churchill was at that time so disturbed by Moscow's relations with the general that he wrote to Stalin counselling caution, at least until the aims of de Gaulle's new French Committee of National Liberation were unmistakably at one with those of the allies.[14] But Stalin's reply merely affirmed that the refusal to give de Gaulle due recognition would be offensive to the French. In the end, the three major allies waited until two months after Churchill's letter before finally recognising the general's new, enlarged committee (23 August 1943). However, the differences between the terms in which they did it were significant. The United States merely acknowledged the committee's power to administer the territories which recognised its authority. The London statement went somewhat beyond that, considering the committee as qualified to conduct the French war effort. The Soviet Union, on the other hand, said that the new body represented the national interests of the French Republic and was the only proper mouthpiece for all French patriots fighting against Hitler.[15] Within a month the committee was enlarged to take in representatives of the resistance movements inside France, including Communists. That the Communists participated was not only de Gaulle's tribute to Moscow, but also the result of the successful conclusion of an internal argument within the PCF,[16] where some sections had been maintaining that they should go all out for the conquest of power in France, while others, led by Thorez, had advocated at least temporary collaboration with other parties. The acceptance of the Thorez view was to lead the PCF also to take part in the first French postwar governments.

The policy followed by Moscow towards de Gaulle nevertheless showed that, at least most of the time, it recognised his relatively limited use to it. Given his circumstances, the most that could be hoped for from him was some kind of nuisance value with the United States and Britain. The Russians were well aware where real power lay. But despite the fact that they were basically interested in recreating a France that was strong enough to stand up to the United States as well as to help contain postwar Germany, the Russians very early showed that they had misgivings about such strength because it was likely to encourage the French to resume an active interest in the central and eastern European states where they had been very active in the past. Here the Russians were no longer prepared to tolerate interference. On this kind of reasoning one can understand why Stalin, in any case allegedly impressed only by strength, tended to prefer to deal with Washington and London.[17]

De Gaulle was not consulted by any of the allies about the Italian armistice, nor about the decision to have the Italians declare war on Hitler. And though the Russians claimed that they had been responsible for allowing Couve de Murville to represent France at the Inter-Allied Commission for Italy,[18] they were no keener than the other allies to have France attend the Teheran Conference in December 1943 at which, among other things, future zones of influence in Europe were to be decided. Indeed, in the absence of French representation at Teheran, Stalin seemed to feel free to suggest that France should be deprived of her overseas possessions, with the implicit consequence that the Soviet Union would then be without question the most significant power on the European continent.[19]

After the Teheran Conference, Beneš, the Czech leader, reported to de Gaulle that his recent conversations with Stalin had made it clear that Czechoslovakia would, after the war, be within the Soviet zone of influence.[20] The fact that Poland – like Czechoslovakia under strong French influence before the war – was also to be within the Soviet sphere brought an open clash between de Gaulle and Moscow. Polish gold had been transported to Paris at the outbreak of war, and later sent to French West Africa. De Gaulle put this gold at the disposal of the Polish government in exile in London, having refused it to the Soviet-sponsored rival government. At this the Russians protested,[21] as well as over an article in an Algerian newspaper which showed a map of Poland with the borders of August 1939. De Gaulle's reply to the charge of ingratitude was that there often appeared to be a difference between diplomatic theory and diplomatic practice, recalling that the Soviet government had done nothing to have France at Teheran in spite of the Soviet Union's recognition of France's European interests.

It took the three major allies two months to recognise the provisional government de Gaulle set up in Paris after its liberation in August 1944. Some weeks later, on their visit to the French capital, Churchill and his foreign minister Eden informed de Gaulle that, at their recent Moscow talks, they had reached an agreement with the Soviet government on the Soviet Union's borders with Poland, as well as on the division of zones of influence in eastern and southern Europe.[22] It appears that de Gaulle at once got in touch with the Soviet government, suggesting a visit to Moscow. At any rate there is a letter from Stalin to Churchill, dated 20 November 1944 – that is ten days after the Churchill-Eden trip to Paris – in which de Gaulle's request is reported.[23] On 2 December 1944 Stalin, in another letter,[24] asked for Churchill's advice about what should be said to de Gaulle about a Franco-Russian pact and frontiers in eastern Europe, issues he was sure to want to raise. Roosevelt was similarly sounded out by Stalin.

A week after Stalin's first note to Churchill about de Gaulle's desire to come to Moscow, the general stated in the Paris Consultative Assembly that France was now in a position to demand that she be represented at all international discussions of major importance. He added that France would not feel herself bound by decisions she had not helped to make.[25] In that mood he went to Moscow.

As expected, in Moscow de Gaulle asked for Soviet support against Britain and the United States – particularly in his views on postwar Germany – and a pact with the Soviet Union on the lines of the treaties of 1892 and 1935. Perhaps the greatest attraction of a close relationship with the Soviet Union was that it would bring France international status, without – given the geographical distance between the two countries – involving the kind of overwhelming and inhibiting pressures inevitably set up by the United States' presence in western Europe. His problem was that he had little to offer the Russians in exchange. He was ready to accept the Oder-Neisse frontier for Germany and Poland, but the Soviet Union hardly needed de Gaulle's approval. In fact, a traditional French reflex caused him to adopt a position on the political future of Poland which in its obstinacy annoyed Stalin intensely. Ignoring the obvious reality that the Soviet Union had a free hand in eastern Europe, de Gaulle made a great fuss about wanting all Poles, including the London exiles, to have a say in the making of postwar Poland. In the end, after a good deal of pointless histrionics, a twenty-year Franco-Soviet treaty emerged, directed only against Germany. On 21 December 1944, eleven days after its signature in Moscow, Georges Bidault, de Gaulle's foreign minister, told the Consultative Assembly that the alliance was based at once on reason and on sentiment.[26]

The Franco-Russian treaty did not mean much to the Soviet government. Throughout de Gaulle's stay in Moscow, Stalin had kept in touch with Churchill about the talks. The Soviet and British governments would have preferred a pact with which Britain was also associated. But de Gaulle rejected the idea out of hand, not only because he would have been a kind of junior partner, but also because he was deeply affected by current British efforts in the middle east to oust France from the area. Moreover, neither reason nor sentiment had made the Russians breathe a word to de Gaulle about the imminent Yalta Conference (2–12 February 1945) between Stalin, Roosevelt and Churchill, at which their future policy on Germany was to be decided. In a radio broadcast, three days after the opening of the Yalta Conference, de Gaulle again stated that France would not be bound by any decisions she had not helped to make.[27]

It was Stalin who, at Yalta, was the most scathing about de Gaulle's international pretensions. He completely rejected the French demand that Germany be dismembered, and was very much opposed to Churchill's suggestion that the French be accorded an occupation zone. Churchill's reason would not have commended itself to Stalin: it was that Britain needed the support of a not too demoralised or weak France against Soviet pressure in Europe once the United States had withdrawn its forces from the continent; an occupation zone for the French would help to give their morale a boost. When the Soviet leader finally agreed, it was only on the understanding that the French occupation zone would come out of the Anglo-American area. Soon, in Berlin, the Russians were to try to prevent the French from signing the armistice.[28]

That the Franco-Soviet treaty was of small importance to the Russians was also the conclusion reached by General

Catroux,[29] who had taken up his post as French ambassador to Moscow in February 1945. Catroux thought the Russians were suspicious of the kind of government France was going to have under de Gaulle, and had therefore no wish to bolster him up, even against the Anglo-American allies. There seemed no way at that time of inducing the Soviet leaders to treat France as an equal, and Catroux's appeal to the two-months' old treaty proved useless when the Russians refused to have the French on the Reparations Commission for Germany. Similarly, French protests in Moscow about their being excluded from the Potsdam Conference in July 1945 were unavailing. De Gaulle took it hard that France should not have been called to meetings which were to decide on problems like the delimitation of occupation zones in Germany, reparations procedures, denazification, war crimes and population transfers.[30] In the event, de Gaulle did not find it too difficult to accept the Potsdam decisions, except for the provision that Germany should have a central administration. Even that provision, however, turned out to be a less serious reverse for French policy than might have been expected: not only did the French do what they could to keep their own occupation zone detached from the rest of Germany, but the large Soviet zone was also soon to be treated as a separate unit.

Stalin's increasingly open disdain for him may have prompted de Gaulle, during his visit to President Truman in Washington in August 1945, to use a new argument to press his case for a weak Germany: if Germany ceased to be a threat to her neighbours, he said, the Soviet Union would soon have trouble with its satellites in eastern Europe. De Gaulle based this view on the assumption that only the threat posed by a strong Germany could hold the eastern bloc together under Soviet hegemony.[31]

After his return from the United States the general gave an interview to the London *Times* which was to unleash a violent campaign against him in the Soviet Union.[32] He had advocated the creation of a western bloc which would closely collaborate in the building of the postwar world. But the Russians had not waited for this interview to give further proof of their lack of appreciation for his government. Already during the spring they had added to their anti-French activities by objecting to the French presence in the Levant and, very much more unkindly, had made it difficult for the French to discover the whereabouts of French prisoners of war liberated by the Red Army.

Thus the first anniversary of the Franco-Soviet treaty was no occasion for celebrations. In fact it was marked by a petty diplomatic incident of dubious origin. De Gaulle, in a telegram to Stalin, had addressed him as 'Marshal' and not 'Generalissimo', which elicited a sour comment from the head of Soviet protocol. On the whole, one expected de Gaulle to know what he was doing; it is therefore not clear how far a slight was intended. *Pravda* limited Soviet rejoicings to the reproduction of extracts from an article by the French Communist Pierre Cot, in which he deplored that de Gaulle, with his plan for a western bloc, had violated the spirit of the treaty.[33]

But already before these latest manifestations of hostility de Gaulle had decided to send a mission to Moscow to improve relations. It was led by Hervé Alphand, at the time director-general of Economic Affairs at the Quai, with the double intention of trying again to secure Soviet support for French policy on the Rhine, and to promote trade between the two countries. The mission was not a success. Molotov was non-committal on the Rhine issue, while a lesser official told the French ambassador, Catroux, that such support would have to be reciprocal, requiring at least French assistance in reinforcing the Communists' position in Poland.[34] As for trade, Mikoyan was entirely negative, and shortly afterwards signed a commercial treaty with Britain.

At that point General de Gaulle resigned from office.

1946–7: FRENCH ATTEMPTS AT AN INDEPENDENT FOREIGN POLICY

After de Gaulle's resignation, Georges Bidault remained foreign minister. During the many meetings in 1946 between the representatives of the victorious states, he tried to play the role of arbitrator. It was one possibly efficacious way in which to strive for a prominent international place, when that of sheer power was impossible. But the worsening relations between the Soviet Union and the Anglo-American allies allowed little scope for arbitration. Prime Minister as well as foreign minister from June 1946 until December, Bidault was unable to make any real impact on the negotiations that were to lead to peace treaties with Italy, Bulgaria, Rumania, Hungary and Finland. These treaties were signed in Paris on 10 February 1947. In the Ramadier government which inaugurated the Fourth Republic (the first general election under the new constitution had been held in November 1946), Bidault was again foreign minister. The signing of the Dunkirk treaty with Britain in February hardly helped to endear him or the French to the Russians, because the treaty looked to them like just a further strengthening of ties among the western countries.[35] If, finally, the Truman doctrine (12 March 1947) – warning the Soviet Union to remain within its existing zones of influence – heightened tension between the western countries and the Soviet Union still further, and consequently made the largely unproductive French attempts at arbitration increasingly irritating at least to Britain and the United States, it still took Bidault until April before he was prepared to acknowledge that his 'independent' policy had failed.

But his policy had failed not only because of the increasing rift between the superpowers. By April 1947 the recognition had dawned upon the French that even their basic economic needs could be satisfied only if they gave their full support to the United States and Britain. Their urgent need for Saar and Ruhr coal and for economic aid had made independence a luxury they could ill afford. That they would receive no help from the Soviet Union had been clear for some time. It was made still clearer at the Moscow Conference of foreign ministers (March–April 1947), where Molotov was again to brush aside French claims in the Rhineland and the Saar. When the British and American foreign ministers, outside the conference, offered Bidault their support in his major demand for French control over the Saar, he accepted. It was an acceptance which not only spelt the end of diplomatic independence, but also the beginning of France's accession to the western bloc.

It had been interesting to see how little the active participation of the French Communist Party in the government of France had affected Soviet policy towards Paris. It might have been thought that the spectacle of as dedicated a member of the PCF as Billoux in charge at the French Ministry of Defence would have appealed to the Kremlin, and that it would have gone out of its way to ensure the continuation of Communist membership of French governments. Whatever the reasons for the Soviet Union's apparent lack of interest, the Saar agreement with the United States and Britain had not only the direct effect of driving France firmly into the Anglo-American camp, but also the indirect effect of driving the Communists out of the Paris government. In May Ramadier got rid of them. It must be said that there had been considerable pressure from the United States for him to do just that. But it must also be said that the dismissal of the Communist ministers was not an unmitigated blessing for France. Out of office, the PCF began to indulge in the most disruptive tactics which not only deeply hurt the French economy but also, as a consequence, kept the country disunited, weak, and the poor relation in the western alliance for much longer than the effects of the war alone would have warranted. There is of course no saying how long the Communists would have stayed in the government in any case, nor what their tactics within it would have been if they had stayed.

1947–53: THE COLD WAR

For at least a decade Franco-Soviet relations were now to be little more than part of Soviet relations with the west as a whole. The first major manifestation within France of this fact, with its anti-Soviet as well as anti-Communist features, came, surprisingly, from the independent-minded head of the wartime Free French movement. At about the time of Bidault's acceptance of the Anglo-American offer on the Saar, General de

Gaulle – out of office since 1946 – founded his *Rassemblement du Peuple Français*. One of the chief characteristics of the new movement was its violent anti-Communism, and the target for its virulence was the Soviet Union as much as the Communist Party in France. For the next few years de Gaulle was to lose no opportunity of inveighing against the twin enemy. Although he was unable directly to affect government policy, his supporters were at times influential in Parliament. Moreover, this phase of his career must be of relevance to any assessment of his policies when he was again in power from 1958 to 1969. For, if his detestation of Communism was really genuine, and the Soviet system as deeply repulsive to him as he claimed in the RPF period, he must have undergone an extraordinary conversion between then and 1964, when his overtures to the Soviet Union again became insistent. The alternative explanation could only be that his subsequent policies towards the Soviet Union were merely displays of opportunism. There was never any evidence of a conversion.

During the summer of 1947 – despite an all-time low in pettiness between the two countries, in which there were mutual accusations that they were holding on to each others' citizens (Moscow for this purpose treated citizens of satellite states as Russians)[36] – Bidault joined the British foreign minister in inviting the Soviet Union to discussions on the Marshall Plan. The meetings took place in Paris between 27 June and 2 July 1947. The Moscow government was deeply suspicious of the plan, seeing it as a United States trick to enable it to interfere in the affairs of other countries. Moreover, Molotov stated that the Soviet Union could accept aid only if it was reserved for victims of Hitler's aggression. Perhaps the Russians genuinely believed in that principle. But the Cold War had already reached the stage at which worthwhile collaboration between the Soviet Union and the west was unlikely. In any case, Molotov bravely affirmed that the Russians had a plan of their own.

The reaction of the French Communist Party to the Marshall Plan was entirely attuned to that of Moscow. A series of PCF-inspired strikes hit France in the final part of 1947, and in

Belgrade the PCF helped to found the Cominform, in which the Communist parties of eastern and western Europe were to be linked in their common defence against the capitalist system. Within France, violent anti-Communism now raged. De Gaulle's RPF swept to victory at the municipal elections at the end of October, and the government was unable – and probably unwilling – to resist the widespread desire for a tough attitude towards the PCF at home and the Soviet Union and her satellites abroad. November and December saw typical consequences of the resulting tensions. Arms were allegedly found at a Russian repatriation camp; nineteen Russians were expelled from France for having participated in strikes; General Catroux was kept in Paris until the end of January 1948 on the assumption that Moscow was about to recall its ambassador in Paris. Not wishing to be outdone, the Soviet Union recalled its repatriation mission from France, and expelled the French counterpart from the Soviet Union.[37] Catroux asked to leave his Moscow post, and returned home in April 1948.

Things went from bad to worse. Partly because the London Conference of foreign ministers (25 November 1947) had produced little more than irritation in Bidault over constant Soviet accusations of bad faith, the foreign ministers of the three western countries decided to meet on their own in London in February 1948. At about the same time the countries of the Communist bloc met in Prague and accused France, the United States and Britain of contravening the Potsdam agreement. Next, the Russian representative, referring to what he called the 'illegal' London Conference of February (since it had been held without the Soviet Union) suddenly broke up the Four Power Control Commission meeting in Berlin on 19 March, thus ending the last joint east-west effort to implement the Potsdam arrangements for the postwar government of Germany. In July 1948 the Russians began the Berlin blockade – ostensibly because the western allies had, without consulting them, introduced a currency reform in the western zones – that made the situation decidedly serious, because no one could foresee what would happen if the western allies tried to force supplies through to Berlin on land. They had certainly made it clear that they had no intention of allowing themselves to be evicted from their occupation areas in the former German capital. In the event, they chose to avoid a direct confrontation with the Soviet Union by supplying Berlin by air, and the Russians did not interfere. The blockade, which lasted for nearly a year – it ended in May 1949 – marked the hottest point in the Cold War in Europe.

There had been other reasons for friction during 1948. The French in particular had been badly shaken by the Communist takeover in Czechoslovakia in February 1948. Despite their 1938 Munich deal with Hitler, they still liked to think that Czechoslovakia had some special significance for them. This latest Soviet *coup* caused France, Britain and the Benelux countries to alter their plans for a meeting in Brussels in March 1948. Having intended primarily to work out projects for economic and cultural collaboration, they now spent much of their time also arranging for military cooperation. Their pact in Brussels was signed on 17 March; it pledged, among other things, that they would assist each other in case of military danger to any one country or to several of them; the cursory reference to Germany in the preamble deceived no one about where they thought the real threat was at that time. Soon after the treaty was signed the French foreign minister, Bidault, asked the Americans and other states to join it. This step marked the beginning of the North Atlantic Treaty Organisation.

At about the same time, the Rumanians closed their French schools and the French Institute in Bucarest. The Paris government responded by expelling a number of Rumanian citizens from France and by forbidding the importation of certain Rumanian periodicals. Bulgaria and Poland followed Rumania's (or, more probably, the Soviet Union's) lead. At the Danube Shipping Conference in Belgrade in August 1948, the French and Russians clashed again. The Russians wanted to restrict the control of the Danube to countries bordering on it, while the French, who had important interests there since the interwar years, insisted on sharing it. There was a moment at the conference when Vishinsky was so outraged by French claims that he referred to France as a 'little cock jumping about behind the Anglo-Saxon powers'.[38] Unappeased, the French refused to sign the convention.

The slight easing of east-west tensions that came with the lifting of the Berlin blockade had been foreshadowed since January 1949. The veteran French Communist, Marcel Cachin, had begun the new year by stating in the National Assembly that Communism and Capitalism could coexist. The following month saw the representatives of the Soviet Union and the United States talking together at the United Nations, which almost certainly led to the announcement at the end of April that the four foreign ministers would meet again. They did meet, eleven days after the end of the Berlin blockade, on 23 May 1949 in Paris. Meanwhile Molotov had been replaced by Vishinsky, not altogether the happiest choice for the *coq gaulois*.

The easing of tension coincided with the creation of NATO* in April 1949. But, as had been the case in 1947 with the Marshall Plan, this major western show of solidarity in the face of the Soviet Union also had its effect on the PCF and, therefore, directly on the internal situation in France. In a speech to the Central Committee of the PCF, Maurice Thorez threatened, some weeks before NATO came into being, that if war were to come between NATO and the Soviet Union, French workers could not be expected to fight her.[39] Although the degree to which such talk reflected reality can be exaggerated, there is no doubt that French relations with the Soviet Union to some extent governed the political, social and economic situation in France.

Shortly before the NATO treaty was signed in Washington on 4 April 1949, Moscow radio claimed that the treaty marked the end of French independence.[40] Certainly, it has been shown that since 1947 France's policy towards the Soviet Union had been increasingly aligned with that of her western partners, who tended at that time to present a monolithic front in their dealings

* It included Belgium, Canada, Denmark, France, Britain, Iceland, Italy, Luxembourg, Holland, Norway, Portugal and the United States.

with Moscow. At the end of March 1949 the Soviet Union sent notes to all the signatories of the NATO treaty asserting that the alliance violated the United Nations charter, the Anglo-Soviet treaty of 1942, the Franco-Soviet treaty of 1944, and the agreements of Yalta and Potsdam.[41]

The setting up of NATO was followed, early in April 1949, by the decision taken in Washington by the United States, Britain and France to grant autonomy to their part of Germany, without prejudice to their rights as occupying powers. It was a further step in the consolidation of the western bloc. The unilateral Washington decision was communicated to the Soviet Union when its foreign minister met his colleagues from France, the United States and Britain in Paris on 23 May 1949. Unable to change that decision, the Soviet Union in reply set up the Council of the German People in Berlin and, in October 1949, transformed their own occupation zone into the German Democratic Republic (DDR).

Though some of the heat had been taken out of the east-west conflict since the end of the Berlin blockade, the early 1950s saw no change in the rigidity with which both sides clung to their positions. Unsurprisingly, the Soviet Union and Communist China gave *de jure* recognition to the 'rebel' government of Ho-Chi-Minh in Indo-China, at a time, in 1950, when the French were beginning seriously to feel the strain of their commitments in that area. At the outbreak of the war in Korea six months later, when the Americans began to press for German rearmament, Soviet reaction was also predictable. Early in November the Soviet government protested to the Security Council of the United Nations about it. The French, with their own misgivings about German rearmament, could not resist taunting the Russians with the fact that the Soviet Union had itself allowed rearmament in its own zone. While West Germany would never be allowed to become a base for aggression against the Soviet Union, they said, they could feel no certainty about the consequences of the Soviet rearming of the DDR.[42]

The same dreary slanging continued in 1951. The PCF duly called a strike when General Eisenhower arrived in France in January to take up his post as NATO commander-in-chief. The French government retaliated by seizing PCF newspapers and banning some foreign Communist periodicals. The strikes did the Communists little good: they were not very effective and were no doubt in part responsible for the PCF's poor showing at the general election in June 1951. In September the Soviet Union refused to sign the peace treaty with Japan because the United States, having had the major burden of the war in the Pacific, had insisted on having most of its own way over the arrangements for peace.

1952 began no more auspiciously. In March the Soviet government imposed travel restrictions on western diplomats in the Soviet Union. The western countries imaginatively replied in like coin. In the same month the Russian foreign minister, Gromyko, proposed negotiations for a German peace treaty. There should be, he said, an all-German government before the negotiations began, and the Germany that emerged from the treaty should be neutral, though it could have an army; to which the west replied, as before and again later on a number of occasions, that the Soviet suggestion was no more than a move to delay the effectiveness of NATO, that before there could be an all-German government there must be free all-German elections, and that, in any case, the Russian should for a start help reactivate the four-power organisations set up after Potsdam. Although a joint east-west solution of the German problem might indeed have made German rearmament (as well as NATO) unnecessary – and the French detested the very thought of German rearmament – the French government adopted substantially the same negative position on Gromyko's suggestion as its allies.

That the Cold War, by that time, had shown itself to be little more than a petty and tragically expensive pantomime in a world that found it impossible adequately to nourish the majority of its population, rather than the first step towards a third world war, could also be seen from Stalin's behaviour shortly before he died in March 1953. Although the so-called thaw between the east and west is often taken to have started with his death, Stalin himself had expressed the belief that war was not inevitable, in an article in *Bolshevist*,[43] and had shown by his subsequent efforts to stop the war in Korea that while he was not averse from pushing his opponents hard, he had no desire to court national extinction. The French, unable to come up with anything that could end the rigid and impoverishing posturings of the Cold War, nevertheless distinguished themselves from their allies at the time of Stalin's death. On the day of the official announcement that the Soviet leader was dead, the French minister of defence ordered flags to be flown at half-mast. He was promptly taken to task by some of his countrymen for thus 'insulting' the men fighting in Indo-China to keep it within the 'free' world.

1953–6: EAST-WEST THAW

Malenkov and Khrushchev, apparently jointly taking Stalin's place, were invited by the British prime minister, Churchill, in April 1953 to discuss outstanding problems at a summit conference. As an immediate consequence, meetings were held in Berlin at foreign minister level from 25 January to 18 February 1954. France was represented by Bidault, the Soviet Union by Molotov. But Molotov merely repeated the well-worn Russian demands that Germany be neutralised, that both Germanies be treated as equals in negotiations, and that negotiations about Germany be preceded by the withdrawal of all foreign troops. As a result, apart from arrangements for a conference at Geneva on Asian problems, nothing useful emerged from the Berlin marathon.

However, if the Berlin meetings were still apparently cast in the Cold War mould, the immediate post-Stalin period provided a number of illustrations of a relaxation of tension. Since, as has been seen, it had been at the petty level at which east-west hostility had shown itself most clearly, it was also at that level that the relaxation most clearly showed itself. On 5 April 1953 seventeen Soviet sailors were allowed to go on shore leave from their ship at Rouen and travel to Paris. At about the same time, French and British civilians were allowed to return home from North Korea via Moscow. Restrictions on the movement of foreign diplomats in Moscow were eased. At the end of April, economists from east and west met in Geneva to work out ways of increasing trade between their respective areas. In June, French and Russian talks began for a commercial and payments agreement. Rapid progress was made, and an agreement was signed on 15 July 1953.[44]

Moreover, fears in the west that the Berlin rising in June 1953 would make the Soviet leaders hesitate over further relaxation of tension were shown to be unfounded. Admittedly, western suggestions to Moscow in July that discussions should be resumed on current problems brought a dead-pan refusal in the form of a reiteration of well-known Soviet attitudes. But the rebuff was largely explicable by the fact that this was the time when EDC debates among the Atlantic allies were getting hotter, as France was being pressed with increasing impatience by the United States to ratify the treaty so that German rearmament could get under way. In their reply of 4 August 1953 to the western invitation, the Russians specifically objected to the prospect of German rearmament, and shortly afterwards Malenkov seemed to address himself particularly to France when, in a speech on 8 August, he said that EDC meant the handing over of France to German revanchism, Germany being 'the mortal enemy of France'.[45] Malenkov was voicing a fear that was also to be heard in France, even among non-Communists, that any military alliance which included both France and Germany would sooner or later be dominated by the Germans. The Soviet leader went so far as to offer France an alternative to EDC, if the purpose of EDC really was to provide a safeguard against future German aggression. He offered Russian help against Germany whenever it was needed, and reminded the French of the existence of the Franco-Soviet treaty which, he said, could be the guarantee of future European security. A week later, on 15 August, the Soviet government issued another protest against the rearming of Germany.[46] On the same day it announced that it possessed the hydrogen bomb.

German rearmament was apparently so unhappy a prospect for the Soviet Union that, on the eve of the French National Assembly debate to decide on the principle of EDC at the end of November 1953, the Soviet government agreed to come to another four-power conference after all. This provided the many French opponents of EDC with useful support for their habitual hope that, somehow, an understanding with the Soviet Union would come about which would make the whole hateful business of German rearmament unnecessary. The problem was to find out how genuine Russian fears about rearming the Germans were, and how genuine were their suggested alternatives. It was seen in the previous chapter that the reluctance of the French to see the Germans rearmed was deeply felt and widespread; but their difficulty was that they were uncertain about Soviet intentions in Europe which, if aggressive, would for most of them make the controlled rearming of the Germans preferable to Soviet domination. The four-power conference, held in Berlin at the end of January 1954, failed to reassure the French about Russian intentions. When it broke up, on 18 February, the representatives of the western powers were left with the Soviet proposal for a European collective security treaty that did not include the United States. This they understandably refused to accept. Georges Bidault, the French foreign minister, insisted that NATO remained a necessary part of the European defence system.[47] The Soviet Union's reply was a piece of high comedy. On 31 March the three western ambassadors in Moscow were told that the Soviet Union wanted to join NATO. It took the French some six weeks to compose their reply, in which they spoke of the 'absolutely unreal character'[48] of the Soviet request before, like their partners, turning it down – which made Moscow accuse France of supporting the warmongers in the United States. A week before their request to join NATO, the Russians had recognised what they termed the 'diplomatic sovereignty' of the German Democratic Republic.

But the French were grateful that the Soviet Union had not changed its mind about wanting to end the war in Indo-China. By 1954 it had become an intolerable burden for the French, but also a nuisance for the Russians, who were committed to helping the Indo-Chinese Communists without any certainty of imminent victory after nearly a decade of fighting. At the end of April 1954, in Geneva, five-power talks began (the four 'big' powers and China) to bring the war to an end. If it took until July to reach agreement, this was more because the French found it difficult to concede complete independence to the states in Indo-China than because of Soviet or Chinese unhelpfulness.*

The question of German rearmament continued to preoccupy both the Soviet Union and the western governments throughout the remainder of 1954. EDC having been rejected by the National Assembly in Paris, the Soviet government tried hard to bring about also the rejection of the agreements that were to replace it. It pointed out that if the French agreed to the rearming of Germany they would be guilty of going against the spirit of their 1944 treaty with the Soviet Union. Furthermore, it asked for another conference. Mendès-France, who was then prime minister, having presented his allies with the National Assembly's rejection of EDC after four years of variously contrived French delays, somewhat impatiently told Moscow to stop playing games.[49] He accused the Russians of merely wanting to impede the ratification of the London and Paris agreements which, since the French Parliament was assumed to be prepared to accept them, were finally to bring about the conditions for controlled West German rearmament. Two weeks before the last ratification debate in the National Assembly the Soviet Union, on 16 December 1954, stated in a note that if the Paris agreements were ratified it would annul the 1944 treaty.[50] Mendès-France thereupon sought to persuade his countrymen that such Soviet pressure was intolerable, that it was being exercised in this way only because the internal political weaknesses of France made it appear that such pressure might succeed, and in support of this thesis pointed out that similar pressure was not being put on the British government which also had a treaty with the Soviet Union and was also a signatory to the Paris agreements.[51]

The French National Assembly ratified the agreements on 30 December 1954. In his summing up,[52] Mendès-France stated that the agreements in no way affected the 1944 treaty with the Soviet Union. He also implied that if it were really argued that

* See below pp. 190–1.

the agreements did affect it, then the Russian rearming of the DDR in previous years must also have affected it. In addition, Moscow was reminded that, although the Soviet Union had rearmed the DDR, the French for their part had never threatened to annul the 1944 treaty. Government changes in the Soviet Union delayed a reply, Bulganin replacing Malenkov in February 1955. But on 7 May 1955 the Soviet Union denounced the Franco-Soviet treaty of 1944 as 'having lost all value'.[53] A week later, apparently in answer to the incorporation of the German Federal Republic into the now more cohesive western military grouping, the countries of eastern Europe concluded their own, military, Warsaw Pact. But, to show that east-west relations were not thereby meant to be frozen again, the Soviet government joined the western allies in signing a peace treaty with Austria the day after the Warsaw Pact had been concluded.

In fact, though without illusions about speedy results, east-west contacts continued at all levels. In July 1955 the French prime minister, Edgar Faure, joined Eisenhower and Anthony Eden in their Geneva meetings with Bulganin and Khrushchev. They agreed that exchanges of views between the two sides should be encouraged. (It is true that they agreed on little else.) In September the German chancellor, Dr Adenauer, paid a visit to the Soviet Union which led to the opening of diplomatic relations between the two countries. The French government applauded this first step towards the 'normalisation' of Soviet-German relations, if only because it helped to reduce tension in Europe and was therefore at least to that degree in the French interest. What was particularly significant about the resumption of German-Soviet contacts was that the initiative had come from Moscow.

1956–8: RENEWED ATTEMPTS AT AN INDEPENDENT FRENCH FOREIGN POLICY

After the general election of January 1956 the leader of the French Socialist Party, Guy Mollet, took over the government. There is no doubt that his cabinet wanted to give all possible encouragement to the continuing *détente* with the east.[54] It particularly wished to establish cultural exchanges with the Soviet Union, a step which seemed to make it necessary for Mollet to assure the United States ambassador that the French government envisaged no changes in its foreign policy.[55] But the end of the Indo-Chinese war, and growing prosperity, were making the French feel rather more independent of the United States than they had done since 1947, and the Algerian war was not yet straining French resources. Khrushchev's anti-Stalin speech (25 February 1956) at the 20th Party Congress was an encouragement to the French to multiply their own contacts with the east and to explore the possibilities for a genuine *détente*. The climate became increasingly auspicious. The Cominform was dissolved on 17 April 1956. On the following day Bulganin and Khrushchev arrived in England for a state visit. In May Tito came to France, the first visit since the war by the head of a Socialist state. During the same month a delegation of the SFIO went to the Soviet Union, having chosen its own programme.

Emboldened by their own successes so far, as well as by the continuance of the east-west thaw in general, Mollet and Pineau, his foreign minister, ventured upon a five-day visit to the Soviet Union – beginning on 15 May 1956 – during which they had political and economic talks with the Soviet leaders. The communiqué issued on 19 May[56] contained the usual platitudes about support for the United Nations, peaceful coexistence, and non-interference in the affairs of other countries. On disarmament, the Soviet Union stated that it would unilaterally demobilise 1,200,000 soldiers; the French wisely dwelt on the need for international control in disarmament. So far as Germany was concerned, Mollet came away with the conviction that the Soviet government was happy to adjourn reunification indefinitely.[57]

However, it soon became clear that the Soviet leaders' regard for France was still not very great. For example, Mollet had apparently been told privately that his country needed the Soviet Union in order to be able to cope with the Germans,[58] but Adenauer was invited by Khrushchev a few weeks later to collaborate with the Russians against the 'American' west and

China.[59] Again, Mollet had tried in Moscow to gain Soviet understanding for France's problems in Algeria. The Russian leaders had said reassuringly that Algeria was a purely French problem. Yet the Russian representative at the United Nations voted in favour of the discussion of the Algerian problem in the United Nations General Assembly. And within one day of the publication of the Franco-Soviet communiqué at the end of Mollet's stay, Khrushchev had gone to a reception in the Soviet capital and publicly drunk a toast to all peoples fighting for their freedom.[60]

The replacement of Molotov by Shepilov as foreign minister early in June 1956 was to be the last manifestation of that phase of the east-west thaw. There were two major reasons for the coming change. First, Shepilov's appointment coincided with a visit to Moscow by Tito; it was assumed that the Yugoslav leader's presence in the Soviet capital was connected with the increasingly difficult disciplinary problems the Russians were encountering in several of the east European satellite countries, particularly in Poland and Hungary. These problems tended to make the Soviet Union more inward-looking, while the repressive policies to which they gave rise silenced western advocates of a *rapprochement* with Moscow. Second, on 26 July 1956, President Nasser of Egypt announced the nationalisation of the Suez Canal. To this act Russia gave its support, although it was a direct challenge to the interests of France and Britain.

The 'disciplinary problems' in Hungary, and Franco-British reaction to Nasser's Suez *coup,* quickly brought the relations between Paris and Moscow close to breaking point. Egypt refused to attend the international conference in London in August where the nationalisation of the Suez canal was to be discussed, and the Soviet Union firmly opposed compromise suggestions for the internationalisation of the canal. Furthermore, at the Security Council the Soviet Union vetoed the proposal that the canal should be run by a users' group.[61] Tension between Israel and Egypt was also increasing at this time.

Undeterred by Soviet hostility, on 30 October 1956, the day after Israel attacked Egypt, France and Britain confronted Cairo with an ultimatum, having sounded out neither their closest ally, the United States, nor the United Nations on their proposed use of force to settle the Suez canal problem. Paris and London informed Egypt that unless her forces withdrew sixteen kilometres from the canal, France and Britain would see to it that her war with Israel would not be able to interfere with navigation in the Suez canal. Egypt rejected the ultimatum. At the same time the Soviet Union was preparing to crush its enemies in Hungary. On 4 November the Soviet army began to batter the country into submission. On the following day French and British troops invaded Egypt. During the previous night, that is after the Soviet attack on Hungary and at the beginning of Franco-British operations in Egypt, Bulganin had sent notes to France, Britain and Israel in which he said that the war in Egypt could spread to other areas and turn into a third world war. In addition, he said explicitly that the Soviet Union was prepared to use force in order to crush the aggressors and restore peace in the middle east, and that it had already asked the United Nations to intervene militarily.[62] The French prime minister's reply did not suggest that he was particularly impressed by these Soviet moves. Mollet, on 6 November, told the Soviet government that the threat to use long-range weapons on the countries in conflict with Egypt was unlikely to solve the problems of the middle east; that what it was doing in Hungary gave the Soviet Union no moral right to brandish slogans of liberty and independence; and that if the Soviet Union had used its influence in the middle east to reduce tension in conformity with its alleged desire, events would have turned out differently.[63] However, at 18.30 on the same day, a ceasefire came into force along the canal. This was not because Mollet had suddenly been frightened or converted to the Soviet view, but because Britain had been successfully bullied by Eisenhower into abandoning so anachronistic an adventure. During a foreign affairs debate in the National Assembly in December 1956, the French foreign minister, Pineau, complained about the United Nations' double standards, which caused it to concentrate its thunder on the British and French while leaving it at rather platonic declarations when it came to Soviet repression in Hungary.[64]

In 1957, Franco-Soviet relations were largely restricted to a series of minatory messages from Moscow. As the EEC treaty was being ratified by its future members, the Soviet government sent each of them a note stating that they were about to become even more dependent on the United States than they already were as members of NATO. In April, as the United States was proposing to equip NATO countries with atomic weapons, under American control, Moscow declared that these countries should appraise the risk of retaliation. Then, on the anniversary of Mollet's Moscow visit (18 May), Bulganin wrote to the French premier to express his concern about United States' bases in France.[65] At the same time he renewed the Soviet offer of a non-aggression treaty between the Warsaw pact countries and NATO, but linked it with a demand for the withdrawal of foreign (i.e. American) troops from Europe and the ending of nuclear testing. Bulganin also advised Mollet to end the war in Algeria 'in France's own interest'. In conclusion, the Soviet leader asked for more cultural and scientific exchanges. To these objurgations, Mollet could apparently find nothing new to reply, but reminded the Soviet government of earlier French reproaches about its attitude over the middle east.[66]

Probably one of the main reasons for the diplomatic holding operation of the Russians in 1957 was to be found in their own internal political difficulties. That there was a leadership struggle became clear when in the late spring talk about 'anti-party' activities was to be heard in Moscow. One of the more diverting consequences of this struggle was the appointment of Molotov, that embodiment of Stalinist rigour and perennial scourge of the world of international diplomacy, as ambassador to Outer Mongolia. Earlier, in February, Shepilov had been replaced as foreign minister by Gromyko.

But by now France's own internal problems were increasingly demanding the attention of her governments. The war in Algeria could no longer be ignored, and the threat to the very survival of the regime of the Fourth Republic was becoming patent. As a result, French foreign policy became less overtly independent than Mollet had wanted it to be, especially after his disgust with Eisenhower's sermonising over Suez. But the decision to go ahead with the production of a French atom bomb was not re-scinded, in spite of growing financial difficulties. Moreover, the United States, on whom in the last analysis French security was known to depend, was experiencing a high degree of demora-lisation, and thus adding to the preoccupations of French gov-ernments. In August 1957 the Soviet Union had successfully tested an intercontinental ballistic missile, and in October had managed to send its Sputnik into space. Having so far only failures to record in the latter realm, the United States seemed to go into a kind of despondency, at a time when the Russians – the leadership problems apparently resolving themselves – were beginning to be more self-assured than ever. It looked as if the days of unchallengeable American-led western superiority were over. A kind of balance of power between east and west seemed to be establishing itself.

At the end of 1957 the Polish foreign minister, Rapacki, put forward a plan which in effect would have left the whole of Europe at Russia's mercy. It is unlikely that his proposals had not received prior Soviet approval, unless of course they had actually originated in Moscow itself. The plan advocated the setting-up of a nuclear free zone in central Europe, which would allow for a united Germany, and for the creation of that zone to be accompanied by the withdrawal of United States' forces from Europe. Thus, it was suggested, tension would be eased and the German problem solved. At the end of December 1957 Félix Gaillard, the French prime minister, in an interview with *United States News,* rejected the plan, largely on the grounds that it would make no contribution to French security, since once the United States had repatriated their forces, Soviet forces would still be where they had been since 1945.[67]

As the internal political position deteriorated in France, Soviet respect for her governments, never conspicuous, seemed to de-cline still further. On 9 January 1958 Bulganin sent notes to a number of countries inviting them to increase east-west contacts, especially commercial exchanges. There was a particularly inso-lent tone to the note directed to Paris. 'So far as is known,' Bulganin wrote,[68] 'French business circles are far from satisfied with the one-sidedness of French external trade, which limits the economic development of the nation and has an unfavourable influence on the balance of payments.' Even if the phrase 'one-sidedness of external trade' was not entirely clear, the tone was. At the same time the Soviet leader also proposed an early summit meeting. The Gaillard government dutifully followed its western partners in rejecting an early summit meeting but, given its preoccupations, wanted to close no doors, and in its reply was less firm than before about the Rapacki plan.[69]

On 31 March 1958, more confident of itself than ever, the Soviet government announced that it would, unilaterally, end all nuclear testing. In France, the gesture barely made an impact. The country was almost entirely absorbed with its internal problems. The aftermath of the French bombing of the Tunisian village Sakhiet, with its political implications, was to lead to the fall of the Gaillard administration on 15 April.

Then came the final agony of the Fourth Republic, the 13 May revolution, and the return to power of General de Gaulle through the good offices of the French army in Algeria.

1958–63: DE GAULLE'S ANTI-SOVIET PHASE

De Gaulle formed his first government after the May revolution on 1 June 1958. He took as foreign minister Maurice Couve de Murville, a career diplomat – not a politician – whose last post had been that of ambassador to Bonn. The Soviet government, as will be shown, saw the 13 May revolution as a Fascist *coup,* but at first avoided invective. The new French government's early statement that it reserved the right to have its own atomic weapons left the Soviet Union ambivalent; it did not like nuclear proliferation, but to the degree to which France became self-reliant in nuclear defence she would also be likely – under de Gaulle – to assert her independence from the United States and NATO. And whatever weakened NATO was welcome to the Soviet Union.

But it is doubtful whether de Gaulle did want to weaken NATO. In fact, it is likely that at this time his anti-Communism would have been a decisive motive for his wanting a strong

NATO. His threat in 1958 to refuse the United States launching sites and rocket dumps in France if his country were not given more responsibility in NATO was less an assertion of independence from the Atlantic alliance than a demand for a bigger say in its decisions. Indeed, the threat accompanied his note of 24 September 1958 to Britain and the United States in which he actually asked for greater NATO coordination and a re-examination of its defence plans. The note also demanded a reallocation of commands so that the French could be given greater responsibilities, commensurate with their involvement in Algeria. De Gaulle was here following the many French politicians and army officers who had been suggesting for some time that the war against the Algerian FLN was an integral part of the struggle of the west against World-Communism, where North Africa had to be seen as the southern flank of the NATO area. De Gaulle's quarrel with the United States could therefore not, as yet, provide the Soviet Union with much joy.

In fact, not only was de Gaulle at this stage refusing to allow his desire for equality of rank in the western alliance to bring him closer to the Soviet Union, but his response to Soviet pressure on NATO was capable of being more violent than that of the United States. For example, when the Soviet Union in November 1958 demanded that West Berlin be 'free' and demilitarised, and followed this up in January 1959 with an ultimatum that the question must be settled by a conference within two months, his reaction, to the overt delight of the Federal Republic, was more uncompromising than that of the British and Americans.[70] The Soviet government professed to see this as a piece of anti-Soviet collusion between the Germans and the French, just when it was also claiming that the constitution of the Fifth Republic was turning France into a Gaullist dictatorship. On 27 January 1959, at the beginning of the 21st Communist Party Congress, Khrushchev said:

That France is heading towards a military dictatorship has now become clearer: democratic liberty is being trampled underfoot, as are the gains the popular masses had managed to make in the past. The headlong rush into reaction in France, a country celebrated for its democratic traditions, fills with anxiety all those who value democracy and progress.[71]

But already in September 1958 Khrushchev had commented in an article:

Three or four months ago all Europe could hope that the new [French] government, having de Gaulle at its head, would have the will and power to control the Fascists, end the unjust colonial war against the Algerian people, and maintain the Republic in France . . . Vain and dangerous illusions.[72]

Unimpressed, de Gaulle at his press conference in March 1959 rejected the Rapacki plan[73] – already dismissed by the United States in May 1958 – on the grounds that it would kill the Atlantic alliance. Not content with that, de Gaulle turned his attention to the DDR, whose recognition by the west the Russians had unceasingly demanded since they had set it up in opposition to the Bonn regime in 1949, and in his most scathing accents said:

We are not prepared to recognise the Pankow system as a sovereign and independent state since it was merely created, and continues to exist, as a result of Soviet occupation and thanks to an implacable dictatorship.[74]

A few days later, at a NATO conference, Couve de Murville remained true to the current Gaullist anti-Soviet line by enjoining his colleagues to be firm and not to be misled by apparent changes in Soviet diplomacy which, he said, were only changes in tactics, the ultimate aim always remaining the same.

Nevertheless, before the year was out, at his press conference in November 1959, de Gaulle foresaw that one day the Soviet Union would regard itself as a European power whose fate was closely bound up with that of the other European powers. He was thinking in particular of the pressure which China would soon be exercising on Russian interests and territories in the far east.[75] It was likely that in the face of that pressure the Soviet Union would want to secure her western borders. There, the only country with an interest in upsetting the *status quo* was Germany. To gain her ends, the Soviet Union could either come to an agreement with France which would commit both countries to controlling Germany, or it would seek a direct understanding with Bonn, outside the context of NATO in general and France in particular. De Gaulle must have preferred the first solution. But for a start the Soviet Union had to be induced to act as if it recognised its need for peace in the west, and to see France as an essential element in the promotion of that peace.

However, at that stage de Gaulle was still greatly preoccupied with the permanent threat to his regime from a combination of Algerian settlers and army officers. His ability to take initiatives in foreign affairs was therefore limited. Even so, he continued to take a rather more inflexible line with the Kremlin than his western allies. The May to August meetings in 1959 of foreign ministers of the 'big four' produced no agreement on Germany. But they paved the way for Khrushchev's visit to the United States in October. Characteristically, de Gaulle was unenthusiastic about the proposal for a big four summit meeting which emerged from Khrushchev's American visit. On 21 October 1959 he agreed in principle to attend but insisted, and again repeated at his press conference on 10 November, that signs of a lessening of tension in east-west relations had to be a precondition for such a meeting.[76] No doubt fearing that given the precarious state of his government he would not cut much of a figure at a meeting with the other three heads of government, de Gaulle would have preferred it to take place in the more distant future. That this was weighing with him was shown at least indirectly by his additional point that before a summit there should also be more consultations between the different governments, and that in particular he should meet the Soviet leader, who had after all already met his United States and British counterparts, Eisenhower and Macmillan. Somewhat surprisingly, de Gaulle at the same press conference paid a tribute to Khrushchev, saying that the Soviet leader had recognised the importance of peace and human happiness. The tribute – perhaps based on Khrushchev's grandfatherly gestures in the United States – came strangely from the head of a government which had only a short time before warned its western allies that changes in Soviet tone amounted to changes in tactics, not in ultimate aims. In its turn, the tribute itself can hardly have been more than a change in tactics, helping the general to keep his powder dry.

On 31 October 1959 it was announced that Khrushchev was to visit France. He was to come in March 1960. 'Objectively,' Khrushchev wrote to de Gaulle, 'the interests of our two nations clash nowhere in the world, and it could of course not be said that it was only by chance that we were allies in two world wars.'[77] It looked as if at least a marriage of convenience might be arranged. Long resentful of the importance of the Anglo-American bloc within the western alliance, de Gaulle might already have been edging over to see what the Soviet Union had to offer. And the Soviet Union was unlikely to object.

For the French it was an impressive coincidence that they succeeded in exploding their first atomic bomb during Khrushchev's visit (23 March–3 April 1960). The Russian leader officially regretted that the explosion had taken place, and hoped that the French would now sign the test ban treaty; a vain hope, because de Gaulle had much catching-up to do. Khrushchev also made it clear that he was unhappy about Franco-German relations. This was understandable, if only because the Bonn-Paris link, were it really to become an established feature of European life, would necessarily weaken the Soviet position in Europe. It has already been noted in the previous chapter that de Gaulle was not only aware of this but actually intended it to be one of the main objectives of his relationship with Adenauer. An understanding with the Soviet Union, at least at that time, seemed to have lower priority than a Paris-Bonn axis. The Soviet leader's irritation with this aspect of French policy exploded at a lunch given for him at Reims. 'Your speech,' he told a minister in de Gaulle's government, 'was so diplomatic that I do not know whether, in your view, the Germans came to you as aggressors or as guests. For our part, we cannot forget the German attack on the Soviet Union.'[78] The communiqué issued at the end of the visit enumerated the main international problems over which the Soviet Union and France disagreed; it provided no answers but looked forward to the summit conference to be held, in Paris, in May.[79]

But the summit was a mess. On 1 May an American reconnaissance aircraft had been shot down over the Soviet Union. President Eisenhower showed none of the contrition over the flight the Kremlin considered appropriate after all the talk about peace during Khrushchev's American visit and the great hopes the four heads of governments had said they had of the coming summit meetings. When Khrushchev arrived in Paris on 14 May he immediately went to see de Gaulle. On the following day he presented the general with three conditions for his own participation in the summit meetings: the United States had to apologise for the plane incident, had to promise that those responsible for it would be punished, and had to undertake that nothing like it would happen again. Eisenhower confined himself to giving an undertaking that there would be no more such flights during his presidency; this was not good enough for the Russians, who promptly left Paris after farewell visits to de Gaulle and Macmillan.

On 31 May de Gaulle stated in a radio and television talk that, in his view, the plane incident had not been an adequate reason for abandoning a summit conference in which the problems of the world were to have been discussed. At this the Russians withdrew into their former defensive invective. Already overtly critical of de Gaulle's treatment of Guinée – it had opted for independence in 1958 and had instantly had all forms of French assistance completely cut off – the Soviet government now loudly accused de Gaulle of practising neo-colonialism in Africa, not least in Algeria. Gromyko, addressing the Supreme Soviet on 23 November 1960, said: 'Just as Hitler's atrocities did not succeed in making Germans, or even half-Germans, out of Frenchmen, so neither the crimes nor the actions designed to crush the national liberation struggle of the Algerian people can make Algeria French, or half-French'.[80] Already in July, however, the Soviet news agency Tass[81] had accused the French of complicity in what it called the colonialist plot in the former Belgian Congo where civil war had broken out. That Franco-Soviet relations were back in their most virulent state was finally exhibited by de Gaulle himself in his end-of-the-year message on 31 December 1960.

Expressing the hope that the new African countries would enjoy order and peace in 1961, the general said that this could only happen in spite of what he called the Soviet empire: 'This [empire] is not content with colonising forty million Asian and Caucasian Muslims, and enslaving a dozen or more peoples which are entirely foreign to it, but it also encourages and exploits every difficult situation in order to gain a foothold in the already stricken country.'[82]

In 1961 relations between France and the Soviet Union remained bad. Khrushchev's attempts to bully President Kennedy when the two met in Vienna in June seemed to make Kennedy less cross than de Gaulle.[83] The American president had been told that unless a peace treaty were signed with both Germanies by the end of the year, and the status of Berlin modified in accordance with Soviet wishes, the Soviet Union would unilaterally conclude a separate treaty with the DDR. The result of such a Soviet step would be that the DDR would become responsible for allied access to West Berlin, a demand the west had hitherto resisted because the occupation arrangements outlined at Yalta had led to the 1945 four power occupation statute which made the Soviet Union herself responsible for western access to Berlin. It would also have implied some kind of western recognition of the DDR – which was anathema to them – if they had been forced to treat with it over access to the former German capital. Notes containing the Soviet demands were also sent to France and Britain on 16 June. On 18 July the three western countries sent the Soviet Union a collective refusal.

But the Russian diplomatic offensive continued. In a note dated 3 August 1961, Khrushchev taunted de Gaulle with the contradiction which permitted the French on the one hand to demand the Germans' right to self-determination and on the other hand to refuse the Algerians their's.[84] It may well be that all this diplomatic frenzy hid a deep malaise in the Soviet government about the way the German problem was going for them. Not only were France and West Germany drawing still closer together, and Adenauer's Federal Republic increasing its political confidence and economic strength through its connections with the United States and its membership of EEC, but the population of the DDR was brutally showing its preference for its capitalist brother across the Elbe by rapidly speeding up its migration to it. To put an end to the exodus of its people, the DDR, if not actually at the behest of the Soviet Union then at least with its connivance, built the Berlin Wall in August 1961. At the same time travel restrictions to and from Berlin were imposed. The response to this renewed threat to western interests in Berlin was immediate. The United States sent reinforcements to Germany, and the French, though hard-pressed in Algeria, transferred a whole division from there to Europe. As a final fling, the Soviet Union announced at the end of August that it was resuming nuclear testing.

That de Gaulle saw the Soviet government's bluster in part as a reaction to its difficulties with the eastern satellites as well as with its own people – demands for greater freedom were being heard with increasing frequency in the east – he made clear at his press conference on 5 September 1961. His recipe for dealing with the Kremlin was, as has been seen, less indulgent than that of his allies. While Britain and the United States were inclined to go on discussing Germany's future with the Soviet Union, de Gaulle – backed by the Federal Republic – counselled the postponement of talks until the Kremlin had given up issuing threats.* As if to vindicate de Gaulle's hard line, during the 22nd Congress of the Communist Party of the Soviet Union, on 17 October 1961, Khrushchev withdrew his time limit (31 December) on the conclusion of a German peace treaty. But, contrary to the immediate reaction of France's allies, who wanted at once to sound out the Kremlin's latest intentions, de Gaulle was against action prompted by hasty relief and advised a delay until all Russian threats had ceased. [85]

Preliminary soundings having nevertheless been undertaken by his allies, and found to have been unsuccessful, de Gaulle, cock-a-hoop also over the imminent end to the Algerian war,

* See above, p. 144 (note 83).

congratulated himself in a radio and television talk on 5 February 1962 in the most buoyant prose:

> Having acted on the assumption that it would be wrong to negotiate either over Berlin or about Germany while the Soviet Union was still issuing threats and peremptory orders to the west, and while she had not brought about a real international *détente*, we are certain that we have avoided the worst for both our allies and ourselves, whether that would have been in the form of a catastrophic climb-down, a dramatic break-down, or a tragi-comic bogging-down, one of which would surely have been the result of such a conference.[86]

The Soviet Union for its part did nothing to improve relations with de Gaulle. The Evian agreements, providing for a referendum likely to lead to Algerian independence, had hardly been signed (18 March 1962) when the Soviet government gave recognition to the FLN's provisional government. At that stage French sovereignty over Algeria was still theoretically intact, and de Gaulle decided to make heavy weather over this breach of protocol by the Soviet Union. Vinogradov, the Soviet ambassador in Paris, was gravely asked for an explanation, and de Gaulle recalled his own ambassador from Moscow for 'consultations'. The Soviet Union waited until the end of March before rhetorically asking de Gaulle who he thought he was in telling Moscow whom it might or might not recognise.[87] By then, however, the referendum in Algeria had taken place, her independence decided upon, and the incident, overtaken by events, was closed. But it had underlined again that, between Moscow and Paris, little love was lost at that time.

The next clash came over the resumption of disarmament talks among the new Nineteen-Nation Commission, the Soviet Union having withdrawn from the previous Commission of Ten in 1960. Khrushchev suggested a summit conference to discuss, for a start, a nuclear test ban. On 10 February 1962 de Gaulle declared that he refused to participate in such a ban – France was still well behind Russia, the United States and Britain in the atomic field – but said he would welcome the destruction of all nuclear vectors.[88] The Soviet Union showed no interest in such a self-denying act, and proceeded to attack the French for their policy of *rapprochement* with Bonn. Indeed, the Franco-German honeymoon was reaching new ecstasies. In July Adenauer was to pay a state visit to France, and in September de Gaulle made his triumphal progress through the Federal Republic. The general's speech to the German War College in Hamburg* went down particularly badly with Moscow, and the Soviet government claimed that the Paris-Bonn axis was aimed against it. The exaltation of German military achievement by the president of France could plausibly be interpreted that way.

Then the Russians bungled themselves into the Cuban missile crisis. There had for some time been a build-up of Soviet missile installations in Cuba. By October 1962 the United States government considered that the threat to its country from these installations had become intolerable. Consequently, when a further twenty-five Soviet ships were on their way to Cuba, presumably with more equipment, President Kennedy ordered a blockade of the island and instructed the American navy to sink whatever vessel did not stop on its orders. De Gaulle instantly pledged his support to the American president.[89] Within four days of Kennedy's imposition of the blockade the Soviet government, on 28 October 1962, stated that it had ordered the transfer of its missile equipment from Cuba to the Soviet Union. Kennedy could certainly have managed without French support. But it was significant that de Gaulle instantly promised it.

Soviet fears of a Franco-German *entente* were strengthened in January 1963 when the Paris-Bonn treaty was signed. Moscow already professed to see the influence of the treaty in de Gaulle's refusal, in February 1963, to allow the broadcast of a French radio interview with Khrushchev and Malinowsky on the twentieth anniversary of the battle of Stalingrad. The interview turned out to be not merely an attack on the Germans but also on the Bonn government. On 5 February the Soviet government officially protested against the treaty,[90] claiming that its military clauses contravened the Paris treaty of 1956, especially since it

* See above pp. 85–6.

contained no reference to arms restrictions. Moreover, at his press conference on 14 January, de Gaulle had said that the Federal Republic was free to choose its own defence policy.[91] The Russians were now asking specifically whether the Bonn government might benefit from French atomic weapons. If this were so, then the Soviet government would consider this 'an immediate threat to its vital national interests and oblige it at once to take the necessary measures'.[92] At the end of March the French government replied that the Franco-German treaty signified no change in the military situation in Europe; it could only help peace.[93] Some six weeks later Moscow sent Paris one of those notes which, depending on the international situation, either capital could have composed for the other: on 17 May 1963 the Soviet government reminded de Gaulle of the facts of geography and history which, it said, had made the French and Russians 'natural allies'. The note added that if the two countries could get together, then 'no force could arise to change the new map of Europe'.[94]

1963–8: A PARIS-MOSCOW AXIS?

It took a number of factors to change de Gaulle's attitude to the Soviet Union. Perhaps the most important consideration was his growing distrust of the United States. Kennedy seemed to be working for a direct understanding with Moscow, and was doing so without consulting his allies as much as de Gaulle thought appropriate. The nuclear test ban treaty, signed in Moscow on 5 August 1963, was a case in point. France did not like its terms and had refused to have anything to do with it, along with China and Albania. At his press conference on 29 September 1963, the general was to wonder how far Moscow's problems with China were going to affect its relations with the west in general, and with the United States in particular. 'The United States,' he said, 'since Yalta and Potsdam have really no outstanding problems with the Soviet Union, and [the Soviet Union's difficulties with China] are opening up tempting prospects for Washington. Hence, for example, all those separate negotiations between the Anglo-Saxons and the Soviets . . . so far in the absence of the Europeans which, it goes without saying, goes against the wishes of France.'[95] On this same occasion de Gaulle also came out with his condemnation of the 'two hegemonies' which, he maintained, threatened the independence of nations. The hegemony of the Soviet Union he still qualified as 'odious', but that of the United States – though a friend and ally – was also unacceptable if it amounted in any way to a kind of protection. The general followed this up with two appeals, one to the 'Third World' to remain independent of these two hegemonies, and the other to the satellite countries of the Soviet Union to emancipate themselves and help in the making of 'Europe'.

It is arguable that his distrust and dislike of the United States led de Gaulle into his own exploration of Franco-Soviet possibilities. After Adenauer's retirement in 1963, the realisation that relations with Bonn might not after all have the heady consequences hoped for provided another reason. It is even possible that his recognition of the Communist regime in China on 27 January 1964 was calculated to add to his weight with Moscow. If Red China was really beginning to be a worry for the Soviet Union, and if his recognition of China brought him the economic and political pull with her which he hoped for, then de Gaulle might turn out to be doubly useful to the Soviets. He would not just be a disaggregating influence in NATO, but conceivably the only likely 'honest broker' between the two Communist colossi. But perhaps this is fantasy, and it may just have been a coincidence that Peking received French recognition when it did. At any rate, it predictably annoyed not only the United States and other NATO countries – West Germany in particular since, despite the provisions of the Franco-German treaty, she had not been consulted – but also the Soviet Union, though the Kremlin nobly gritted its teeth and congratulated de Gaulle on his realism.[96]

At the end of January 1964 the French finance minister, Valéry Giscard d'Estaing, visited Moscow. In February the Soviet vice-premier in charge of scientific questions, Rudniev, came to Paris. From 25 February to 5 March the French entertained a Soviet parliamentary delegation led by Podgorny, and speeches during that visit repeatedly brought out Franco-Soviet agreement on three international questions: that the 1954 Geneva agreements should be applied to end the war in Vietnam; that Laos and Cambodia should have their neutrality respected; and that the functions of the United Nations – including those of the Security Council – should be reappraised. The ice had been broken. There then followed exchanges of good-will messages on every conceivable occasion. The Soviet government sent a note in August on the twentieth anniversary of the liberation of Paris. The French government sent one in October to celebrate the fortieth anniversary of France's belated recognition of the Soviet Union, in which de Gaulle, deliciously converted, said that 'despite the accidents of history, our two nations are linked in depth by a durable friendship'.[97] Perhaps the general was here making his famous distinction between nations, which he thought were the products of long historical processes, and their institutions, which for him were superficial ephemera.

Khrushchev's dismissal from power in October 1964 failed to affect Franco-Soviet explorations. On 9 December, Kosygin told the Supreme Soviet that 'our policy towards France is guided by the fact that the Soviet Union and France are the two most powerful nations on the European continent and therefore have a very great responsibility for the security of Europe'.[98] That de Gaulle was encouraging the satellite countries of the Soviet Union towards greater independence made no obvious impact on Moscow. In July 1964 the Rumanian prime minister visited France, and on 22 November, in Strasbourg, the general referred to his expectation that the demand for human dignity and national independence would make itself increasingly felt both inside and outside what he still called the 'eastern totalitarian bloc'.[99]

One of the first concrete results of the Franco-Soviet *rapprochement* was the conclusion of a five-year commercial agreement in October 1964. There was much scope for improvement, for French trade with all the Soviet bloc countries amounted to only 2.7 per cent of all French exports and only 2.5 per cent of all French imports.

At his press conference on 4 February 1965, de Gaulle still showed himself rather cautious in his attitude to the Soviet Union. But at the same time he demonstrated that his international pretensions were just as great in relation to the Soviet Union as in relation to his western allies. He was not averse, he said, to Soviet participation in the settlement of the German problem, but Russia had to change first. 'Russia,' he stated, 'must develop in such a way that she sees her future no longer in terms of totalitarian constraint imposed both upon her own country and others, but through progress brought about in common by free men and peoples.'[100] Not content with this piece of stern advice, he went on to unburden himself of a vision of a new Europe which would incorporate Russia, though apparently stripped of her lands east of the Urals: 'Europe, the Mother of modern civilisation, must establish herself from the Atlantic to the Urals through cooperation, in order to be able to develop her immense resources, and so that she may, together with her daughter America, play the part that is properly hers.' Ten days later *Pravda*,[101] in a commentary, reproached the general for his lack of realism, oddly exemplified for it by his omitting to acknowledge the existence of two Germanies, and told him that he had no right to make a European settlement dependent upon developments in the east that might be to his taste. Even so, in March 1965 Vinogradov was replaced as ambassador in Paris by Zorin, who was higher in the hierarchy of the Russian Communist Party.

The Soviet Union continued to woo de Gaulle in spite of his apparent aberrations. In April Gromyko, the Soviet foreign minister, spent five days in the French capital. But the final communiqué[102] showed that the major policy differences had not been resolved. The Russians were not prepared to accept the principle of free determination in Germany, and the French were still opposed to Soviet policy in the middle east where Moscow favoured the Arabs. Moreover, de Gaulle maintained his refusal to sign the nuclear non-proliferation treaty. Progress was, however, to be recorded in other spheres. Even before Gromyko's visit, at the end of March, the two countries had signed an agreement on scientific cooperation, the

Soviet Union having gone so far as to propose adopting the French system of colour television. Then, in May, an agreement on cultural exchanges was initialled. At the end of October, the French foreign minister returned Gromyko's visit, spending five days in the Soviet Union in a most cordial atmosphere. Soviet solicitude reached a poignant climax at the end of 1965. During the French presidential elections de Gaulle, to the Kremlin's surprise, was forced into a second ballot. Moscow, in its growing Gaullist ardour, actually went so far as to reproach the leader of the PCF, Waldeck-Rochet, for hostile remarks he had made about the general.

In 1966 Franco-Soviet relations reached their most exalted state. At the beginning of the year it was announced that de Gaulle was to pay a state visit to the Soviet Union at the end of June, repaying that of Khrushchev to France in 1960. In February NATO countries – the Federal Republic in particular – which had already viewed the progress of Franco-Soviet relations with some alarm, were made even more apprehensive when the French declared that they would leave the integrated command structure of the Atlantic alliance. In March the French government stated that its troops in Germany would be withdrawn from NATO command, and asked that NATO headquarters should leave French territory. Paris denied, however, that it intended to take France out of the Atlantic alliance altogether, which signified, among other things, that France still wanted to be able to claim the protection of United States weaponry. Even so, that in the circumstances there should have been much talk about a French reversal of alliances is understandable. De Gaulle's prime minister, Pompidou, denied that this was the case in the National Assembly.[103] He said that it was all a matter of *rapprochement* and that the future of peace depended on it. But the imprisonment in the Soviet Union of Daniel and Siniavsky in February 1966 for their critique of the Soviet system had shown that Moscow had not yet fulfilled the conditions de Gaulle had set it in his February 1964 press conference before it could be an acceptable partner.

On 20 June 1966 General de Gaulle began his state visit to

the Soviet Union. It lasted ten days, and he was accorded the most deferential treatment. He was even taken to see the launching of a Russian communications' satellite, the first western eyewitness of such an event. On Moscow television he spoke of his presence in the Soviet Union as 'the visit of eternal France to eternal Russia', another illustration of that distinctively Gaullist doctrine that underneath political regimes lie the deeper realities of nations. On the day before his departure a number of agreements, already initialled on 16 June in Paris, were signed in Moscow. They related to cooperation in spatial, atomic, scientific, technical and consular affairs. A mixed permanent economic commission was also created, which was to meet at least once a year and was to ensure the proper working of the 1964 commercial agreement. Finally, to make sure that honour was seen to be satisfied, the Soviet Union agreed to install a direct teleprinter for use in international emergencies between Paris and Moscow, just like the one they had with the United States. On 1 July 1966 de Gaulle returned to Paris.

Also on 1 July 1966 de Gaulle's withdrawal from NATO became effective. But the French state radio ensured that the citizens of France were aware that their country could still depend on the United States nuclear deterrent for their protection. The French government had merely divested itself of most of the major responsibilities that might have been thought to follow from that protection.

Exchanges between the Soviet Union and France continued to multiply during the remaining months of 1966. The Renault and Peugeot motor manufacturers established themselves in Tashkent. A Franco-Soviet Chamber of Commerce was founded. Finally, at the end of 1966, Kosygin came to France for nine days and was given an impressive welcome.

Had it not been for the complication of the six-day war between Israel and the Arab states, 1967 would probably have been a splendid year for improved Soviet relations with the west as a whole. Whether the alleged Chinese threat was responsible for it or not – the first Chinese hydrogen bomb was exploded on 17 June 1967 – the Soviet Union multiplied its friendly efforts in many western countries. Podgorny, the president of the Praesidium of the Supreme Soviet, visited Italy in January and, though he must have been seen as Anti-Christ by faithful Catholics, was even received by the Pope. In February Kosygin went to Britain. At the same time the Soviet satellite countries were stirring. Some of them were actually making contact with the German Federal Republic, Moscow's favourite whipping boy, and Chancellor Kiesinger let it be known that he was ready for the journey to Moscow itself. But the June war in the middle east proved to be a setback. The Soviet Union, in its resolute support for the Arab cause, instantly became estranged from most western European countries, which, in common with the United States, tended to sympathise with Israel. To Moscow's delight, de Gaulle was to prove to be the exception.

Although the Soviet Union had indeed succeeded in improving its relations with a number of western countries in 1967, contacts with France had remained privileged in the sense that they had been particularly frequent and diverse. The end of January had seen the first major meeting of the economic commission set up in Moscow during the de Gaulle visit. The Russians had sent a vice-premier, Kirillin, to Paris, who, with Debré, the French finance minister, was jointly to chair the meetings. In April 1967 the two countries signed a maritime agreement and, in time for the Mayday celebrations, the French Chief of the General Staff, Ailleret, paid a visit to the Soviet Union. It was said that there were to be no military talks, but General Ailleret was given the honour of being allowed to watch the customary parade from the official stand.

Then, in June, the Soviet Union and France together took the Arab side during and after the six-day war. For France this was a new attitude, her support for Israel having so far been steady, as well as profitable to both sides. The military link went back to the Suez affair in 1956, the emotional link much further. It is not clear what caused de Gaulle to rally to the enemies of Israel. His 'realism' might have swayed him, the political and economic advantages of links with the Arab world outweighing, in his calculations, those to be gained from continued collaboration with the Jewish state. Or it might have been pique at having had his advice not to go to war ignored in Tel-Aviv. Or he might have considered it desirable for some other reason at that stage to align himself with the Soviet Union on a major international issue. Whatever the cause, France joined the Soviet Union at the United Nations in condemning Israel's action. Kosygin, both on his way to the United Nations meeting and on his return, called on de Gaulle in Paris. But the discussions that ultimately mattered to a solution of the middle east conflict had already begun between Kosygin and President Johnson in the margin of the UN debates and without France, a fact de Gaulle must have found highly unpalatable. French pressure for four power arbitration was unsuccessful, if only because it was difficult to see in what way France was neutral in the Arab-Israel confrontation. It may be noted in passing that de Gaulle's conversion to anti-Israeli policies was unpopular in France.

In July the French prime minister and foreign minister, Pompidou and Couve de Murville, spent five friendly days in the Soviet Union. During the same month, perhaps persuaded that he had reached the mighty international position for which he had so long striven, de Gaulle, during a visit to Canada, unleashed his 'Vive le Québec libre', an astonishing affront to his hosts. In September, however, the general was back in the east, paying an official visit to Poland. Addressing Polish parliamentarians, he again evoked the vision of a 'Europe' from the Atlantic to the Urals,[104] while Gomulka cautiously underlined Poland's basic need for a continued alliance with the Soviet Union. The visit was followed in October by the first combined Franco-Russian space shot. It coincided with NATO's last meeting in Paris, before its move to Belgium. Finally, as 1967 was ending, the Six, meeting in Brussels, recognised that French objections to British entry into EEC were as strong as ever.

It looked as if de Gaulle had made his choice. The Franco-German *entente* having yielded little of its initial promise for France, and EEC visibly not transforming itself into the French-led association of states he had hoped for, the general seemed to have chosen collaboration with the Soviet Union as the high road to international significance.

Moreover, in January 1968 it looked as if the liberalisation of the Soviet bloc that de Gaulle had been demanding was actually beginning in earnest. In Czechoslovakia Dubček was replacing Novotny as first secretary of the Communist Party, a change that was interpreted as foreshadowing a rather more liberal regime. In March the head of the Hungarian government paid an official visit to France, which at least showed that contacts with non-Communist countries were now possible for his country too. In May, General de Gaulle went to Rumania, where he called the Soviet Union an 'essential pillar' of Europe. In June the Prague Parliament passed a law allowing the rehabilitation of those earlier condemned for political offences; then it abolished censorship.

At the same time the Soviet Union and the United States were also improving relations with each other. Though this did not always lead to agreements of which de Gaulle approved, his country could reasonably expect to benefit from the resultant relaxation of tension. For example, the joint Russo-American project against nuclear proliferation, presented at the Geneva disarmament conference in January, was found unacceptable by de Gaulle, but France had much to gain from the self-denial of states which refused to have nuclear weapons. In April, encouraged by the Soviet Union, North Vietnam agreed to hold talks with the United States on ending the war in south-east Asia. De Gaulle had for many years clamoured for the end of that war, and can only have been flattered that the talks were to be held in Paris.

1968–9: DISILLUSIONMENT

In the summer of 1968 everything suddenly went wrong with de Gaulle's hopes. In May and June he had to contend with a revolutionary situation at home which shook the foundations of his regime, and in July and August the Soviet Union abruptly decided that it could not accept the consequences of liberal developments in Czechoslovakia and sent its armies to occupy it. De Gaulle's internal problems, which had ironically come to a head while he was preaching his gospel in Rumania, were to lead to his disappearance from active politics in April 1969. The Soviet invasion of Czechoslovakia in August 1968 seriously checked the entire movement towards an east-west *détente.*

What was perhaps in the long run more serious, the Russian subjugation of Czechoslovakia came at a moment when it seemed possible that democratic Socialist parties, notably in France and Italy, could for the first time in living memory (if not for the first time ever) seriously think of collaborating with the large Communist parties in their respective countries. The Soviet move killed the hope that, through such collaboration, the Left in those countries could make for greater internal political stability by providing, at last, a credibly united political movement. Democratically trustworthy Communist parties could have helped to do that, and in the process have added to the political stability not only of their own countries but also of international politics.

It is true that to begin with the reaction of the French Communist Party to the Soviet invasion of Czechoslovakia was more violent than that of the French government. While the PCF openly expressed its reprobation, de Gaulle's foreign minister, Michel Debré, was trying to pass it off as a minor accident; the general himself initially put it down to the deplorable existence of the two blocs. However, by the time of the November foreign affairs debate in the National Assembly, the PCF had become more circumspect in its condemnation of the Soviet Union, while Debré voiced the revulsion of a large number of his compatriots by insisting that '*détente* is built on liberty and leads to liberty'.[105] The embarrassment of the French government could, however, already be seen in the tortured communiqué issued after the meeting of the council of ministers on 23 October 1968.[106] The communiqué ended:'French policy must continue along the lines it has followed, which means *détente*. This amounts to the refusal to accept the existence of blocs. But, at the same time, it entails the determination to bring about the recognition that each country must have the possibility of determining its fate.'

The machinery for Franco-Soviet cooperation that had been set up during the previous years continued to function. At their meeting in January 1969, the Kirillin-Debré commission noted that France now had a favourable trade balance with the Soviet Union. In fact, France had overtaken West Germany as Russia's biggest supplier of capital goods. Raw materials were France's principal imports from the Soviet Union. Everything pointed to the desire of both sides to expand their exchange still further. On 26 May 1969, the 1964 trade pact was renewed for another five years, with more ambitious objectives.

Nevertheless 1968 brought about a distinct change in de Gaulle's foreign policy attitudes. It showed itself mainly in his dealings with EEC and NATO. When, on 4 February 1969, the general talked to Christopher Soames, the British ambassador in Paris, about the possibility of enlarging the Common Market through the inclusion of Britain and other countries – indiscretions concerning this interview led to the so-called Soames affair – he was clearly thinking along lines that a few months earlier had been anathema to him. Even if this new thinking was prompted more by the growing strength of Bonn than by Moscow's latest repressive policies, and even if doubts cast on the firmness of de Gaulle's suggestions to Soames[107] are justified, there can be no doubt that from the end of 1968 the French government showed renewed interest in EEC. Moreover, it has to be recalled that the Soviet Union was not enamoured of the Brussels organisation, so that the new Gaullist line was, in a sense, an act of defiance of the Soviet Union.

De Gaulle also showed a friendlier attitude towards NATO. This was explicable not only in terms of the obvious doubt engendered by the hardening of Soviet policy in the east. It was also connected with cut-backs in the French defence budget, made necessary by the consequences of the May-June riots. In January 1968, when de Gaulle had proclaimed that France must have a world-wide strategy *(tous azimuts)*,[108] the expectation had been that by the mid-1970s a submarine-based nuclear deterrent of some credibility would be available. However, at the end of 1968 and in 1969 drastic cuts in all forms of military expenditure had to be made. From the strategic point of view an interesting consequence followed; or if it was not a direct consequence it was at least an interesting coincidence. In the May 1969 issue of the *Revue de Défense Nationale,* General Fourquet, the French army's chief of staff, conceded that in the case of an enemy attack the French might, after all, make a 'graduated response'. Now, that policy had not only been precisely that of NATO, but had for well over a decade been the target of major Gaullist objections. De Gaulle in particular had always maintained that this strategy testified to the readiness of the United States to sacrifice Europe before risking its own cities. Instead, he had demanded that any attack in Europe should instantly bring about massive nuclear retaliation, on the grounds that the Elbe was too close for the principle of graduated response not to result in the early arrival in Paris of Soviet armour. Thus, Fourquet's article showed that there was no longer any difference between NATO and the French on this basic strategic issue.

In any case, already at the end of October 1968, that is two months after the Soviet invasion of Czechoslovakia, the French minister of the armed forces, Messmer, had publicly stated that in a serious international crisis direct arrangements would be made between Paris and Washington concerning the French contribution to NATO forces. At the same time, the French minister confirmed that agreements already existed about the employment of French forces in conjunction with those of NATO.[109] To this must be added the agreements about the use of French forces in Germany that France had made with Bonn when she withdrew from NATO's integrated command structure in 1966.

It may, therefore, be affirmed that the Soviet invasion of Czechoslovakia was followed by greater French interest in EEC and NATO, whether or not these events were causally related. Franco-Soviet attitudes towards each other must have been affected by this renewed French interest. The least one may say is that it indicated, as late as 1968–9, France's continuing adherence to the western camp. This fact was endorsed by a French public opinion poll, held in May 1969, in which 74.3 per cent stated that France should stay in the Atlantic alliance.[110] It was also authoritatively reported[111] that President Pompidou had asked the United States not further to reduce their forces in Europe.

FRANCO-SOVIET RELATIONS SINCE 1969

Before resigning in April 1969, de Gaulle had given the impression that he would have liked to pretend that the 1968 Czech invasion had not happened. Like the May-June riots, it had been too upsetting for his basic policies. It was suggested by a usually well-informed journalist[112] that de Gaulle had even postponed the projected visit to Paris in November of 1968 of Rumania's prime minister Ceausescu in order not to offend the Russians. The Pompidou administration began with a somewhat different outlook. In a speech to the United Nations, Pompidou's foreign minister, Maurice Schumann, pointedly stated that France had an 'equal interest and respect' for all countries of eastern Europe.[113] On the other hand, there were at least three reasons why the French felt the need for a continuing policy of *détente* with the Soviet Union. First, the United States had not interrupted its own, similar policy. Second, the economic benefits of relations with the Soviet Union were considerable. Third, the German Federal Republic under Brandt was making rapid progress with its own attempts at collaboration with the Soviet Union, and the French could not afford to ignore this.

Despite continuing efforts to renew the 'European' concept and give it greater substance within a possibly enlarged framework for EEC – the Hague Conference of EEC heads of government in December 1969 provided an obvious illustration of this – the Pompidou administration therefore also worked for good relations with the Soviet Union. French and Soviet middle east policies still followed similar lines, although France supported the Arab cause in the main only at a diplomatic level (this was enough to bring her great economic rewards), while the Soviet Union did so by supplying a large amount of arms as well. However, French feelings about Soviet involvement in the Mediterranean, which this policy increasingly brought with it, were mixed. The return in strength of the French fleet into the Mediterranean – from which de Gaulle had withdrawn much of it largely as an anti-NATO gesture after the end of the Algerian war – could plausibly be seen as a consequence of French apprehensions at Soviet activity there. So may the French decision to aid the Libyan revolution in 1969, although there were no doubt more materialistic French interests at work too.

The first major foreign policy discussions between the Pompidou administration and the Soviet Union took place during the French foreign minister's visit to Moscow in October 1969. Then, as during the subsequent visit to the Soviet Union of the secretary general of the Quai d'Orsay in January 1970, it appeared that Soviet policy had undergone no material change. Agreement between the two countries continued on a whole range of topics, from the continuing war in Vietnam to the need for a peaceful settlement of Russian problems with China; Chinese intentions were apparently as unclear to the Soviet Union as to the French, who were again making efforts to improve relations with Peking. On the other hand, already during the French foreign minister's visit the Soviet government had mentioned its desire for a European security conference, and about that Paris had many reservations. But when the secretary general of the Quai was in Moscow, he was given to understand that the Soviet Union would want such a conference to be a meeting of independent countries, not of blocs. While this made the project more palatable to the French, it seemed to them that there were too many complications for the meeting to take place in the near future.

The secretary general's stay in Moscow had also been used to make arrangements for a series of visits. Gromyko was to come to Paris in April 1970; Pompidou was to go to the Soviet Union in October of the same year; Breznev, Podgorny, and Kosygin were to visit France in 1971. It certainly looked as if the flames were to be rekindled.

The Gromyko visit, postponed to June 1970, concluded with a communiqué of customary banality. Having recorded that both countries championed peace everywhere, it did however go on to show that no real progress had been made in converting the French to the idea of a European security conference. But it was noted that the French and Soviet views on Indo-China and the middle east remained similar.[114]

Then, in August 1970, came the Bonn-Moscow non-aggression pact. In so far as it brought home to the French that the Federal Republic had outgrown French tutelage in its relations with the Soviet Union, it made the Pompidou government apprehensive. This was not because they suspected Chancellor Brandt of preparing a deal with the Russians that would harm France, or any western interests in Europe. Even on purely selfish national grounds such a deal, since it would alienate the United States, would have been inconceivable in Bonn in 1970. But growing economic and, sooner or later, political importance might in the future make the Germans more useful partners for the Soviet Union than France. There was also the fear that, somehow, the reunification of Germany might come about in time, if Bonn and Moscow succeeded in working out a mutually useful partnership. And a reunified Germany could scarcely be advantageous to France, whatever French politicians might say to the contrary.

Thus, in 1970, the increasing political importance of the German Federal Republic might well have initiated a significant change in Franco-Soviet attitudes towards each other. Indeed, it might have been the chilling thought of the consequences of a lasting Bonn-Moscow understanding which in November 1970 brought the French foreign minister, Maurice Schumann, to the chastening conclusion that 'without the European community and the Atlantic alliance, we would not count for much'.[115]

4

French Policy Outside the Soviet and Atlantic Blocs

⌈Nothing can have been more irksome and disappointing to the makers of French foreign policy in the period immediately after the second world war than their inability to follow traditional French lines of conduct in the mainstream of international affairs. Constantly subjected to conflicting and paralysing pressures from the Soviet Union and the United States – and increasingly from their own overseas commitments – it was rare for them to find opportunities for independent action⌡Although French governments were to succeed in emancipating themselves from many of these pressures in the 1960s, and consequently in enlarging the areas in which they could attempt to play an independent role, the degree to which they could successfully challenge United States and Soviet influence in the world as a whole was open to much doubt. But this doubt did not deter them from trying.

It will be seen that after 1945 France's desire to maintain and expand her influence abroad, outside the two power blocs, manifested itself in four major ways. First, through a massive effort of cultural proselytising, which was explicitly motivated by political considerations. Second, through a necessarily less ambitious, because more costly, economic and technical aid programme, which was also politically inspired. Third, through the – eventually – skilful use of decolonisation. Fourth, through the assiduous courting of the so-called Third World.

FRENCH CULTURE AS AN INSTRUMENT OF
FOREIGN POLICY

(i) General Principles: Traditionally, French initiatives
abroad are to a considerable degree founded on the belief
that France has something uniquely valuable to contribute
to the world as a whole. This valuable contribution is French
culture. Nor do the French have to do very much to export
it; there appears to be an avid demand for it in many parts
of the world. Since French began to supplant Latin as the
international language in the post-Renaissance period, the
language of France as well as the literature which uses it
came to be greatly esteemed by intellectual elites everywhere.
The 1789 Revolution added a new dimension to the appeal
of France. The Revolution was seen by many as the culmination of Cartesian thinking, which had not only exhibited
complete faith in the rational faculty of man as a guide to
truth, but had also taught that this rational faculty was
democratically distributed in all men. As in Descartes, but
much more radically so, the doctrine led in the eighteenth
century to a disdain for all mere authority and, by extension,
to the demand for the abolition of what were deemed to be
inequities. Man, *qua* man, was thought to have worth because
he was rational, and anything that was not defensible at the
bar of Reason diminished man and was therefore bad.
Oppression, inequality, selfishness were held to be irrational;
liberty, equality, fraternity were rational. Moreover, since
Reason was the highest faculty of all men, and not merely
of Frenchmen, its demands were thought to be universally
valid for mankind as a whole. The French Revolution was
therefore the Revolution of all men, its principles laws to
all men. It was periodically to be a feature of official French
policy abroad that it sought to persuade others of the excellence of this philosophy although, without official encouragement, it had already made headway abroad before 1789.
There is, for example, no doubt about the influence exercised
by this outlook upon Europe and the United States of
America in the eighteenth century.

The politico-moral message of 1789 might have helped to make foreign countries also receptive to other aspects of French culture. But the message might not have been needed, because much of the outside world had for a long time shared with the builder of Versailles and his spiritual heirs the view that France was the Athens of the modern world. Even if there have been many French governments since 1789 which have shown minimal enthusiasm for the propagation of the gospel of Reason, they nevertheless sent French teachers around the world, in their thousands, to alert it to the splendours of Racine and the language that had made him possible. Any attempt to understand French foreign policy must take into account the strong proselytising compulsion that demands from the educated Frenchman that he acquaint the barbarians with the achievements of his country's thought and culture. It helps to explain his air of superiority which has infuriated Boeotians the world over, but his successes are measured by the seemingly uncritical adulation which – however reluctantly – educated foreigners reserve for his country in which their heart somehow always beats a little faster.

There is no cultural equivalent of the 1963 Jeanneney report on French foreign aid, no attempt to evaluate to what degree the propagation of French culture is a disinterested affair. It would, however, have been surprising if the thought had not occurred to French policy-makers to exploit the appeal of French culture for more narrowly political French ends. Indeed, there is a good deal of evidence that the possibility of such exploitation has been assumed by them. For example, M. Claude Lebel, a high official in the French Diplomatic Service, has placed the cultural work of his Ministry on the same level as its political work:

> However indispensable the various other departments [of the Quai d'Orsay] may be, no one can deny that the twin pillars that are essential to the Ministry of Foreign Affairs are the General Directorate of Political and Economic Affairs and the General Directorate of Cultural and Technical Affairs. The former provides the basis

for government policies so far as France's political and economic *relations* with the rest of the world are concerned: the latter organises and conducts France's *action* abroad, with the full weight which, today, cultural or artistic and technical expansion must have because it has replaced action by gunboat.[1]

The official report on the French Second Quinquennial Plan for Cultural Expansion of the General Directorate of Cultural Relations at the Ministry of Foreign Affairs records:

The spreading of her language, her culture, and her ideas, the attraction of her literature, science, technology, and art, the merits of her ways of forming men, all these are for France essential means of action in her foreign policy through the influence she exercises because of them. Cultural action is closely linked with political and economic action, both of which it precedes. Cultural action therefore directly contributes to the power of our country in international affairs.[2]

This attitude to cultural expansion, as the spearhead of political penetration, explains the immense increases in expenditure for that specific purpose which successive French governments have allowed since the end of the second world war. Nor was it merely a matter of proselytising work abroad. Recognising that the war had left them with little prestige in the world, the French deliberately set out in 1945 to entice foreign students into France, at a time when their resources to do anything abroad were still minimal. But the scale on which this kind of activity has since expanded may be gauged from the fact that while in 1946 the number of scholarships granted to foreign students was six hundred, in 1967–8 it had grown to 15,731. If the latter figure is broken down, it will be seen that significantly larger numbers of scholarships were provided for countries in which the French either had traditional grounds for providing them, or had particular political intentions behind the gesture. For example, that African states should have obtained nearly one-third of the available scholarships is understandable in terms of the long French involvement on that continent; but the rapid expansion of scholarships in South America between 1959–60 (302) and 1967 (2,366) is explicable only by General de Gaulle's wish, at least since his visit to that continent in 1964, to gain influence there.

But by far the most important aspect of cultural proselytising has been the teaching of the French language abroad, which is an obvious first step to other forms of penetration. Although even before the advent of the Third Republic fitful attention was paid to this kind of activity, it was not until 1911 that a special office within the Quai was created, much of whose function was precisely the organisation and expansion of the teaching of French abroad. In 1920 this office became the *Service des Oeuvres,* which was raised to the status of a General Directorate in 1945 and much expanded.

The ambivalence about this kind of work has nearly always been total. There are times when it is presented as entirely altruistic, French and French culture assuming the status of free gifts from Paris for the culturally needy, and bestowed quite disinterestedly. At other times, as has already been shown, disinterestedness loses its place to the recognition of the benefits for France that flow from cultural exports. Outrey sums up the ambivalence with masterly naivety: 'It was a sign of the originality and excellence of French foreign policy [after 1920] that it recognised before other countries what great advantages could come to our country's political influence from a policy of disinterested action in favour of the works of the spirit.'[3]

By 1968–9 there were 33,814 French teachers abroad, nearly three times as many as nine years earlier, and most of them taught French. They were either seconded to teaching establishments within the local educational framework of the foreign country, or helped to fill places in the various French-run institutions abroad, which range from small schools catering for the children of French families to French institutes with very much higher academic ambitions, via the unique *lycées* system where foreigners too can be given a typically French education. At the end of the 1960s, about one-third of French teachers abroad were doing their national service that way; but they were qualified teachers like all the others who are sent to foreign countries. In fact, French commitments of this kind have grown so spectacularly that in 1970 serious doubts have been expressed by French experts about the ability of their country to maintain the level of this kind of export. Nor was it thought that this form of cultural expansion was necessarily the most efficient. Highly trained French teachers, it has been suggested,[4] would be better employed training elites rather than natives in the bush; the same point has been made about the vastly expanded system of scholarships for foreigners in France. But such criticisms merely underline the basic assumption that the French civilising mission must be carried on in the most effective ways possible.

Yet, given the fact that some two hundred million people live in countries where French is either the national or official or educational language, the educational effort undertaken by the French has not been successful in giving their language a wide distribution; or at least not as wide a distribution as their effort would have led one to expect. For example, it is estimated that in Africa south of the Sahara, where the French have been for a century, only about one or two per cent of the population speak the language fluently. However, this assessment acts merely as a spur to further action. There is now to be greater concentration on work among the foreign elites, who will in their turn provide the teachers at the lower levels. Elsewhere, to increase the spread of French, new buildings for *lycées* have been opened in recent years in many foreign cities, for example in Barcelona, Brussels, Teheran, Montreal, Mexico, Bogotà, while new *lycées* were established in Lima, Athens, Ottawa, Tokyo, Washington, Caracas, Copenhagen, Costa Rica, Quito, and Buenos Aires.

Apart from direct teaching activities, all kinds of other aids to expanding French cultural influence abroad are used today. Not only in the thirty-one countries where French is the mother tongue or the official or educational language, but also in most of the seventy-five countries with which France has concluded cultural agreements, the distribution of French books, films and other cultural products is carried on with much determination. The cultural fund of the Ministry of Foreign Affairs is used specifically to help with book exports, and credits as well as subsidies are provided for especially important markets; the Soviet Union, for example, is given a special discount of 70 per cent, and Quebec receives a discount of 30 per cent. In 1968 alone the Quai d'Orsay sent more than half a million volumes around the world, as well as some ninety thousand text books to Algeria and the rest of Africa, and half as many again to cultural centres abroad. In the same year a total of 15.5 million francs was spent on distributing books in foreign countries, the biggest total reached by any nation except the United States (20 million francs).

(ii) Geographical distribution of French cultural activities: Although facts and figures make tiresome reading, some factual information on French cultural activities abroad is a necessary background for an understanding of the scope of the French effort.

(a) The former empire: France tends to be most active in her efforts to maintain and expand her cultural influence in countries with which she has been traditionally associated. In the first instance this means her former colonial empire. Quebec, North Africa (Algeria, Tunisia, Morocco), Indo-China (Cambodia, Laos, Vietnam), Lebanon, and the fourteen African and Malagasy Republics all still use French at least as the major teaching language, although some countries (Algeria, for example) are trying to reduce the influence of French. Thus, Africa alone (Maghreb and Black Africa) in 1968 took all but some five thousand of the thirty-four thousand teachers France had sent abroad, while Asia-Oceania, the near east and North America accounted for a further two thousand.

General de Gaulle's visit to Quebec in 1967 produced a startling increase in that province's awareness of its French antecedents. The French population of Canada had on the whole always retained its suspicions of the Anglo-Saxon majority in the country, not least because it had with some justification considered itself to be exploited by that majority. But there had also been the religious link with Catholic France, for the Republican regime that had been installed in Paris in the nineteenth century had seemed to French Canadians, despite its anti-clericalism, to be less of an evil than the Protestantism of the rest of Canada. Already before de Gaulle's visit, there had been, since 1965, a considerable increase in Franco-Quebec exchanges. But with the French president's undiplomatic cry 'Vive le Québec libre' a new impetus was given to the relationship between the Canadian province and Paris: the number of teachers increased from 110 to 623, technical cooperation missions from 15 to 450, and university scholarships for French Canadians in France from 15 to 235. It can readily be understood that the Canadian government viewed General de Gaulle's interest in the already troubled Quebec province with distrust and some dismay. By 1971, the Pompidou administration had shown no sign of wanting to alter de Gaulle's policy in Quebec, though it clearly intended to undo the damage de Gaulle's Quebec affront had done to Franco-Canadian relations.

In the Maghreb of North Africa, although there has been much emphasis on Arabisation since it attained independence, French continues to play a significant role in the educational systems of all three states. In 1967 France still provided nearly a quarter of all primary teachers in Algeria, but in 1962 this figure had been 40 per cent. On the other hand, French teachers in secondary and higher education actually increased during that period. The picture is broadly similar in Tunisia and Morocco, where the numbers of French teachers in 1967 (that is, eleven years after the two countries' independence) was higher than ever before. It may be noted that while Arabic remains the main teaching language in the first two years of primary education in Tunisia, and bilingual instruction the rule thereafter in primary and secondary education – with French alone the language in higher education – both Morocco and Algeria have still to come to a firm decision on the respective places within their educational systems of Arabic and French. Meanwhile, French is the only language for secondary and higher education in Algeria (the study of Arabic culture excepted), while in Morocco no firm rule seems as yet to exist.

In Vietnam French is now only taught as a foreign language, but the remainder of what used to be French Indo-China has retained French as the language of instruction at least in higher education. In addition, Laos teaches French at the primary level, while French is also the teaching language at secondary level. In Cambodia attempts are now being made to introduce Khmer progressively into secondary education, although technical as well as higher education is dispensed entirely in French. Furthermore, French teaching institutions remain in all three countries, and their elites still send their children to them in considerable numbers. French *lycées* in Vietnam and Cambodia educate well over ten thousand pupils, most of them children of local parents, and the number of French teachers seconded to the area from metropolitan France increased from 734 in 1960 to over one thousand in 1968. A good deal of French assistance is also given in the form of scholarships, textbooks, teaching techniques, and teachers' training.

In sub-Saharan Africa education has expanded very greatly since independence. Thus primary education has doubled and secondary education has trebled since 1960. In fact, it has been held by some observers that education in Africa has expanded too much in relation to economic growth, because relatively well educated adults have for some years found it difficult to obtain work commensurate with their training.[5] French has remained the official language of all these states, although it shares that status with English in Cameroun and with Arabic in Mauritania and the indigenous language in Madagascar. The demand for French teachers has therefore vastly increased since independence, as well as the need for financial assistance to improve educational systems. A good deal of work has been devoted to the production of syllabuses appropriate to the different states, which nevertheless do not ignore the cultural heritage of France, whose excellence is said to be the very foundation of the ideal of *francophonie*.

(b) Francophonie: When, at the end of the second world war, General de Gaulle insisted that French should be one of the three official languages of the United Nations Organisation, the intention was clearly that this should help to restore French prestige in the world.[6] The care with which subsequent French governments orchestrated that policy is not at first reconcilable with the caution Paris reserved for the phenomenon of *francophonie*. In 1962, the president of the former French colony Senegal, Léopold Senghor, proposed that the states of the regional *Union Africaine et Malgache* should, in concert with France, create a 'vertical organisation, solidly yet flexibly structured, with a view to promoting especially close cooperation in Africa'.[7] Two years later, Senghor defined *francophonie* in terms that do not allow one to forget that he himself has written a good deal of poetry (in French). He said that it is 'that kind of integral humanism which works itself out over the entire earth, the symbiosis of the dormant energies of all the continents, all the races, who are awakening to their complementary warmth.' The idea was taken up by the president of Tunisia, Habib Bourguiba, who translated it into a project for a 'Commonwealth à la française'. By June 1966 the suggestion had hardened into the proposal that Senghor, and Hamani Diori, president of Niger, should explore possibilities with all French-speaking countries. In September 1966 and January 1967 Hamani Diori conveyed the attitudes of the African states to General de Gaulle, although by then even countries like Haiti and Canada (Quebec) had become involved in the discussions.[8] Meanwhile, in metropolitan France, a high committee for the defence and expansion of the French language was set up by a decree of 31 March 1966. But the French government seemed to be in no haste to take other initiatives of its own, largely because – or so it was often said – it tended to distrust 'theoretical' organisations, did not want to be accused of neo-colonialism,

did not want non-African states to have the opportunity of interfering in what it took to be its rightful sphere of influence in Africa, and was worried about the hostility with which countries like Algeria treated the whole idea.

Even so, France joined twenty other French-speaking countries on 20 March 1970 at Niamey in creating the *Agence de coopération culturelle et technique,* which comprised the following: Belgium, Burundi, Cameroun, Canada, Chad, Ivory Coast, Dahomey, France, Gabon, Haute Volta, Luxembourg, Madagascar, Mali, Mauritius, Monaco, Niger, Ruanda, Senegal, Togo, Tunisia and South Vietnam. The Agency gave itself a Canadian secretary general, but precisely what it was expected to produce remained unclear. In any case, it was only the last of a number of organisations to be created for the express purpose of furthering collaboration among French-speaking countries. The United Nations already had a *groupe francophone* of thirty members; since 1962 there has been in existence a Conference of *francophone* ministers of education which meets twice a year and is composed of French, African and Malagasy members, plus, more recently, Quebec and Canada; since 1969 there is also a Conference, similarly composed but without Quebec and Canada, of ministers for youth. In addition to these governmental organisations there is a large number of unofficial groups which are similarly inspired, ranging from university and parliamentary organisations to broadcasting companies.

(c) Other areas: In the rest of the world, too, quite apart from a vast effort in the west and the Soviet Union, there has been a specially active French campaign since the late 1960s to multiply cultural agreements. An agreement signed in October 1968 with Bulgaria increased the number of scholarships in France for Bulgarian teachers of French; it also expanded a wide range of other cultural arrangements between the two countries.[9] In May 1969 an agreement with India created an Institute for French Studies in that country which is to be part of the Nehru University in Delhi. The French expressed the desire that the Institute should con-

centrate on training teachers of French. More generally, it was agreed that cultural relations between France and India should be increased at all levels.[10] France has also encouraged contacts with Cuba, despite the absence of any formal agreement between the two governments. Since 1968 an officially unspecified number of Cubans have taken up scholarships in France[11] and French instructors have gone to Cuba; in both cases the stress was on technical aid, although the more traditional cultural activities were not neglected.

The middle east has also seen an expansion of French cultural activity. In March 1968 the French signed a cultural agreement with the United Arab Republic, which among other provisions was to bring about a considerable increase in the teaching of French language, culture and civilisation in Egypt, as well as reciprocal arrangements in France. The desire for similar improvements in Franco-Syrian relations was expressed in Damascus at the end of the visit there in April 1968 by the director of cultural affairs at the Quai d'Orsay. At about the same time, in May 1968,[12] Israel signed a cultural agreement with France which was to lead, within eighteen months, to a 10–15 per cent increase in the number of Israeli students learning French. France and Ethiopia decided, in August 1968, to implement the cultural agreement reached between the two countries during General de Gaulle's visit to Emperor Haile Selassie two years earlier, by making French the compulsory foreign language in twenty-two secondary schools during the last four school years.

This analysis of French efforts in the field of cultural expansion is far from complete, but in greater detail it would clearly make for drearier reading. However, without some detail, the determination with which French governments have sought to increase their influence abroad through cultural expansion might well be underestimated. Moreover, it will have been noted that the French have pursued the policy of cultural expansion particularly assiduously among nations which have not overtly thrown in their lot with either the United States or the Soviet Union. It is an interesting reflection of French thinking that a recent analysis by a member of the Quai d'Orsay[13] of the spread of French culture should be looking forward not only to there being 100 to 150 million French speakers in Africa and Asia by 1990, but also to French having by then become the official language of the Common Market.

FRENCH ECONOMIC AND TECHNICAL AID
AS AN INSTRUMENT OF FOREIGN POLICY

(i) General principles: It was not until after the second world war that French governments began to provide systematic economic and technical aid outside metropolitan Frânce and Algeria. In the realm of such aid, as in that of cultural aid, the priorities from the beginning tended to be settled in terms of political objectives. As a result, for at least a decade after 1946 no economic or technical aid found its way outside French territories overseas.

Before the second world war France had expected her overseas territories to be profitable to her, or at least self-sufficient. Although these territories were generally allowed to borrow on the French financial market, they were given no special privileges and received little official assistance for development. The situation in the Maghreb countries of North Africa was somewhat different, because the proximity of France had caused French settlers to move there. But it could hardly be said that such settlement was a significant advantage to the native populations, since the French tended to take over the best land and certainly ran the rest of the economy largely for their own benefit too.

After 1945 the French abandoned the earlier concept that overseas territories should subsist on their own resources, a concept which in part reflected the extreme reluctance of many Third Republic politicians to acquire an empire at all. It was replaced by the doctrine that all such territories were part of a French Union, and were henceforth to be considered as interdependent. As the 1946 Constitution of the Fourth Republic put it:

> The French Union is composed of peoples and nations who pool their resources and their efforts to develop their respective civilisations, increase their well-being, and ensure their security.

In accordance with that new outlook, French aid to the countries of the union was explicitly not meant to make those countries self-sufficient. A ten-year plan, beginning in 1946, was intended to promote the social and economic development of the French Union as a whole. The plan was to be partly financed through annual grants from the French budget, but the overseas territories and departments were to contribute 45 per cent from their own resources. It soon appeared that a 45 per cent contribution was quite out of their reach, and the figure was progressively reduced until it reached 10 per cent by 1955, mostly raised by loans carrying low interest (not more than 2 per cent). In addition, the overseas territories benefited from funds made available for research projects that were also expected to be useful to metropolitan France. Special agencies were created to administer the funds. No clear records of French aid exist until 1961, but it is estimated that between 1946 and 1963 funds to the equivalent of 9,813 million new francs were provided.[14]

The Fourth Republic's *loi cadre* of 1956, which was intended to lead to a measure of independence for many overseas territories, transferred the receipts of individual territories to the respective local governments. But the implementation of the *loi cadre* in no way diminished the dependence of these governments overseas on subsidies from Paris. Indeed, one of the recurring criticisms of French aid was that it tended to make its recipients increasingly dependent on its renewal. That was not merely because such aid became addictive, but much more significantly because it continued to be dispensed with little concern for the increasing self-sufficiency of receiving countries. There was no need to wait for the Jeanneney report of 1963 to be told that, at least under the Fourth Republic, aid had often been politically motivated when overseas representatives in the French

Parliament had their support solicited by Paris governments in need of votes. But a much more important objection to the manner in which aid was given concerned the use to which it was put. Prestige projects (airports, administrative buildings) were undertaken when basic agricultural and industrial development would have been infinitely more desirable for the economic health of the country; and highly paid, sophisticated local elites were encouraged to model themselves upon their Parisian counterparts with scant regard for the social and economic requirements of their own populations. Given the low base from which they started, such advances as the tripling of the coffee exports of West Africa and the doubling of its groundnut exports between 1947 and 1957 were 'as unimpressive as the fact that the great majority of the investments in the French Union had been in non-productive sectors.

The special status of French overseas territories as part of the franc zone has on the whole been to their advantage. Paris governments have tended to pay high prices for the few exports of countries within that zone, despite the growing belief among French economists that the corresponding ease with which French exports were finding their way into these countries may well have been positively detrimental to French competitiveness in the increasingly important world market outside the franc zone. Certainly, the Jeanneney report was sceptical about the continuing economic usefulness of the franc zone to France, although financial aid made available by Paris within the franc zone is generally spent in France and thus brings French industry the usual benefits of an increased market.

The first plan for the development of the French Union (1946–56) had perhaps been more open to the criticism of non-productiveness than the second plan (1956–66). But the difference was not very significant, since projected expenditure on production and social development increased by only 15 per cent, while infrastructure expenditure remained

at the high figure of 49 per cent. However, the period of the
second plan coincided with the rapid accession to independence of most of the states of the French Union; the latter,
after the creation of the Fifth Republic in 1958, became the
ephemeral French Community. By 1962 the French government was, officially, responsible for only a few small and
scattered overseas territories which, in Africa, amounted to
no more than the area around the port of Djibouti. Thus,
between 1954 when Indo-China severed its connections
with France, and 1962 when Algeria gained independence,
the data on which the concept of aid had been based – that
is, that of a French Union of interdependent countries – had
drastically changed. It is not surprising that efforts were
made to change French policies on aid too.

*(ii) Geographical distribution of French economic and
technical aid:* The most important fact about French aid
policy after 1962 is that despite the alteration in the balance
of this aid in favour of what are officially designated as
'traditionally foreign countries' (that is, countries that had
never been ruled by France), aid programmes to former
French territories in Africa (south of the Sahara) continued
at a high level. Indeed, the State Secretariat in charge of
Cooperation, originally set up in 1961 as a separate Ministry
to deal with aid to the fourteen African and Malagasy
Republics, continued after its integration with the Ministry
of Foreign Affairs in 1966 to administer lavish funds for the
development of those countries. Independent of the political
Directorate in the Quai responsible for African and Malagasy
affairs, the State Secretariat maintains the closest contacts
with the African governments, which rely heavily on the
funds, personnel and advice it provides. It was typical, however, of de Gaulle's philosophy of *'coopération'* that Guinée,
which opted for independence from France in 1958, was
virtually cut off from all French aid, while the countries which
agreed to retain connections with France continued to enjoy
rich benefits from those connections. Already linked by the
ideal of *francophonie,* most of the fourteen countries also

have defence agreements with France and have generally tended to align their attitudes in international politics with those of France.

At least until the end of the 1960s France devoted a greater proportion of her national income to foreign aid than any other country, including the United States. But in terms of the proportion of the national income, French aid has since 1966 been diminishing, like that of other countries. Although there are differences in the official figures published for 1967,[15] between 1962 and 1967 the proportion dwindled from 2.51 per cent to around 1.6 per cent. But despite the discrepancies in the published statistics, it appears that at least one-third of all French aid habitually went to the African and Malagasy Republics.[16] It is worth noting, however, that as state aid from France decreased, private aid tended to increase, at least for the last year (1968) for which figures are available at the time of writing. For private investment in the African and Malagasy Republics, the French government introduced a special form of guarantee in 1970.

Through their links with France, the African and Malagasy states have also considerably benefited from EEC. French insistence, when the treaty of Rome was being negotiated, that the Common Market should take an active interest in the development of the overseas territories of member nations brought them many advantages. The extent of the EEC commitment turned out to be lavish, to the point where at the end of 1968 Senegal, one of the more prosperous African countries, received more aid from EEC through the European Fund for Overseas Development (for which France provides one-third of the resources) than from direct French public aid. It may be noted, incidentally, that the first instalment of EEC aid (1960–4) was, just like direct aid from France, used in the African and Malagasy states to a large extent (44 per cent) for infrastructure expenditure. But the second instalment (1965–9), probably more usefully, placed greater emphasis on the modernisation of agriculture (45.2 per cent of aid). The 1969–75 period, which will be coextensive with that covered by the second convention signed at Yaoundé in 1969, will provide aid and loans totalling 900 million dollars, an increase of 170 million dollars over the preceding period, nearly all for the former French states. The Yaoundé conventions, the first of which dates back to 1963, brought these states the additional benefit of preferential tariff arrangements with all Common Market countries.

French aid to Algeria, independent since 1962, has a motivation which is rather different from that governing aid to the African and Malagasy Republics. Although there can be little doubt that the motivation here, too, is primarily political, the specific considerations are nevertheless very different. In terms of trade alone, Algeria is France's fourth most important partner, coming ahead even of Great Britain. Thus, while French economists have had little hesitation in discounting the economic benefits to France of her association with the African and Malagasy states, French economic interests in Algeria remain considerable. French natural gas and oil interests in Algeria are substantial. Algerian oil – payable in francs, for Algeria is in the franc zone – provided France with 37 per cent of her needs in 1964, and with 26.8 per cent in 1970 in a greatly expanded market. It is well known that Algeria has succeeded in exacting unusually high returns for allowing France a large share in the exploitation of her oil resources, but the French have clearly thought the price worth paying. The independence it brings France from the Anglo-American controlled oil market is certainly one attraction. The hope for continuing French influence in Algeria, one of the leading countries of the so-called Third World, is another.

Franco-Algerian understanding on oil and gas no doubt also helped to bring about the five-year agreement (1966–70) which led France to provide a total of one billion francs as aid to Algerian industrialisation. Although this is well down on the level of previous aid, which as a result of the 1958 Constantine plan at first provided that same amount each year, it continues to account for a sizable slice from the French aid budget; in 1964 aid to Algeria still took a quarter of all French foreign aid. Although in later years French public aid to Algeria declined, private aid increased considerably, rising by as much as 157 per cent between 1967 and 1968, particularly to help exploit Algeria's gas and oil resources.

But there is also a sense in which the Algerians need the French as much as the African and Malagasy states do, so that mere political and economic self-interest on the part of France may not alone account for continuing French aid there. An average of half a million Algerians have been working in France at any one time since Algerian independence, and they have been sending home considerable sums of money which are useful to the Algerian economy. And Algerian exports to France, especially wine, are important to Algeria. On the fifth anniversary of the regime of Colonel Boumediène in 1970, *Le Monde* still qualified Algeria's economic relations with France as 'fundamental' to his government.[17] Even so, a large part of the rest of the world which so far receives little or nothing from France could find such aid 'fundamental' too; the fact that it does not receive it is the result of a deliberate political French choice.

A special Secretariat of the Quai d'Orsay has, since 1962, dealt with all Algerian matters, including aid. There is consequently here a much closer organisational link between political and aid questions than in the case of the African and Malagasy Republics; it has been seen that aid to the latter is administered by the Secretariat in charge of Cooperation while political relations are dealt with by the requisite Directorate at the Quai. This difference affects the whole tone of the relations between France and the countries concerned, and there is little of the informal dropping in of officials in the Algerian section of the Quai that one encounters with such frequency at the former Ministry for Cooperation.

The other major territories formerly under French rule, Morocco, Tunisia and the three Indo-Chinese states, also have such aid as they receive administered directly by the Ministry of Foreign Affairs. Since they gained their independence in the middle of the 1950s, most aid to them has been technical aid, and this, in the Quai, has since 1956 been the responsibility of the General Directorate of Cultural and Technical Affairs. It was not until 1960 that a financial loan was actually made to one of the countries (Vietnam), but in 1963–4 this was followed by loans to Morocco, Tunisia and Cambodia, and all the loans have been administered by the Treasury in exactly the same way as loans to other countries that have never been under French rule. None of these countries, however, receives any form of aid on anything like the scale of Algeria or the African and Malagasy Republics.

That the largely technical aid given to the former Indo-Chinese states, Morocco and Tunisia is politically motivated has been publicly acknowledged by the Ministry of Foreign Affairs itself. For example, the report for 1963 of the General Directorate for Cultural and Technical Affairs of the Quai stated that the purpose of its work is to 'defend economic and cultural positions in a rapidly changing world by maintaining an original form of contact and activities in developing countries'. In the following year, the report defined the mission of the General Directorate as the training of the professional and educated classes in developing countries.[18]

An idea of the relatively small budgets involved in technical aid to these countries, when compared with Algeria and sub-Saharan Africa, will be conveyed by the fact that in the mid-1960s Tunisia and Morocco received an allocation of around 33 million francs a year and the Indo-Chinese states some 25 millions. At the same time Algeria received 200 millions a year for industrial aid alone. The reasons for the comparatively low level of French aid to these areas have, of course, not been officially stated, but it may be thought that the demonstrations of independence from France which the countries concerned have at times given are not irrelevant considerations. The Indo-Chinese states and Morocco have developed relationships with the United States, while Tunisia under President Bourguiba has not always shown itself a pliable partner for France. What distinguishes Tunisia from Algeria in this respect is largely that Algeria has much more to offer Paris, even though it is hardly more accommodating than Tunisia.

So far as the rest of the world is concerned, France provided no technical aid at all until 1956 and no financial aid until 1961. The reason for this is almost certainly that until the end of the 1950s France simply did not have the means with which to finance an aid programme outside the areas for which she was directly responsible. But when she did venture further afield, political considerations clearly determined where the aid went.

Technical aid for 'traditionally foreign countries' is not only administered by the relevant General Directorate at the Quai d'Orsay – as is the case for such aid to the three Indo-Chinese states, Morocco and Tunisia – but also by a similar department at the Ministry for Economic and Financial Affairs. Roughly speaking, the Quai is responsible for cultural, educational, scientific, social, administrative and agricultural aid, while the Ministry for Economic and Financial Affairs deals more with economic, commercial and industrial aid. According to the report of the French Economic and Social Council published in 1965, the aid activities of the two Ministries have been somewhat haphazard. But the first five-year plan for technical aid, in force since 1962, had already begun to give a much clearer direction to their work, and both Ministries have since then collaborated in an increasingly coordinated programme. The 1962 plan unambiguously set out the political considerations upon which the technical aid programme was to be based. It said that small, scattered operations were to be avoided in favour of a limited number of objectives selected in accordance with political or cultural priorities. Nor were technical aid programmes in future to be restricted to the underdeveloped areas of Africa and Asia, but they were to be extended to Canada, eastern Europe and South America too. In those three areas, the political motivation was particularly obvious.

In fact, since 1963 agreements on technical aid have been signed between France and a large number of 'traditionally foreign countries'. This is reflected in the increasing proportion of budgetary provision for aid to countries outside the franc zone. By 1968 that proportion had increased by 10 per cent to 36 per cent as compared with 1964. South America, after de Gaulle's visit there in 1964, and the Arab countries of the middle east after 1967, were areas in which the French became particularly active. Between 1963 and 1965 budget allocations for the two Ministries administering technical aid to traditionally foreign countries more than doubled (to 97.2 million francs from 43.2 millions) while those for former French-controlled states like Tunisia remained more or less stable, or in the case of Morocco actually declined; and it was in keeping with General de Gaulle's objectives in the former Indo-Chinese states that during the same period French technical aid there nearly doubled (to 24.7 millions from 13.8).

It has already been seen that official financial, as distinct from technical, aid was furnished by France relatively late to traditionally foreign countries. Chile was the first such country to be granted an official loan in 1961. Since then, this side of French aid has considerably increased, reaching 150 million dollars for 1969.[19] Although the considerations governing the granting of a loan are usually political, the negotiations are carried out by the Ministry of Economic and Financial Affairs, which also later administers the loan. Most loans are made to cover purchases of French goods. In that sense it is true that 'official financial aid to traditionally foreign countries has so far . . . merely supplemented private export credits'.[20]

On the subject of aid in general, it must finally be said that French aid has nearly always been bilateral. That fact, more perhaps than any other, underlines the political motivation that has governed French aid projects. In that respect France is not of course alone; United States aid, for example, has followed the same tendency. Nevertheless, M. Pompidou, when he was prime minister, placed particular emphasis on the nationalist element in France's wish to keep aid as bilateral a concern as possible. In the National Assembly he put it like this:

> It remains true that multilateral aid, in the way it is handled in the big international organisations, ends up by reinforcing the English language. And I repeat, we, as Frenchmen, feel a kind of need to maintain the French language. This is a fundamental reason for maintaining bilateral aid.[21]

Even so, the proportion of French multilateral aid is roughly the same as that of the United States, Britain and Germany, although it includes aid administered by the EEC's European Development Fund, most of which goes to the former French overseas territories. The French contribution to the United Nations technical assistance and relief programmes is substantially less than that of the other main contributors. In 1962 it amounted to 3.6 million dollars, compared with 95.9 million supplied by the United States and 15.4 million by the United Kingdom. It is likely that General de Gaulle's dislike of the United Nations Organisation, which until Algerian independence was most outspoken in its condemnation of French 'colonialism', played at least some part in France's reluctance to participate in its aid programmes, just as France had usually refused to help pay for its peace-keeping efforts.

DECOLONISATION AND ITS IMPLICATIONS FOR FRENCH FOREIGN POLICY

Despite France's redoubled efforts after the second world war to impress the world with her language and cultural traditions, and despite the new philosophy which governed her relations with her overseas territories in the French Union, her governments failed to gain any sizable political influence among the countries outside the Soviet and American alliance systems. Although the reason for this was in part the same as that which had inhibited France's political progress within either alliance system – namely her manifold weakness under the Fourth Republic – it was also to a very considerable extent because of the obstinacy with which she refused to decolonise, a fact that was in any case much to blame for the political precariousness of the regime itself. It was not until decolonisation had finally been forced upon her, and completed with Algerian independence in 1962, that France became an acceptable partner for the countries of the so-called 'Third World', many of which had only recently won their own independence from colonial rule. Since the manner in which independence was attained by the countries that had been under French rule to a considerable extent determined their future relations with France, as well as the attitudes of other countries to France, the evolution of French colonial policies since 1945 has to be examined.

(i) The background: It is typical of the universalist tradition of the French that the first modern colonial doctrine they evolved should have been that of assimilation. It maintained that the 'rational' ideals which had informed the French Revolution are universally valid, and implied that it would be selfish to deprive colonial subjects of its benefits. The doctrine did not simply make it a humanitarian duty for the French to civilise others, but also to see to it that the mission was properly completed before they abandoned their part of the task. Since the Jacobin belief in administrative centralisation had been the political and constitutional consequence of the rational ideal, Paris was taken to be the centre from which the civilising mission had to be directed. Thus the most recalcitrant colonial subject would eventually be brought to the moral and intellectual outlook of the most sophisticated Parisian.

The doctrine sounds generous, especially when it is as vibrantly proclaimed as it had been by the French Revolution; in 1794, Boissy d'Anglas had declared that 'The French Revolution was not only for Europe but for the universe . . .

since we have found the right way of administering European countries, why should ... the colonies be deprived of it.' But Ferry, the man as much responsible as anyone under the Third Republic for French colonial expansion, seemed to state with very little compunction in 1895 that 'the declaration of the rights of man was not written for the blacks of Equatorial Africa'.[22] At least he was honest. Although assimilation seemed to be a highly respectable even if intellectually hazardously grounded doctrine, in the light of actual colonial policy it turned out to be little more than a squalid rationalisation of inexcusable exploitation. This is not the place to go into a detailed analysis of French rule in the colonial empire before 1945, but the recognition that the noble ideal of assimilation had not been implemented was largely responsible for the fact that the concept of a French Union was created.

(ii) Colonial policy, 1944–58: The new era is generally taken to have begun with the declaration at the end of General de Gaulle's Free French Brazzaville Conference in January 1944. The motivation behind the declaration was no doubt complex. The many statements made by the leaders of nations fighting Germany and Japan had for some time contained generously worded generalities about freedom from all kinds of evil, including exploitation, and these must have played some part in the Brazzaville pronouncements. But the role a number of French overseas territories had played in furthering the cause of General de Gaulle's Free French movement was no doubt also an important consideration. And, in January 1944, metropolitan France was still occupied by the Germans, so that colonial susceptibilities had in any case still to be appeased. In the absence of reliable accounts of what was behind the Brazzaville declaration, it has at least to be noted that it said 'We want the colonies to enjoy great administrative and economic freedom', and that 'their feeling of responsibility [should be] gradually formed and increased so that they might be associated in the public administration of their countries'.[23] Similarly, in

his report of a conversation with President Truman, de Gaulle wrote in his *Mémoires*[24] that he told the president, 'We intend to bring the countries under our control to the point where they will be able freely to decide their future.'

But what 'freedom' meant in that context was soon to be made clear by de Gaulle himself. The Brazzaville declaration, as well as the *Mémoires,* qualified the degree of independence that might be accorded to French territories overseas to such an extent that it fell very far short not only of the aspirations already expressed by many French colonial subjects, but also of the hopes pressingly voiced by the United States. The Brazzaville Conference had concluded that 'the goals of the French civilising mission in the colonies cannot be reconciled with any idea of autonomy or with the prospect of an evolution outside the French empire. The self-government of the colonies even as a remote possibility is to be rejected'.[25] Without being as categorical, the *Mémoires* nevertheless also preclude real decolonisation: 'After what has happened in our African and Asian possessions it is unlikely that we can maintain our empire there in the same manner as before. If we want the peoples for whom we are responsible still to remain with France tomorrow, we must transform their present status as subjects into one of autonomy. But with the proviso that we hold firmly to our values . . . and demand that such countries keep their word to us.'[26] Even if de Gaulle's meaning seemed unambiguous at the time, subsequent events showed that he wanted such countries to remain open to French political influence; the fate of Guinée after 1958 illustrates that point.

The Brazzaville declaration was therefore not the liberal charter announcing decolonisation that subsequent Gaullist hagiography has made of it. It would have been remarkable if it had been. General de Gaulle had spent most of his time since the defeat of his country in 1940 defending the territorial integrity of France and its empire, and the very possibility of giving up any of it must have been the last thought to occur to him at that stage. His not altogether mistaken suspicion that Britain – if not the United States, too – was anxious to replace the French at least in the middle east would have clinched matters for him. As he said himself, 'If overseas territories cut themselves off from metropolitan France . . . for how much would we count between the North Sea and the Mediterranean?'[27]

In fact, in 1946, the year of de Gaulle's departure from power, the concept of assimilation played an important part in the allocation of 63 seats of the National Assembly (out of 600) to representatives of the French colonies and protectorates. The overseas representatives were elected by local French residents and certain categories of educated natives, although in Tunisia and Morocco only French citizens voted. It can, of course, be taken for granted that the educated local inhabitants who had the vote had received an essentially French education. Even the French Communist Party advocated a policy of assimilation, which was understood to entail the granting of French citizenship and representation in the Paris Parliament. At that time only the Algerians and Madagascans spoke out against that principle and openly asked for independence. But they met with only hostile response, and when shortly afterwards some of their countrymen tried to achieve independence by taking up arms against France, the repression which followed was reported to have brought about the death of 'many thousands [of Algerians] . . . and the very few Algerian leaders were arrested and put in prison'.[28] That was as early as 1945. In Madagascar it was not until 1947 that the nationalists openly rebelled: eighty thousand local inhabitants were killed. Both Algeria and Madagascar therafter remained quiet for several years. But the rebellion which began in Indo-China at about the same time did not finally come to an end until 1954, and then only after the French armies had been beaten and forced to leave the country. In any case, the veteran Radical leader Edouard Herriot had already in the debate on the Constitution instituting the French Union demonstrated the unacceptable logic which the policy of assimilation entailed. It is worth quoting him in full:

Let us have a look at article 67: 'The nationals or natives of metropolitan France, of the overseas departments and territories

enjoy the liberties and rights that go with French citizenship.'
How many citizens will there be in the territories overseas? According to many, there will be more than in metropolitan France ...
As one of my friends put it to me amusingly yet profoundly, France
will thus become the colony of her former colonies.[29]

Leopold Senghor, the future president of Senegal, whose
soldiers were soon to help the French with the massacre of
the natives in Madagascar, thereupon exclaimed that Herriot
was guilty of racialism. Perhaps he was, but the fact that a mere
sixty-three seats in the National Assembly had been given to
representatives from overseas – a large proportion of whom
represented only white settlers – showed quite eloquently
enough that the concept of assimilation was not likely to
be translated into hard political fact in the near future.

Although, as has been shown, Paris Parliaments in the
period after 1945 were enormously more generous than their
predecessors in the financial and technical contributions
they made to the development of France's overseas territories,
the sluggishness of progress towards real assimilation was
a significant reason for the increasing overseas demands for
independence. But another important reason was that the
concept of assimilation itself was repugnant to nationalist
elements overseas. Nowhere more than in the so-called
associated states of Indo-China was it clear that assimilation
meant nothing; it was a fact recognised in Paris, where
even in 1946 no attempt was made to have the states represented in the National Assembly. That in itself tends to
make the French refusal to countenance independence at
least for the associated states after 1945 difficult to defend.

There is no need here to go into the many promises and
counterpromises made by the French to Ho-Chi-Minh and
other Indo-Chinese nationalists between 1945 and 1954.
The strenuous efforts of the Fourth Republic to retain intact
the Jacobin conception of the Republic One and Indivisible,
if necessary by deception that was sometimes presented as
Reason of State, have been studied in detail by others.[30]
Two points must, however, be brought out. First, the demand
for independence by the Indo-Chinese states was resisted

by all Paris governments until the physical defeat of the
French armies in 1954, particularly at Dien-Bien-Phu.
Second, the French army had played an important political
part in persuading Paris governments to resist that demand.
The consequences of these two points for the future history
of French decolonisation and foreign policy were, first,
that France was consistently reviled at the United Nations
and shunned by most of the newly independent states, and
by others which intended to be on good terms with these
states; second, the French army's bitterness at its defeat in
Indo-China led it to blame its own ineptitude on the regime
of the Fourth Republic which had allegedly starved it of
supplies; the bitterness was to increase with Tunisian and
Moroccan independence, finally to reach breaking point over
Algeria in 1958.

Had there not been a good deal of difference between the
approaches of the French army and the population of
metropolitan France to the problem of Indo-China, it is
doubtful if Pierre Mendès-France could have made peace
with the Indo-Chinese even in 1954. But the lack of interest,
and in the end the distaste, of the French for the Indo-
Chinese war helped to make the Geneva agreements of July
1954 possible. The same kind of indifference on the part of the
metropolitan French enabled Mendès-France to begin the
decolonisation process in Tunisia and Morocco. In both
these countries the previous governments of the Fourth
Republic had played the same ambiguous game about
independence as in Indo-China. Sometimes they had made
hopeful promises, then they had blown cold again and tried
to play it tough. It was not so much a matter of bad faith
on their part, though that was not always obviously absent,
as a token of the weakness of the regime as a whole. Whenever a 'liberal' solution seemed possible, either the French
settlers in the two countries or French politicians of the
extreme Right at home would seek to destroy a possible
settlement, and they generally got their way because the
various factions of the National Assembly only rarely succeeded in agreeing on policies that would have enabled them

to put up a united front against the defenders of colonialism.

In fact, until the Mendès-France administration briefly asserted the rights and duties of the Paris government, the local settlers both in Tunisia and in Morocco had tended to call the tune, to which Paris then found itself condemned to dance. It had been the settlers who had pressed on the official representative of the French government in Tunis, the resident, the arrest and deportation of Tunisia's prime minister, at a time in 1952 when negotiations with Paris might just have succeeded; and the resident acted in accordance with their demands without first bothering even to consult his government. In Morocco, the settlers had presented Paris with a similar *fait accompli,* except there they had gone further still. In 1953 the representative of the French government had actually been induced to depose the sultan without first sounding out Paris. Even so, Mendès-France negotiated a settlement with the Tunisians in 1955, and this led to complete independence within a year; and the next prime minister, Edgar Faure, having restored the sultan to his throne, initiated the process which brought about the independence of Morocco in 1956. Neither the loss of Tunisia nor that of Morocco caused much of a stir in France, except among a number of politicians of the Right and Jacobin veterans of the Left.

The revolt which broke out in Algeria in 1954 was a rather different matter. The number of French settlers in Tunisia and Morocco had been larger than in Indo-China, but small in comparison with the million white French nationals who had made their life in Algeria. Even the population of metropolitan France had long been in the habit of looking upon Algeria as an integral part of their country. Unlike Tunisia and Morocco, Algeria had not been a 'protectorate' but, so the fiction ran, a region composed of departments like any region in the metropolitan French Republic. But the discriminatory treatment reserved for the non-white Algerians belied this description. Voting procedures were heavily weighted against the eight million Muslims, and the economic and social benefits of close association with France went very largely to white French nationals. The point here is not that the Muslims derived no benefit from the association of their country with France, for that would be a manifestly false assertion, but that the benefits they did derive were very small indeed when compared with those enjoyed by the million white settlers. In fact, there is a sense in which it was precisely some of the major benefits the Muslims did derive from French rule which eventually led to the expulsion of the French from Algeria. For it was largely from the French-educated elite of Algerian Muslims that the nationalist leaders were drawn. It was they who most felt the need to bring French universalist theories into some kind of working relationship with practical Algerian realities.

The question of Algerian independence was further complicated by the presence in the Maghreb of an increasing number of French army units that had seen service in Indo-China, and defeat. It had been no boost to the morale of the army that its first major independent operation since 1940 should have ended as it had at Dien-Bien-Phu. By 1956, when Tunisia and Morocco had obtained their independence, the bases which the French army had retained in those countries contained many officers who found it intolerable to have to operate in the kind of confinement the new order imposed on them. What was worse, the Tunisians and Moroccans could not fail to sympathise with their Muslim neighbours across the border in Algeria, and as the war between the Algerian nationalists and the French increased in scope and bitterness, relations between the French and the populations in Tunisia and Morocco deteriorated at all levels. In October 1956 the French military command in Algeria, on its own initiative, intercepted a plane carrying a number of leaders of the Algerian rebellion who had been on their way from Morocco to Tunisia. It was another one of those actions on which the Paris government had not even been consulted, and it increased the ill-feeling against the French throughout North Africa. It also led to the resignation, by way of protest, of the French ambassador in Tunis and of one of the secretaries of state in the government led by Guy Mollet, who had lamely accepted the *fait accompli*. And it was responsible for the massacre of some thirty Europeans in Meknès.

Part of the reason for the enthusiasm of the French government about the Anglo-French intervention on the Suez canal at the end of 1956[31] was that it was meant to be a blow to Arab nationalism in general. Egypt, under Nasser, had tried to become the spearhead of the Arab nationalist crusade, and Algerian rebels fighting the French had received every kind of help from Cairo. The fact that the French army thought the politicians in Paris were responsible for robbing it of victory at Suez, just as the same politicians had previously been accused of having abandoned it in Indo-China, hardly encouraged the hope that French forces would be keen to leave Algeria without first having secured a military victory. It was therefore not a surprise to those who knew the mood of many army officers that, when negotiations were taking place between the French government and the Algerian nationalists, many of these officers were driven to the brink of rebellion, and some well over the brink.

Against that background, soldiers and settlers combined to destroy the regime of the Fourth Republic, in the expectation that it would be followed by a government that would safeguard the 'honour' of the army and the interests of settlers by keeping Algeria an integral part of France, *Algérie française*. And indeed the Fourth Republic disappeared in the face of the threat of an invasion of metropolitan France by the French army from North Africa, while the Algerian Muslims who were not actually fighting the French were being pushed into the streets of Algerian towns by extremist settlers and zealous soldiers so that they might demonstrate their eagerness to remain French citizens. At that stage the defenders of the ideal of *Algérie française* recalled General de Gaulle from his political retirement, which had never been passive, and the politicians who had given the Fourth Republic its ethos capitulated before most of his demands so that he could take over the government of France with a semblance of legality.

(iii) Decolonisation, 1958–62: That was in May 1958. One of the preoccupations of those who were working out the Constitution for the next Republic, the Fifth, was the future status of the overseas territories. The 1946 concept of a French Union was no longer politically viable in 1958. Indo-China, Tunisia and Morocco had become independent countries. The Sudan had attained independence in 1956, the British Gold Coast had lost its colonial status to become Ghana a year later, and several other British territories were expected to follow suit in the near future. Besides, the 1955 Bandoeng Conference of countries non-aligned with either of the super powers had greatly increased international pressure against the remaining traces of old-style imperialism. In the summer of 1958 the question was how far France would go in the direction of decolonisation, given the delicate situation in Algeria and the morose watchfulness of the army.

Already in 1956, when defending projected colonial reforms, Gaston Defferre had asked the French Senate 'not to let it be thought that France only thinks of making reforms once blood has begun to flow'.[32] As it turned out, General de Gaulle's Constitution for the Fifth Republic went well beyond the establishment of local assemblies granted by the Defferre measures. The French Union became the new Constitution's French Community, and the former colonial territories were referred to as states and given internal autonomy. However, foreign affairs, defence, and other important attributes of statehood were to remain in the hands of the French Community which, in effect, meant the government in Paris. Had this been all, the provisions of the new Constitution would indeed have been an improvement on previous French colonial policies, but not a radical improvement. But it also contained Article 86, which said that any overseas territory could have its independence, provided that the territory's legislative assembly had a vote to that effect confirmed by the local population in a referendum. Metropolitan France and the French overseas territories were called upon to accept the new Constitution in a referendum in September

1958, and it was understood that any overseas territory voting 'No' would automatically be deemed to have opted for immediate independence.

There has been much speculation about de Gaulle's reasons for adopting such a liberal colonial policy. It is unlikely that there will ever be a reliable answer. His *Mémoires* had already tried to perpetuate the myth that the Brazzaville declaration had been a clear indication that he intended to pursue a policy of decolonisation, but it has been shown* that it was no such thing. And even though many of his admirers, not least intellectuals from the former French colonies, have seen Brazzaville in that light too, that is no reason for ignoring the actual text of the declaration. In fact, there had been nothing in de Gaulle's record before 1958 which would have allowed one to predict that his colonial policy would take the form it did. Perhaps it should not be held against him that most of his followers in the 1940s and 1950s were among the most rabid defenders of French colonialism. But it was while he was still head of the government that, in 1945, Algerian nationalists were killed in their thousands, and it was not until the final months of the agony of the French army in Indo-China that he seemed to come firmly round to the idea of independence for the associated states. And despite his friendship for the sultan of Morocco whom French settlers there had removed from the throne – before Edgar Faure had him brought back – General de Gaulle's closest reactionary collaborators were convinced that he detested the granting of independence to the two North African protectorates as much as they all detested the thought of an independent Algeria.

It would be tidy if de Gaulle's conversion to more liberal colonial policies could be accounted for by his reading of the Bandoeng Conference. Having since before the end of the war despaired of being able to make an impression on the policies of either of the super powers, it would have been rational for de Gaulle to want to promote France to the

* See above, pp. 187–8.

leadership of the Third World, whose hazy and amorphous existence had manifested itself at Bandoeng. Tidiness, of course, proves nothing about the truth of a hypothesis, but it was not before the signal from Bandoeng that the apparent change in de Gaulle's outlook became visible. Scarcely three months after the Bandoeng Conference, de Gaulle spoke of an association between France and Algeria in a wider community 'with all the political participation of the Algerians which such integration entails'.[33] This was not very explicit, but it went further in the direction of conceding some kind of political responsibility to the Algerian Muslims than any of the robustly nationalist talk of most of the prominent politicians of the Fourth Republic. Even Mendès-France, who had helped Tunisia and Morocco to independence, did not openly disavow his earlier insistence that Algeria had to remain an integral part of France until May 1956, when he resigned from the Mollet government that had surrendered to the repressive demands of the Algerian settlers.

In the volume of his *Mémoires* published in 1970, de Gaulle stated that he had no hand in the revolt that overthrew the Fourth Republic.[34] He certainly made no public utterance during the final months before his return to power in 1958 that could have suggested that he was whole-heartedly behind those who, like his admirers Michel Debré and Jacques Soustelle, were prepared to sacrifice everything to keeping Algeria French. He had not openly condemned torture in Algeria, whether inflicted by the French army or the rebels, but neither had he accused of lack of patriotism those who condemned the army for practising torture, as apologists for *Algérie française* had tended to do. Thus, the first clearcut statement of de Gaulle's position on decolonisation in 1958 came in the project for the new Constitution, with the option of independence for overseas territories.

But Algeria's special status as an integral part of France meant that it was precluded from obtaining its independence merely through the rejection of the new Constitution. On the other hand, de Gaulle was later to state that on his return to power in 1958 he had been completely convinced that 'there was no alternative to according the Algerians the right of self-determination'. *Algérie française* he thought a 'ruinous utopia', and he excluded 'from the realm of possibilities all ideas of assimilation'.[35] The concept of 'integration' which he had himself used – for example in the 1955 press conference* – was for him no more than an 'astute and empty formula'.[36] If the general's recollections in 1970 can be taken at face value, and there is no convincing counter-evidence, then it appears that his thinking on Algeria was already in 1958 a reflection of the doctrine of optional independence clearly contained in the new Constitution. Only tactical considerations could in that case be said to have prevented him at that time from giving the same kind of publicity to his proposals for Algeria as for those contained in Article 86 of the Constitution. There is no doubt that such tactical considerations had, in 1958, to weigh heavily with him, since the army as well as its Algerian settler friends and their allies in metropolitan France were for many months after their *coup* powerful enough to make de Gaulle's position very precarious.

Meanwhile, the sub-Saharan territories had been enthusiastic about de Gaulle's return to power, and the projected new Constitution confirmed for them that their Brazzaville-endorsed admiration for the general had been well-founded. Before the referendum on the Constitution de Gaulle made a tour of Africa and Madagascar, and the reception he received there was predictably impressive. He took the opportunity to explain the aspects of the Constitution which allowed for independence, but he also warned that if any state actually went so far as to demand it by voting 'No', France would instantly sever her connections with it.

It was probably at least as much the attachment of the elites of sub-Saharan Africa and Madagascar to the values of the French cultural tradition as the fear of losing French aid which prompted nearly all the states of the area to approve the new Constitution in September 1958. Only

* See above, p. 197.

Guinée voted 'No', and had its aid from France instantly cut off. But this led to a complete, and quite unexpected, defeat of de Gaulle's latest colonial doctrine. The exemplary punishment meted out to Guinée paradoxically had the opposite effect from that intended. First the Soviet Union and then the United States came to Guinée's aid, which was hardly what de Gaulle had wanted. Then, when the other African states which had voted to remain within the French Community saw that French aid might not be irreplaceable, and had before them the example of a fully independent Guinée, they found it difficult to convince their peoples that they were not ripe for independence as well. As a consequence, in 1959 and 1960 all the sub-Saharan states and Madagascar asked for complete independence, too. Already persuaded that he had blundered in presenting Guinée to the Soviet Union and the United States, de Gaulle made no fuss about granting them independence, and continued France's relationship with them at all levels. Mali, federated at the time with Senegal, began the rush to independence in September 1959, Madagascar was next in December, and in 1960 the remaining states completed it. Thus, within two years of the creation of the French Community it had ceased to exist, at least in the form in which it had first been intended.

But though the Community had disappeared, something much more valuable to France had come into existence instead. Whether the Bandoeng hypothesis is right or not, the transformation of sub-Saharan French colonies into thirteen independent republics and the, by then, growing conviction that a similar solution would be reached by de Gaulle in Algeria, turned France almost overnight into the blue-eyed girl of the west, at least for the countries of the Third World. Moreover, the population of metropolitan France had not merely taken the independence of the African and Malagasy states with equanimity – just as it had hardly objected to the 1956 *loi cadre* – but it had also become so sick of the murderous antics of the Algerian settlers and their friends inside and outside the army that the future independence of Algeria had begun to appear to it as a positive boon. Therefore, once de Gaulle had survived the various attempts at assassination and army revolts in Algeria, and yielded independence to the Algerians at the Evian Conference in 1962, France's colonial slate was clean before the world. De Gaulle almost immediately put the new situation to international use.

RELATIONS WITH THE 'THIRD WORLD' SINCE 1962

There is no evidence that the 'uncommitted' nations which make up the so-called Third World were, in spring 1962, anxiously waiting for France to join them, let alone for her to lead them. India, Yugoslavia and China, for example, were all quite capable of looking after their own international interests; indeed, so far as China was concerned, France did not even have diplomatic relations with her at that time. In addition, Pakistan, like the countries of the Arab League with which it is in sympathy, had not yet forgiven France the Suez adventure and subsequent aid to Israel, and all were keen supporters of Algerian independence. Yet within a month of the Evian agreements, the Arab League Council was beginning the *rapprochement* of the Third World with France by voicing the hope that Franco-Arab relations could now improve. Exactly a year later diplomatic relations were restored between Cairo and Paris, a relationship enhanced by the fact that in the course of the next three years, France granted the United Arab Republic credits amounting to 100 million dollars. That de Gaulle's foreign minister, Couve de Murville, was known to have opposed the Suez invasion was also in France's favour at that time.

There were, in any case, a number of factors which now made France an acceptable partner for countries of the Third World, quite apart from the satisfaction of Arab states that French colonial policy in Africa had changed under de Gaulle. To begin with, there had never been any mystery about the general's dislike of United States power in international affairs, at least when it clashed with his own designs for the world. Also, having been lectured by Americans since the middle of the second world war on the evils of colonialism, it was perhaps not unnatural that he should take the first opportunity, once his own house was in order, to castigate United States involvement in Vietnam. He did so from 1963 onwards, and as might be expected received the approval of the Third World for it. De Gaulle's dislike of Soviet power and its use outside Russia – if only because, with that of America, it had prevented France from exercising any real influence in the world since the war – also appealed in the Third World, as well as in some of the countries in eastern Europe. In fact it was in eastern Europe that the two Gaullist bids for leadership – of the Third World and of a 'Europe' that was wider than EEC – both made their impact.

However, it may well have been less for political than for economic and technological reasons that Gaullist France was valued by the Third World. For it was in those realms that help from a country avowing Gaullist aims would be most useful and welcome. De Gaulle's repeatedly stated doctrine that nations should not seek to interfere in the internal affairs of others, and that assistance should be given without political strings, sounded right in the ears of countries which distrusted the aims of both super powers. The technological and industrial skills of France, as well as her increasingly healthy economy – though obviously very much less capable of meeting the demands of others than those of the United States or the Soviet Union – made her offers of help particularly welcome to governments which were still new enough to independence to view with special suspicion similar offers from the superpowers.[37] At this point, therefore, de Gaulle's political designs in the Third World connect with our earlier analysis of the evolution of French cultural and technical aid abroad.

(i) Relations with former French colonies in Africa: An analysis of French policies towards the Third World since the independence of the French colonial empire shows that France's continuing deep involvement in sub-Saharan Africa and Madagascar remained a constant factor, while

there was much more fluidity in other areas. It was in sub-Saharan Africa and Madagascar that the desire of the French to maintain and expand their influence abroad was at its most outstandingly successful. Earlier in this chapter* it was seen to what extent the area benefited from French cultural and technical aid, and from its continued membership of the franc zone. No doubt the higher level of aid was a reflection of the political links which the states of the area maintained with France. And these links remain close. The treaties they signed with France on gaining independence even went so far as to have Paris represent them abroad wherever they did not have their own representation. Although this kind of provision saves the newly independent countries a good deal of money, it also automatically perpetuates France's role as their foreign relation's mentor. Moreover, consultations between France and the new states on foreign policy issues were also provided for in the treaties, and since their independence this has had the effect that on most international problems the sub-Saharan and Malagasy attitudes have been similar to, if not identical with, those of France.

French ties with the African and Malagasy states have also remained close in matters of defence. France retained garrisons in Madagascar, Ivory Coast, Senegal and Chad, and promised to train the armies of the various states. In addition, French arms were to be made available to them, and de Gaulle undertook to maintain an active interest in their external and internal security. In return, France was to be given first choice in the buying of strategic raw materials which in fact has mainly meant Gabon's uranium. And, as has been noted, French remained the official language of all the countries in the area.

If it is argued that the degree of dependence which the sub-Saharan and Malagasy republics exhibit in their relations with France is scarcely compatible with real independence, the answer must be that there is nothing to prevent any or all of the states concerned from successfully denouncing their

* See above, pp. 169–73 and 177–80.

ties with Paris at any time. But at the beginning of the 1970s the emotional dependence on France – quite apart from dependence in other fields – was still so great, that at least their governing elites seemed to be incapable of even contemplating the severance of ties. Admittedly, much of the emotional dependence was closely connected with General de Gaulle, whose decolonisation policy had made him into a father figure for many of the native politicians. But since de Gaulle's death in 1970 there have been no signs that the State Secretariat in Paris which deals with Cooperation has ceased to be the incarnation of the Gaullist word that it had been for them in the 1960s.

(ii) Relations with Mediterranean countries: Despite the efforts made by both General de Gaulle and his successor at the Elysée, Georges Pompidou, to foster good relations with Algeria, French political influence there has remained minimal since independence. The massiveness of aid, economic, technical and cultural, that France has pumped into Algeria since 1962* was an obvious sign that Paris wished at all costs to establish close collaboration between the two countries. The Algerian government could break one undertaking after another, the French hardly ever went beyond the level of a protest in response; that should be contrasted with French reactions to disagreeable moves from Tunisia or Morocco, for example, which almost invariably elicited instant reprisals. Somehow, in Algeria, the nationalisation of French firms, the growing difficulties put in the way of the French making easy profits from Saharan oil, the morosely independent Algerian political line in international affairs, all of these have failed to deter the French from pursuing a friendly policy. To a considerable extent this may be accounted for by the fact that Algiers is not merely one of the most militant capitals of the countries in the Third World, but also that its place in the Arab areas of North Africa and the middle east is of some significance. The French desire, particularly since the 1967 Israeli-Arab

* See above pp. 170–1 and 180–1.

war, to expand their role in the Mediterranean can hardly be adequately fulfilled without Algeria's good will.

What became known in 1970 as France's Mediterranean policy was not necessarily the result of disappointment with the wider policy of bidding for the leadership of the Third World. The two policies imply no contradictions, and may be seen as complementary. But French policy after 1969 in the Mediterranean could also be compatible with the supposedly realistic bent of President Pompidou, which might have made him abandon de Gaulle's more sweeping cosmic visions on the ground that they were chimerical. However, if the reasoning behind the Pompidou policy is uncertain, its manifestations are clear.

De Gaulle, having in 1967 gained the good will of 100 million Muslims after having discarded that of $2\frac{1}{2}$ million Israelis, had provided his country with new possibilities, both economic and political. Trade prospects with Muslim countries immediately improved, and in the first half of 1969 French exports to Egypt, the Sudan, Libya and the other Muslim countries had increased by 45 per cent over the volume prior to the June war in 1967. In the year 1968–9, trade between France and the Maghreb countries increased by 20 per cent. The Franco-Arab Chamber of Commerce, created in 1970, expected to be able to double the volume of trade between France and the Arab countries within five years, thus making those countries second only to Germany in importance for French exports. Understandably, the first nine months of 1969 saw a decline of French trade with Israel, by some 35 per cent.[38]

But the wooing of the Arabs did not merely bring France commercial benefits. Her political influence among them increased too, at least in the sense that her vigorous political activity in the Mediterranean was received with rather more interest than that of the United States and Britain, both of whom remained tainted by their refusal to break with Israel. Thus the pro-Egyptian revolution in Libya, in September 1969, led to the expulsion of British and United States forces from that country, but to an apparently privileged position for France. For example, American and British oil interests in Libya were harassed while French oil interests were encouraged. France, as a result, offered Libya military air-craft and other arms which she had previously refused Israel. Nevertheless, by the beginning of 1971 it was clear that the Arab countries, at least in the eastern Mediterranean, had no immediate intention of substituting France for the Soviet Union as their main military supplier. What France can do for them politically is to help counterbalance the influence of the Soviet Union in the eastern Mediterranean, for the Arabs cannot be anxious to have Soviet military aid accom-panied by political control of their countries. On the other hand, even as a counterbalancing factor, France can only be of limited use. Neither economically nor militarily is she in a position to become a substitute for the Soviet Union, so that the Arab countries could scarcely use French interest in the area as a convincing alternative with which to counter Soviet pressures.

In the western Mediterranean, apart from the Algerian policy already described, President Pompidou began to restore relations with Morocco as soon as he had taken possession of the Elysée in 1969. De Gaulle had severed these relations in a righteous huff in 1966 because members of the Moroccan administration had allegedly been involved in the assassination, in France, of the Moroccan opposition leader Ben Barka. By the end of 1970 the Moroccan General Oufkir, whom reports had persistently associated with the assassination, appeared at an official reception given by the French foreign minister during a visit to Rabat. The 'recon-ciliation' was thus well under way.

So far as Tunisia was concerned, de Gaulle had kept her in 'quarantine' since 1964 because President Bourguiba had nationalised the land held by the remaining French settlers. Although in 1967 de Gaulle allowed contacts with the Tunisians to be slowly resumed, it was left to President Pompidou to encourage the return to a closer relationship. The trade prospects predicted by the new Franco-Arab Chamber of Commerce depend for their fulfilment partly on the continuation of President Pompidou's conciliatory policy in both Morocco and Tunisia.

On the northern coast of the Mediterranean, French relations with Spain have been particularly interesting. Here, France holds at least two trump cards. The first is her key position within EEC, which Spain badly wants to join. The second is that France could help to make the Spanish regime internationally respectable, as she had helped to make Bonn respectable, an aim which even the establishment of United States military bases in Spain had not been able to promote. In October 1970 when, as a result of the new Mediterranean policy, the presumed successor to General Franco, Prince Juan Carlos, was officially entertained in Paris by President Pompidou, both countries used the occasion to advertise the fact that despite a long period of apparent stagnation in relations, France and Spain had for at least ten years annually held joint naval manoeuvres. One positive fact which facilitates political collaboration between the two countries in at least one area is that both General Franco and the French have developed close contacts with the Arab world.

Apart from helping the expansion of French influence in the Mediterranean area, the friendliness shown to Spain since Pompidou's accession to power has also increased French arms exports. Spain joined Libya in placing orders for Mirage aircraft, and at the end of 1970 it seemed probable that Spain would buy French tanks and actually participate in the production of other French arms.[39]

But at the beginning of 1971 there was a return to the former chilly climate. Spain made two strong protests to the French government over the alleged anti-Franco attitude of the French press and radio during a secret trial of Basque nationalists in Burgos at the end of 1970. In January 1971 the Spanish government went so far as to cancel a visit to Madrid of the French foreign minister. The setback was likely to be temporary.

If France made little headway in Italy – the country is one of the more wholehearted members of both NATO and EEC – and showed no obvious desire to come to an accommodation with the military dictatorship in Greece, she did her utmost to

strengthen her ties with Yugoslavia. As one of the more prominent countries of the Third World, Yugoslavia had been receiving special attention from General de Gaulle since 1966. An
earlier *rapprochement* had been made difficult by the fact
that President Tito had been a violent critic of French repressive policies in Algeria, and de Gaulle had found it difficult to
forgive him for having, like the Soviet Union, recognised the
independent Algerian government before the French referendum in 1962 which finally confirmed the Evian agreements.
But in 1966-7 the foreign ministers of the two countries exchanged visits, and early in 1969 the head of the Federal Yugoslav government came to Paris, where de Gaulle paid his
chief, Tito, well-reported compliments. As a result of these
meetings, an intergovernmental committee was set up to expand trade. In 1970 Tito himself came to France on a private
visit to President Pompidou. All was, however, not well yet
between the two countries, because the care taken to avoid
calling it an official visit contrasted with the cordiality of Tito's
earlier 'official' stay in France in 1956. Moreover, Franco-
Yugoslav trade remained at a low level when compared with
Yugoslavia's exchanges with Germany and Italy. Obviously,
similar attitudes to American involvement in Vietnam and the
Arab-Israeli conflict were not enough to persuade Tito that
Paris had a special claim to prominence in his foreign relations.

(iii) The problem of arms sales to South Africa: Tito's reservations about France had also been prompted by the fact that
the French were selling arms to South Africa, in defiance of
the 1964 United Nations resolution. At the Lusaka Conference
of fifty-four non-aligned nations of the Third World, in September 1970, of which Tito was one of the main sponsors, arms
sales to Pretoria were a major topic. It had been common knowledge for some time that France had taken the place of Britain
as the largest supplier of arms to South Africa after the Wilson
government had begun to implement the United Nations resolution condemning such supplies because of South Africa's
racialist policies. Although the French government had stated
on a number of occasions that it was not supplying arms which

could be used against guerilla activity inside the Union, it had remained a constant criticism of France that it was impossible to make a clear distinction between such arms and any others. In fact, between 1960 and 1968 South Africa had become France's third most important client for the supply of arms, only the United States and Israel buying more. Aircraft of all kinds, including helicopters (which it is difficult not to associate with anti-guerilla campaigns), missiles and submarines were the main items supplied, and some one hundred and fifty officers of the South African navy received their training in France.

The supply of French arms to South Africa highlighted the fact that it was not easy to reconcile the 'realism' of both de Gaulle and his successor (one recalls de Gaulle's dictum that nations are the most selfish entities in the world) with the alleged idealism of the Third World. The moral position of France had by 1970 become so exposed that a month before the Lusaka Conference the French took the opportunity offered by the meeting of the Ministerial Council of the Organisation of African Unity at Addis Ababa to announce their intention to reexamine the question of arms supplies to South Africa. That announcement helped to concentrate the wrath of the Lusaka Conference on the Heath government in Britain, which had soon after its election to office in June 1970 stated that it would resume arms shipments to Pretoria. In October 1970 the French implied that they might not renew contracts with South Africa, at least for the supply of helicopters.[40]

(iv) Relations with countries in Asia: Further afield in the Third World, the French were also busy in Asia and South America. In Asia, France had acquired much opprobrium through her reluctance to leave Indo-China, and to a certain extent through her association with Israel between 1956 and 1967: Pakistan, as a Muslim country, had felt drawn to the Arab cause, and the assertion that Israel was a United States imperialist enclave in the middle east had served as an excuse for neutralist India to follow, for once, a Pakistani policy. Even so, and despite the holy indignation of the Third World about French arms supplies

for South Africa, Pakistan had by the end of the 1960s become one of France's most important arms customers. Various kinds of Mirage aircraft, helicopters and submarines have been among the items supplied by France to the Pakistan armed forces.

Already by 1965, Paris had thought it opportune to make a special effort in Pakistan and India. Pompidou, prime minister at the time, visited both countries and ably used their desire to increase trade with EEC to France's advantage. Given the necessarily limited means at the disposal of the French for aid outside sub-Saharan Africa and Madagascar, France had little more as a bargaining point than her position inside EEC. Nevertheless, as noted in the section on French foreign aid, French cultural, technical and financial aid was stepped up. In 1970, when the Pakistani president paid a visit to France, he recognised that by both joining an international consortium and expanding bilateral aid, France had lately increased her efforts in his country. Although in the general context of Pakistan's international trade, the French role remained modest, just as all French trade with Muslim countries increased after the 1967 break with Israel, so that with Pakistan increased as well. After 1967, Karachi began to have a trade deficit with France, which was largely bridged by French credits. However, the fact that France provided no more that 2.3 per cent of Pakistan's imports in 1970 shows that she still had a long way to go before French influence would be significant, and it would be fair to say the same for the political as well as for the economic sphere. In international affairs Pakistan above all needed friends for her permanent quarrel with India, and for that purpose her relations with the Soviet Union, China, and even the United States and Britain (the latter's Labour government had made India largely responsible for the Indo-Pakistani war of 1965) were more immediately relevant than anything France had to offer. For Pakistan's economic needs France could hardly furnish more than a tiny fraction.

French hesitation over leaving their Indian possessions, after Britain conceded India's independence in 1947, had for some years poisoned French relations with Delhi. After 1954, when the French left both Indo-China and the Indian territories, relations improved. However, neither country was particularly interested in creating special links with the other until de Gaulle made his bid for popularity in the subcontinent in 1965. It cannot, however, be said that French influence counted for much in India even at the beginning of the 1970s. Although India wanted to increase trade with EEC countries, and appreciated France's important place in that organisation as much as she also appreciated French disapproval of United States policy in south-east Asia and the middle east, there was no evidence that Paris had any special standing in Delhi. But, as was seen in an earlier section, the French were working on it, to begin with in the cultural, technical and economic fields.

One of the most spectacular international *coups* of the French in the post-1945 period was their recognition of the Communist government in Peking in 1964.[41] So far as one could tell, none of France's allies had been consulted, neither the United States for whom Communist China was a particular phobia, nor the Federal Republic of Germany with which France had only a year earlier signed a treaty of friendship which provided, among other things, for consultation on important foreign policy issues.

Relations between the People's Republic of China (proclaimed in 1949) and France were initially made difficult by Peking's support for the Indo-Chinese nationalists and then by the Chinese involvement in the Korean war. After the Geneva meetings in 1954 which put an end to the French presence in Indo-China, and in which the Chinese took part, trade and cultural links began to develop between the two countries. De Gaulle's open criticisms of American policy in Vietnam created a suitable atmosphere for his subsequent negotiations with Peking for full diplomatic recognition. In January 1964 these negotiations were successfully ended, and in April ambassadors were exchanged. France instantly gained commercially from this. Within three years French exports to China doubled (1964: 269 million francs; 1967: 511 million). In 1965 a cultural agreement allowed for an exchange of one hundred and fifty students, not of course a large number given the population of China. Politically, China's absence from the United Nations and her relative ostracism in international affairs made the new relationship not very fruitful, except in so far as it never displeased General de Gaulle to displease Washington. In any case, by 1967 the 'cultural revolution' in China abruptly ended the *rapprochement,* and in 1969 French exports to China had fallen below the 1962 level, to 232 million francs. Although reservations about the political use to Paris of Franco-Chinese relations remain, since 1969 Peking has shown renewed interest in contacts with France, and this interest the French have encouraged. In so far as French influence abroad is inversely proportional to the domination of the world by the two superpowers, and in so far as the emergence of China from her isolation might be judged to decrease the influence of the superpowers, in so far also has France much to gain from encouraging China's participation in international exchanges of all kinds. French support for Peking's admission to the United Nations in 1971 is explicable in similar terms.

(v) Relations with countries in South America: If it was both unkind and a small exaggeration for United States commentators to maintain that France counted in south-east Asia for no more than did Luxembourg,[42] de Gaulle's much-publicised visits to South America in 1964 scarcely caused France to count for much more on that continent. South America could perhaps not have been left out in any French attempt to impress the Third World, but even de Gaulle was later to throw doubt on the usefulness of those strenuous trips. In April 1964 he paid a short visit to Mexico, and towards the end of the year he went on an extensive tour of all ten Latin American states. If there was one theme which he stressed, it was that France shared with the continent a Latin culture, but that theme was only likely to be politically efficacious if linked with a cheap anti-Americanism, which de Gaulle on the whole had the good taste to avoid. In contrast with the receptions prominent American visitors had

recently received in South America, de Gaulle was warmly welcomed almost everywhere he went. But what he could, concretely, offer as an alternative to resented United States dependence was limited in South America, too. France had chosen to make its maximum aid effort in other geographical areas, as a result of which only a moderate expansion of cultural and technical aid was possible, and the granting of small credits (Mexico, for example received credits of 150 million dollars).

Given the precariousness of South American politics, de Gaulle and his successors were likely to find support only in those countries in the area which happened to have a government that was particularly detested by the United States or that was particularly anxious to reduce American influence in its state for other reasons. In 1965 the Brazilian president found himself in that position, and his visit to Paris was as much welcomed by de Gaulle as was that of his Chilean colleague. Also, by the end of 1970, four Latin American countries (Peru, Brazil, Argentina, Colombia) had contracted to buy some French aircraft. But on the whole France is both too remote and too limited in her resources to counterbalance South America's need of United States assistance.

FRENCH ATTITUDES TO THE UNITED NATIONS ORGANISATION

France's changing attitudes to UNO can usefully be discussed in conjunction with her relations with the Third World, because the changes which those attitudes have undergone have largely resulted from changes in her relations with the countries of the Third World. If General de Gaulle may be believed, he distrusted the United Nations as an international decision-making organisation from the very beginning:

For my part it was with sympathy but not without circumspection that I looked forward to the birth of the organisation. Of course, the universality of its aims was in itself highly estimable and in conformity with the genius of France . . . In any case it was a good thing that from time to time states should make contact with each other in the presence of public opinion. Yet, contrary to what Roosevelt imagined, Churchill pretended, and Stalin allegedly believed, I did not have unduly high hopes of the United Nations . . . It could be assumed that many small countries would automatically be unfavourably disposed towards the big powers . . . Apart from the right of veto which belonged to France as one of the big powers, the original draft of the charter was amended in such a way as to make the General Assembly the counterweight of the Security Council, while at the same time providing a brake for its enthusiasm by demanding a two-thirds majority for its motions.[43]

The constant criticisms which the French had to listen to at the UN because of their reluctance to decolonise had made successive French governments after 1945 equally dyspeptic about the organisation. As the size of the UN rapidly increased with the decolonisation of the British and French empires, de Gaulle was not the only Frenchman to speak slightingly of the 'improvised nations' that now made up its majorities:

The General Assembly now includes the delegates of more than a hundred states – soon there will be one hundred and twenty – most of which, or many of which, are improvised states and believe that it is their duty to stress grievances or claims with regard to the old nations, rather than ideas of reason and progress. . . . So that now the meetings of the United Nations are no more than riotous and scandalous sessions.[44]

That was in 1961, but it translated very well what most Frenchmen had apparently thought of the United Nations throughout the 1950s.[45]

A good deal of this anti-UN sentiment is no doubt explicable in terms of sour grapes. Under de Gaulle, however, there was another reason. When, in 1960, he objected to the UN involvement in the Congo crisis, it was not because of his much advertised aversion from having a country's internal affairs interfered with from outside; that doctrine had almost certainly resulted from attempts by other countries to interfere in French colonial matters. For, when the Congo crisis broke, de Gaulle's first reaction had been to ask for a conference of the western powers, including France, to settle it. This Gaullist reaction made manifest the same attitude as that which had prompted him in

September 1958 to suggest to President Eisenhower that France should join the United States and Britain to create a triumvirate that would direct the affairs of NATO; de Gaulle was clearly of the opinion that France and the major powers should settle the affairs of the world between themselves, without the tedious cooperation of smaller countries. His refusal to take part in the disarmament talks in Geneva, and his hostility towards UN-sponsored aid, were similarly motivated. So was his call for a four power conference when war broke out in the middle east in 1967. The haughtiness thus shown towards the smaller nations, as well as the interference in their affairs it entailed, could hardly have impressed the Third World, any more than the fact that under de Gaulle France had become the biggest arms supplier to South Africa.

But the shunning of the United Nations as a whole ceased after 1962, that is after Algerian independence. Gradually France was represented in New York by ever more senior men, until in 1965 the French foreign minister himself headed his delegation. At the same time the French began to vote for the admission of Communist China, an annual event until the final ousting of the Taiwan delegation in 1971. But that French vote was ambiguous, for de Gaulle still expressed the opinion that the world should be policed by the great powers, in which he then included Communist China.[46] It is therefore unlikely that his newly found interest in the United Nations created undue rejoicing among most countries of the Third World.

Under President Pompidou, French attitudes to the United Nations Organisation appeared to change rather more radically. Apparently devoid of the more utopian visions of grandeur of his predecessor, Pompidou seemed to use his delegation at the United Nations much more as a diplomatic pressure group within the Third World than de Gaulle had ever done. At the end of 1970, the French delegation expressed the feeling[47] that it had played a significant role in the decision-making of the organisation during that year, that it had been much sought after for advice, and that its attitude towards Israel had earned it much respect among the delegations from the Third World. The French gesture of making a voluntary contribution to UN funds, in place of the payment for the Congo peace-keeping mission to which France was still objecting, had also made a good impression, and it seemed at the end of 1970 that President Pompidou intended in the future to treat the United Nations as a potentially useful instrument with which to promote French foreign policy objectives.

PART TWO

5

The Diplomatic Service

PRESENT ORGANISATION

The French Diplomatic Service is part of the French Civil Service. Although its members, particularly its most senior members, are often called upon to give advice to the foreign minister or other members of the government, policy decisions are ultimately the responsibility of the government alone. It is therefore proper to look upon the Diplomatic Service as that branch of the French Civil Service which carries out the policy decisions of the government in the realm of foreign affairs.

In 1970, the Diplomatic Service was responsible for over eight thousand employees, of whom about eleven hundred belonged to Category A which contains the senior posts. At any one time, about three-quarters of Category A diplomats serve abroad while the remainder runs the central administration of the Foreign Ministry at the Quai d'Orsay in Paris. Although it does not seem to work out in practice, in theory at least two-thirds of a diplomat's career is expected to be spent abroad.

THE MINISTRY OF FOREIGN AFFAIRS

Since 1945* the work at the Quai has been divided among its members according to subject matter. At present there are five main divisions: (1) political, (2) economic and financial, (3) cultural, scientific and technical, (4) general administration and personnel, (5) administrative conventions and social

---

* Ordinance of 13 April 1945; decree of 17 July 1945. Changes in the organisation do, of course, occur from time to time, but the information given in this chapter reflects the situation at the beginning of 1971.

affairs; these main divisions are supplemented by sections dealing with protocol, archives and legal matters. At the head of the entire organisation is the secretary general.

(i) The secretary general: The post of secretary general was established in 1920.[1] It is therefore a relatively new post in an organisation which is very conscious of its three centuries' long traditions. The growing complexities of international relations after the first world war had convinced the government that the Ministry of Foreign Affairs needed a permanent head. Despite the fact that the minister of foreign affairs retains ultimate responsibility for his Ministry,* his many duties as a political executive compel him to leave to the secretary general, in the words of the decree creating the post, 'the overall direction of all the departments *(services)*'. It is the secretary general who coordinates the work of the entire Diplomatic Service. He sees to it that embassies and consulates abroad, as well as all sections of the Ministry itself, implement the policies laid down by the government. He keeps an eye on the efficacy of the organisation of the Diplomatic Service as a whole and is responsible for promoting changes in it if these become desirable. Thus, in 1960, he instituted a new Treaty Office under the control of his own office, whose function it is to keep up-to-date information about all treaties and agreements France has concluded with other countries and, where necessary, to see them through the required constitutional channels before they come into force; in 1969 this office came under the general supervision of the enlarged Legal Department.

It must be noted, however, that the secretary general is no mere administrator. If his closeness to the minister of foreign affairs gives him the best possible opportunity to understand the nuances of government policy, and thus expertly to preside over its execution, it also gives the minister the chance to obtain expert advice from the man who is in constant touch with the departmental experts and the embassies and

---

* See below, pp. 239–41, for the role of the foreign minister.

consulates abroad. The secretary general is therefore also a political adviser to his minister.[2]

(ii) The main Departments of the Quai d'Orsay:

(a) The Political Directorate: The Political Directorate is the maid-of-all-work of the Quai. Whenever a problem arises which does not clearly demand the attention of one of the technical departments, it finds its way here. Moreover, since most technical problems have political implications too, the Political Directorate is rarely left out of the work of the other Directorates. It is headed by a director, who is usually assisted by at least one deputy director; since the 1960s a deputy director has from time to time been given the experimental task of policy planning. To cope with its work the Political Directorate is subdivided geographically, but also has sections dealing with atomic questions, defence, space, the United Nations and other international organisations; it also has a press and information service.

The geographical subdivisions and the areas for which they are responsible vary from time to time. Marked changes have occurred in recent years in relation to Africa in particular, since the mid-1950s began the period of rapid decolonisation. As colonies became independent countries, the Ministry of Foreign Affairs had to make provision for dealing with them. At the present time there are five geographical subdivisions: Europe, Asia-Oceania, Africa-Levant, North Africa, America. Each one of these is further subdivided, on the whole in unsurprising ways. For example, Europe is subdivided into central, eastern, southern and western, the latter having responsibility for Scandinavia, the Benelux countries and Great Britain, as well as for the political sections of the various European organisations including the Common Market, the Council of Europe and Euratom. Sensitivity to the need for changes in organisation can be seen in the fact that the east European subdivision now deals exclusively with the Communist states in that area, including Yugoslavia, while Greece and Turkey have been assigned to southern Europe.

The subdivision Asia and Oceania deals with the geographical areas so designated, as well as with the international organisations covering them. The subdivisions dealing with Africa are rather more complex. After many changes since the second world war, Africa-Levant at present has responsibility for Egypt and countries to the east, as well as for English-speaking Black Africa and the political aspects of French-speaking sub-Saharan Africa and the Malagasy Republic; there is a special State Secretariat of the Foreign Ministry which deals with economic and technical aid from France to the *francophone* sub-Saharan and Malagasy states. North Africa deals with Libya and countries north of the Sahara to the west. The geographical subdivisions Africa-Levant and North Africa also concern themselves with the international organisations of their areas.

The American subdivision deals with the whole of the western hemisphere. Its subsections show, as for example did also those of the European subdivision, that ideological boundaries play at least as important a part in the devising of subdivisions as do those of geography. Mexico goes with South America and not with Central America; Canada goes with the United States. Some of the international organisations concerned with this part of the world (but not, for example, NATO) also come under the scrutiny of this subdivision. But, given the worldwide political involvements of the United States, the activities of its government are equally followed by all those other geographical subdivisions of the Quai in whose area American influence makes itself felt.

Apart from the geographical subdivisions, the Political Directorate also contains a section responsible for dealing with the United Nations Organisation and its various subsidiary bodies. Its principal task is one of coordination. In consultation with other interested departments of the Ministry, and where necessary with other Ministries, it seeks to work out coherent policies for the multitudinous United Nations activities in which France has an interest. It is also this division which plays a major role in the designation of French representatives to the United Nations and to meetings sponsored by that organisation. The division thus presides over the implementation of its policies. However, technical (as distinct from specifically political) organisations like OECD and NATO, and even UNESCO, are handled by other Directorates.

The Department of Military Pacts and Disarmament *(Service des Pactes et du Désarmement)* also belongs to the Political Directorate. It deals with all questions concerning the military alliances of which France is a member. The department keeps in close touch with those responsible for the defence of the country and provides the Minister of Foreign Affairs with information about their thinking.

Finally, within the Political Directorate, there is the Press and Information Service. Its importance as a kind of public relations service of the Quai with the outside world has been recognised by the fact that it is headed by a director of senior rank *(ministre plénipotentiaire)*. It is he, not his minister, who holds regular news conferences – daily for French correspondents, weekly for foreign ones – and who briefs the more distinguished of foreign journalists who seek information. The two subsections of the Service, Press and Information, each has its own deputy director. The first is responsible for compiling daily news reports from newspapers and tapes for the minister and his senior officials, assisting the press in France and abroad – as well as the French embassies abroad – in their quest for information about aspects of French foreign policy, and supervising the manner in which the French radio and television services present this policy.

The Information subsection distributes more detailed documentation on current issues, and is in charge of the administration of the Press and Information Department as a whole and of its counterparts in embassies abroad. It also keeps an eye on foreign periodicals and books of a political character that have been imported into France.

(b) The Directorate for Economic and Financial Affairs: Although many other Ministries have departments which have dealings with foreign governments and organisations, the

political implications of economic and financial relations in international affairs have prompted the Quai to set up this Directorate. Its function is mainly to inform the foreign minister of the economic consequences of political decisions, and to advise other Ministries of the political consequences of their economic proposals in the realm of foreign affairs. This is one of the many areas where the Quai feels aggrieved at the difficulties it encounters when it tries to coordinate France's foreign policy. The theory is, however, that in the negotiations of economic agreements with foreign governments, it is the Quai which ultimately provides the guidelines and usually the chief spokesmen, while it is left to the Ministry of Finance and Economic Affairs or other appropriate Ministries to implement them.

The internal subdivision of this Directorate indicates the diversity of its work. There is a section for bilateral agreements between France and individual foreign countries. There is a section dealing with international organisations, whose head is the French delegate to OECD. It also has responsibility for the Common Market. Finally there are sections that concern themselves with all kinds of economic and financial French interests abroad, from oilwells to copyright payments.

(c) The General Directorate for Cultural, Scientific and Technical Affairs: Apart from the Political Directorate, it would be fair to say that it is to the work of this Directorate that not only the Quai but also the government attaches the greatest importance. The provision of French schools abroad, of books, lecturers, teachers and exhibitions had for a long time been a practice when, in the mid-1950s, French overseas possessions began rapidly to transform themselves into independent countries. Because such educational facilities as they had were French, their request for a continuation, and indeed expansion, of educational services was largely met by French governments through the medium of this Directorate. As one French observer has suggested,[3] given that the age of gunboat diplomacy is over, this is the next best way of influencing

people. In 1971, 47 per cent of the Foreign Ministry's budget was earmarked for this Directorate alone.

The size of the responsibility of the Directorate can be illustrated by the fact that in the year 1966–7 it provided Tunisia alone, after a period of disfavour, with over three thousand teachers, seven hundred and fifty experts in the fields of health, justice and industry, over seven hundred scholarships for study in France, and many other services. The Tunisian example also shows that, besides orthodox educational work, the Directorate has a programme of technical assistance. In that field it caters mainly for former French territories, but in recent years it has, in addition, begun to increase its assistance to other underdeveloped countries. The latter activity mainly involves short-time aid programmes, for example the training of agricultural experts in their own country. A more detailed account of French foreign aid can be found in chapter 3 above.

The parts of the Directorate which deal with cultural and technical aid are the Diffusion and Cultural Exchanges as well as the Cultural and Technical Cooperation sections. The latter also cooperates with the relevant international organisations, though by far the greater fraction of French aid is bilateral. The technical experts are recruited by the section itself, and are sent for special training to the Institute for Political Studies in Paris. The section also provides scholarships for young graduates from countries in need of aid in an attempt to help them become technical experts in their own right. These programmes are worked out in conjunction with other interested Ministries, businessmen and industrialists.

The Directorate has in addition a Service for Cultural Exchanges which seeks to ensure the widest possible distribution abroad of French films, particularly of documentaries, as well as of radio and television programmes, designed in many cases to help with the teaching of the French language. Much of its work is done through the medium of French embassies, whose cultural counsellors and attachés maintain contacts with universities, schools and other relevant organisations in the countries in which they operate. Furthermore, the Service arranges for visits of prominent foreign scholars of French to France to facilitate their work, as well as visits abroad of French experts in the cultural fields with which the Service is concerned. French representatives to international conferences in these areas of interest are nominated by it too. One of its sections is responsible for French relations with international cultural organisations.

It is, lastly, the Service for Artistic Exchanges which has the task of organising French exhibitions abroad of all the arts, similar foreign exhibitions in France, as well as exchanges in the realms of the theatre and music.

In 1969 the General Directorate was reorganised, and enlarged by the addition of a scientific section which also gained control over already extant scientific departments inside the Quai. For example, a subsection on space technology, created in 1960 within the Political Directorate, and which works closely with the relevant bodies outside the Ministry, was incorporated in 1969 into this General Directorate. Its function remains, as before, to keep the minister informed of the latest developments, and to explore possibilities of international collaboration in research and its practical application. The Department of Atomic Affairs, fulfilling a similar function in its own sphere, was also moved from the Political Directorate in 1969 to be brought under the aegis of the General Directorate for Cultural, Scientific and Technical Relations. There are also sections concerned with general scientific matters, as well as with more specialised questions from computers to medicine.

(d) The Directorate for Administrative Conventions and Social Affairs: The main concern of this Directorate is the fate of Frenchmen abroad and of foreigners in France. It presides over the activities of French consular representatives abroad, and the negotiation and fulfilment of reciprocal agreements with other governments about the treatment to be accorded to their respective citizens. Within France, it is responsible for refugees from abroad, as well as for those foreign citizens whose own governments give them consular backing, or who are members of international organisations

working in France. Since, in principle, Frenchmen abroad come under French law, the consular services which endeavour to apply it provide this Directorate with much of its work.

(e) The Directorate for Personnel and General Administration: The work of this Directorate covers much more than its name implies. It provides in fact the basic services which enable the Ministry and its satellite organisations (embassies, consulates, etc.) to function. Thus, apart from being responsible for the recruitment, location and administration of staff throughout the diplomatic service, it controls the Ministry's budget at the Quai and in all foreign posts, the premises they occupy, and ensures that all its services are adequate to deal with such new tasks as rapidly changing conditions may create. Further, the Directorate helps with the recruitment of French employees for international organisations, and of those who are to provide technical assistance outside such organisations. It also looks after the professional interests of such employees, even when they are not civil servants, so that, for example, they will not have lost seniority when they return to their old posts.

The rapid increase since 1945 of the number of independent countries has vastly added to the tasks of the Directorate as well as to the number of persons for which it is responsible. In the case of former French protectorates and other territories, the Directorate also deals with the problems of resettlement and retraining of the French personnel which had administered them.

The system of communications between the Quai and its foreign posts, including the services of the diplomatic bag and cipher, is also in the hands of this Directorate.

(f) Other Departments: The other departments of the Quai perform duties which most Foreign Ministries with similar world-wide responsibilities perform in similar ways. The protocol service determines all points of etiquette relating to functions involving the Ministry and the president of the Republic. For example, it decides questions of precedence, makes the arrangements for the visits of foreign heads of state

for whom there is now lavish accommodation within the Quai itself, looks after the privileges of foreign diplomats in France, and ensures that treaties and other international agreements are properly drawn up.

The Legal Department, as one would expect, advises on questions of international law. It also assists with the drafting of agreements and represents France in cases of international legal disputes. The department was reorganised in 1969 and now has separate sections corresponding to four of the Directorates (i.e. all Directorates except Personnel and General Administration). It has already been noted that the Treaty Office came under its control at the time of the 1969 reorganisation.

One of the possessions of which the Quai is particularly proud is the Archives Department. More perhaps than any other of its services, it is this which acts as a constant reminder to the diplomats of the long tradition behind their work. The archives contain diplomatic correspondence and documents of all kinds, including treaties, dating back at least to the seventeenth century. Some of these may be inspected by researchers. Foreign posts of the diplomatic service normally retain their own documents, but the archives of the Quai are formally responsible for them.

In addition, the Archives Department supervises the publication of certain of its documents which are of interest to diplomats and historians. It now also issues a wide range of periodicals and other publications on matters of current diplomatic or general political interest. The large library of the Quai, available to the entire diplomatic service, is one of its subdepartments, as is also the geographical information service.

REPRESENTATION ABROAD

The days when ambassadors could use, indeed had to use, their initiative in the manner in which they represented their country have long been over. When the journey from London to Paris took five days, as it still did in 1815, the degree of supervision a government could exercise over its representatives abroad was clearly more limited than it has since become. Already by 1848 the journey had been cut to twelve hours; the coming of the telegraph did the rest. Today the ambassador is rarely more than a mouthpiece for his government. Indeed, many of the important international negotiations are now carried on between the responsible ministers themselves, since the development of air travel has enabled them to move rapidly from one meeting to another.

(i) Embassies: Most French representation abroad is accomplished through embassies, since the old hierarchy of legations and embassies no longer accords with the egalitarian aspirations of independent countries. At their head is usually an ambassador. However, 'ambassador' is here more likely to be the name of the post than the title or grade conferred upon only a small handful of Quai dignitaries, because the proliferation of such posts would otherwise not only have devalued this highest of ranks in the Diplomatic Service, but would also have been very expensive for the state.

All diplomatic communications from embassies pass through the Quai, even – except in the most unusual circumstances – when they are directed to other embassies. Most of these are telegrams, about three-quarters of which are now sent through the Telex service, automatically coded. Alternatively, couriers, the diplomatic bag or other forms of communications may be used, depending on the circumstances.

Broadly speaking, what is being fed through this elaborate system of communications is, on the one hand, instructions to the ambassador on how to represent his country's policies at any given time, and, on the other hand, the ambassador's reports on aspects of the foreign country which he thinks will be of interest to his government. In the larger embassies the ambassador is assisted in these tasks by counsellors and attachés who specialise in particular sectors (cultural, military, etc.). For administrative purposes these specialists continue to belong to their respective Ministries, although the ambassador exercises political control over them. Even in small embassies the diplomatic staff is likely to subdivide the work into at least four main sectors: administrative and political, economic and commercial, military, and cultural. But, quite apart from these subdivisions, the ambassador represents his country in every way. He is therefore the natural intermediary between those of his countrymen who have interests in the country in which he finds himself, as well as between the citizens of that country and his own. For that reason he also controls the consular services, though on many purely routine matters the latter may address themselves directly to the Quai.

French representation at international organisations is on similar lines. The main difference at the United Nations is that the ambassador does not as of right act as the representative of his country. This is a role reserved for the foreign minister himself, although the ambassador, as the minister's deputy in this post, is likely to take his place when his chief is not present.

The permanent French delegation at the European Economic Community and at Euratom in Brussels in one sense also acts like an embassy, since part of its routine is to inform the foreign minister of the changing state of Community affairs and to act as spokesman for him. On the other hand, in accordance with the Common Market and Euratom treaties, the permanent delegation also participates in the direction of these organisations. As part of the Committee of Permanent Representatives, it helps to iron out differences between the delegations concerning the application of the treaties or problems arising from them. For this work it is, of course, briefed by the Quai, as it is also for its share in the other important task of the Committee, which is the preparation of the meetings (usually monthly) of the Council of Ministers of the Common Market countries. Various subcommittees of experts have also been established, whose members come largely from the permanent representatives of the Six, and in these, too, it is the task of the national representatives to present their government's case. It is in such subcommittees, for example, that the negotiating positions of the EEC in relation to outside parties are decided. Finally, although only about one-third of the permanent French delegation is composed of Quai diplomats –

the remainder being economists and other experts who belong to different parts of the Civil Service – it should be noted that overall political control is exercised by the Foreign Ministry through the ambassador, who is head of the permanent delegation.

(ii) Consulates: There are four categories of consulates: consulates-general (first and second class), consulates (first and second class); each category has some forty offices. Their rank depends on the degree of importance their government attributes to them in terms of size of their territory and business. Consulates normally function in countries with whom France has diplomatic relations. Their task is basically to protect the interests of French nationals in the area for which they are responsible. They also serve as the medium through which French laws may be applied to their nationals abroad.* In addition, consulates often use their position in the heart of the country in which they find themselves – they are no longer confined to ports – to help promote the economic and commercial interests of French firms, if only by giving valuable information on local conditions. From their long past they have also inherited certain legal powers over their nationals abroad, particularly in their notarial capacity. Some routine functions may be delegated to consular agents who need not be French nationals.

Although there is, since 1945, no distinction between the Diplomatic and Consular Services so far as recruiting and general administration is concerned, the differences in function between the two are recognised by the fact that consuls correspond directly with all the authorities with whom they have dealings in their non-political activities; the embassy need only be involved in the case of political activities by the consulates, in which function they act as agents for their ambassador. The political role of consulates is rapidly expanding. They carry their country's official 'image' into provincial areas which, until the recent increase of French public relations activities,

* See above, pp. 223–4: French nationals registered with their consulates elect six Senators to the French Parliament.

had been immune from embassy attention. Conversely, consulates provide valuable local information for their embassy, and thus improve its knowledge of the country as a whole.

CHANGES IN ORGANISATION

THE HISTORICAL BACKGROUND

According to the *Annuaire Diplomatique,* the origins of the Ministry date back to 1589. While it is true that it was in that year that Henri III, for the first time in the history of France, charged one of his four secretaries with all correspondence to foreign countries, there was a period of about a decade before 1626 when these duties were again dispersed among the secretaries. However, since Louis XIII agreed in 1626 to appoint Raymond Phelippeaux as the secretary responsible for foreign correspondence, the duties relating to the post have never again been separated. On the other hand, French consular services, which have a history going back at least to the Crusades, remained under the control of the navy.

Until the Revolution the staff available to the secretary of state for foreign affairs expanded rather slowly. Early in the eighteenth century there was a staff of twelve, at the beginning of the Revolution this had risen to forty-nine. But already by the time Louis XIV was dying, there was the first sign of specialisation within the Secretariat: there was a keeper for the archives. By 1789 there were also legal advisers, cipher clerks, and geographers. Since the beginning, however, the work of the secretariat has been shared out geographically. There emerged two main divisions, north and south, the major European countries being dealt with in the former, their dependencies and the rest of the world in the latter.

Since the Revolution, seventeen ordinances, decrees or regulations have led to major changes in the administration of the Foreign Ministry; there have been many more that have had less important consequences. In every case the changes were to be the answer to the question which is still posed today, namely how best to divide the work of the Department.

The logical possibilities were as clear then as they are now: the divisions could be either geographical – which would give each subdivision a complete view of all the problems of its area – or they could be in terms of subject matter, in which case each problem would be dealt with by an expert in that field who might not, however, have any knowledge of the country which raised the problem. Since Talleyrand's reform of 1814, the organisation of the Foreign Ministry has been a compromise between these two extremes. Political affairs were dealt with geographically, special problems by specialists. While special problems were little more than legal or linguistic ones, this worked perfectly well.

The Foreign Ministry was very slow in adapting itself to world changes in the nineteenth century. This may have been partly because of the general attitude to political affairs of the ruling middle classes. They wanted government on the cheap. The opening up of China in the middle of the century, of Africa a few decades later, the growing importance of the United States of America, all failed to stir the Ministry into a reorganisation of its ancient north-south divisions. It waited until 1907 before finally creating new geographical sections, one for America, one for Asia, another for the Levant, and one global division for Europe, Africa and Oceania. Just before the end of the first world war another reform brought in the four main geographical divisions which remained basically unaltered for the next half-century: Europe, Africa, Asia and Oceania, America.

Among the main specialised departments (apart from the Archives, Cipher and Legal services mentioned previously), the Personnel and Protocol divisions emerged first. The Press and Information services and those for cultural affairs as they exist today were part of the legacy of the first world war and the League of Nations. They were created in 1920, in the same year as was the post of secretary general.

PRESENT PROBLEMS

Among all sections of the French Diplomatic Service there is an awareness that its organisation could be improved. The principal criticism relates to the absence, or at any rate the difficulty, of adequate correlation between the increasing number of Civil Service departments involved in dealings with foreign countries. Not only, it is said, is there inadequate correlation between the Quai and other Ministries, but also between departments within the Foreign Ministry itself. For that reason, much thought is being given to the closer integration of all French activities within the various geographical areas of the world. There is at present no single section at the Quai which has a complete conspectus of any area, although frequent consultation between the specialised departments and the subsections of the Political Directorate palliate this to some extent. One can see the difficulty: a vast multiplication of staff would be necessary to give each geographical area its own range of experts in all fields in which the Quai has to interest itself today. On the other hand, the need for coordination may be illustrated by the fact that of 292 missions authorised by the Quai in 1961, only fifty-three were effected by its own members; the remainder came from seventeen other parts of the Civil Service.[4] It is doubtful, however, if the organisation of the Ministry of Foreign Affairs has ever been better, or if there has ever been a time in its long history when desirable changes could be more speedily or effectively implemented.

PERSONNEL

PRESENT METHODS OF RECRUITMENT AND TRAINING

Paradoxically, the Ministry of Foreign Affairs has no direct voice in the recruitment of those who are most likely to reach the highest ranks fastest. In accordance with the Ordinance of 9 October 1945, its annual intake of about ten to seventeen for the highest staff category (A) has, since 1947, been drawn largely from the *Ecole Nationale d'Administration* (ENA); ENA provides between eight and ten recruits each year. The *Ecole Nationale des Langues Orientales Vivantes,* through a competitive examination organised by the Foreign Ministry, usually provides another seven specialists. Male or female graduates from ENA whose marks and results at ENA's competitive examinations (taken during their studies) were high enough to qualify for entry to the Ministry, and who choose to enter it, cannot be refused a post by the Foreign Ministry. In this the Ministry is in the same position as the rest of the Civil Service. Entrants into Category A from the *Ecole Nationale des Langues Orientales Vivantes* are chosen from the most successful candidates at the competitive examination organised by the Quai. In addition, there is a Category A' from which a small number is regularly selected for promotion to Category A. Entry into Category A' is by a competitive examination, presided over by the Quai, and is restricted to a maximum of some seventeen annually, several of whom come from the *Langues Orientales.*

The standard of those entering the Quai is high: it figures fourth in the list of preferences of the ninety graduates ENA now has each year; only the *Conseil d'Etat,* the *Inspection Générale des Finances,* and the *Cour des Comptes* provide more coveted places. It should be noted that admission to ENA, which is under the aegis of the minister responsible for the Civil Service and not of the minister of education, is in itself an achievement. Two kinds of competitive examinations regulate admission, and even the terms of eligibility for sitting these examinations are demanding. The main examination for two-thirds of each intake is open to graduates, under twenty-six years old, in law, arts, science, economics, or with diplomas of equivalent standard. The other examination, of a more practical character, is for persons already in the Civil Service, who are under thirty-one, and have spent at least five years in such employment.* For every place the school can offer there have lately been between seven and ten applicants. The school itself rates the chances of success at the entrance examination for graduates very low for anyone who has not supplemented

---

* At the time of writing the regulations governing admission to ENA are contained in Decree No. 65–986 of 24 November 1965.

his four years of degree work with at least one year's special study, possibly at the *Institut d'Etudes Politiques* in Paris. It is only as examiners that members of the Quai may have a direct influence on recruitment from ENA, but they never sit alone and may not know what career a candidate has in mind.

Since ENA tends to supply the all-round administrators at the Diplomatic Services' highest levels – the *Ecole Nationale des Langues Orientales Vivantes* providing mainly specialists in its field – the training ENA gives must be of interest to the student of the French Diplomatic Service. To begin with, entry into the school means entry into the Civil Service. In return for a promise to serve the state for a minimum of ten years, students receive a salary and allowances as well as the full status French law accords to civil servants. One of the more important considerations of the originators of this system was that it would help in the democratisation of the Higher Civil Service. Its desired effect on the composition of the Diplomatic Service in particular was to introduce into it the new technocrats rather than the traditional aristocrats. A glance at the current *Annuaire Diplomatique* will show that, if that intention has been fulfilled, the old and new qualifications are not mutually exclusive.

Members of ENA spend twenty-eight months under its direction. Their programme throughout that period is identical, irrespective of the career they hope to be able to take up. Many diplomats deplore this, for it means that new entrants to the Quai in its highest category will have received no training for diplomacy as such, and – except for those who enter from the *Ecole Nationale des Langues Orientales Vivantes* – will not even have shown that they possess any aptitude for a career in it. Since nothing short of a personal disaster of cataclysmic dimensions can ever get a graduate from ENA sacked, there is clearly some force in such reservations. Although the school provides perhaps the best that can be had in general administrative training, the basic argument that its alumni should be 'polyvalent' amounts to comparatively little in practice. It would certainly be most unusual for a member of the Quai to find himself transferred to, say, the Ministry of Finance or vice versa.

The training itself is divided into three successive stages. After a mere month of initial briefing at ENA, new students spend the rest of their first year at a prefecture somewhere in France or overseas, in a region unknown to them. Since they are attached to the prefect himself, they are instantly initiated into the upper reaches of the French administration. At the end of the year they write a paper on an aspect of their experience at the prefecture, and ENA receives a detailed report on them from the prefect. These provide the first marks towards the aggregate that will condition the width of their choice of career.

Most of the second year is spent at the school. Students are directed in their work by a part-time staff of university teachers and civil servants; the school has no permanent academic staff of its own. By means of seminars, lectures and discussions, the students learn more about public administration in France and abroad, economics, international relations, social studies, statistics, accounting, business management, and a modern foreign language. Several examinations taken in the course of that year provide more marks.

Then follows a period of two months in a private firm, where they are at the 'receiving end' of public administration. After this, the students return to ENA for about four months of further study and the final examinations, oral and written. It is the aggregate of all the marks gained over the twenty-eight months, including a test of their athletic prowess, which will then show the students what careers are open to them. Within these limits, the choice will be entirely theirs. If they qualify for and choose the Diplomatic Service, they enter it at the level of Category A (roughly equivalent to the former administrative class of the British Civil Service) which contains counsellors and secretaries of foreign affairs.

LEGACY OF OTHER METHODS OF RECRUITMENT

Although ENA has provided most of the recruits to the senior ranks of the French Foreign Ministry since 1947, their numbers compared with those recruited previously and since by other means are not yet overwhelming. There are three main reasons for this: a residue of staff dating back to the Third Republic; staff acquired with some haste at the time of the liberation of France in 1944–5; and staff transfers from other parts of the administration whose job ended with the independence of French overseas possessions. Many of the key posts in the Diplomatic Service are still occupied by persons recruited in these ways. In 1962 half the eight hundred senior posts were held by diplomats who had joined the Ministry either in the immediate postwar period or as a result of the abolition of their jobs in other branches of the administration. This fact, which is a considerable brake on promotion possibilities among those who have entered the Service in more orthodox ways, naturally causes a certain amount of ill-feeling among those adversely affected. The latter can easily point to their similarly qualified colleagues in other major branches of the administration where promotion is at least twice as quick.

But quite apart from former members of defunct overseas administrations and those who were able to enter the Service in 1944–5 merely because they had been active in the Gaullist movement or the Resistance, there is still a sizable body of diplomats that was recruited through the competitive examinations of the Third Republic. For the senior part of the Diplomatic Service, the annual recruitment at that time was about the same as it is now through ENA. The orientation was, however, quite diffferent. The stress was on the humanities. Moreover, since the reform of 1877 which introduced genuine competitive examinations – from 1880 these were the same for the Diplomatic and Consular Services – there was also an initial probationary period during which the aspiring diplomat was closely watched for his suitability by members of the Ministry. This is one of the features which those who drafted the reforms of 1945 disliked most, and abolished. On the other hand, the style of those who entered the Quai in those days is very distinct from that of the socially more heterogeneous technocratic elite from ENA. The fact that the Third Republic in the end produced diplomats for whom it was not unusual to have degrees in both arts and law as well as a diploma from the *Ecole des Sciences Politiques*[5] does not necessarily make them less attractive.

METHODS OF WORK

In the absence of scientifically-gathered statistical data about the amount of time spent on different tasks at the Quai, the careful observer might well be tempted to agree with the frequently voiced view within the Ministry that by far the greatest proportion of its members spends by far the greatest amount of its time preparing reports for the ultimate decision-makers. The absence of scope for decision-making is particularly commented upon by those who joined the Quai from one of the dissolved overseas Ministries, where they often had considerable responsibilities and executive autonomy.

A minimum of four daily deliveries of telegrams keeps the departments informed of current developments. They have further on hand the selections from newspapers prepared by the Press and Information Service of the Ministry and newspapers from their special area of interest. They receive reports from French embassies, either because they asked for them or because these embassies thought they should be of interest to them. The library keeps them informed of the latest publications in their field. From all these sources and any others that seem relevant they compile their reports for the director of their Department.

Thus briefed, all the directors meet the secretary general once every week, but many meet him daily. At these meetings decisions not involving the special responsibilities of the minister himself are taken, and the relevant tasks are assigned to the various Departments. This leads to the compilation of further reports. There are, of course, routine matters which a Department can settle on its own initiative. For example, if it is engaged upon negotiations for which it has been briefed in a general way, it does not constantly have to have recourse to advice from the secretary general. In all these tasks the

Departments will, wherever necessary, consult each other, other appropriate Ministries or organisations, or their representatives abroad. Contacts with the representatives of foreign countries in Paris can also provide useful exchanges of views which may help in the appraisal of a situation.

At the top of some backstairs, secluded, almost isolated, the Quai harbours the Office of the foreign minister. Perhaps it is a pathetic fallacy, but somehow its location suggests that it should not be there at all. For, at its door, career diplomacy ends and French internal and political considerations begin, or rather, the two become inextricably mixed.

The staff of his Office is chosen by the minister himself. It may be primarily composed of politicians, or non-Quai civil servants, or even members of the Diplomatic Service, depending on the way the minister sees his needs. Certainly, when the minister is a member of a political party, it would be unusual for his Office not to include some members whose presence is explicable in terms of political considerations. The director of his Office *(Directeur du Cabinet du Ministre)* is generally someone very close to the foreign minister, whose judgement the minister values. There have been many cases in which such a director has exerted considerable influence on the formation of policy: Berthelot on that of Briand, for example. Aided by his staff, the director is the minister's link with all those with whom he has to deal, including the Ministry itself. It is, for example, through the minister's Office that the Ministry learns of his briefing needs, whether it be to make a policy decision, to answer questions in Parliament, or prepare a speech. On the other hand, it is also through his Office that the minister remains in touch with his government colleagues, at least with their respective offices, and is sheltered from the public. The minister has, in recent years, generally been assisted by one or two secretaries of state.

Thus screened from the day-to-day detail of foreign affairs, the minister can devote himself to the activity for which he has been appointed: decision-making. But just how extensive his powers may be in that realm will largely depend on the character of his government, and on his own.

Appendix: Decision-Making in French Foreign Policy

In foreign affairs, as in all other realms of public interest, policy-making is an act of sovereignty. According to Article 3 of the 1958 Constitution of the Fifth Republic, national sovereignty belongs to the people and is exercised by it through its representatives or through a referendum. Article 20 implies that the parliamentary majority of the people's representatives has ultimate control over the action of the government, since it recognises that the government is responsible to Parliament. Articles 49 and 50 seek to ensure that the parliamentary majority does not use its powers frivolously, providing opportunities for reflection before a censure motion which, if carried, automatically leads to the resignation of the government. Actual policy, according to Article 20, is made by the government, whose action is directed by the prime minister (Article 21). To ensure that ministers can do their work without having to consider narrow political interests, Article 22 stipulates that membership of the government is incompatible with membership of Parliament; this means that if the prime minister, whose duty it is to select his ministers, decides to offer a post in the government to someone holding a parliamentary mandate, the latter must resign his mandate before he can accept the post.

So much for the letter of the Constitution. In fact, Article 5 of the Constitution which deals with some of the functions of the president of the Republic had, under General de Gaulle, begun to be applied in such a way that effective power to make foreign policy came into the hands of the president. The vague drafting of the article confers upon the president the responsibility for upholding the Constitution, for the proper functioning of the state 'by means of his arbitration', and for ensuring the continuity of the state. Among other powers, apart from such traditional prerogatives as having ambassadors accredited to him and appointing French ambassadors abroad, the president of the Fifth Republic has also regained the responsibility for negotiating treaties (Article 52) which had been exercised by the presidents of the Third Republic at least in theory, and he also ratifies them. The president also declares war.

As a consequence of the amendment of the Constitution contained in Article 6, and which was made through a referendum demanded by General de Gaulle in 1962, the president has since that date been elected by universal suffrage, for seven years at a time, so that his interpretation of the Constitution as putting effective policy-making power into the hands of the head of state has been morally strengthened. Conversely, the fact that ministers may not hold a popular mandate puts them, since 1962, at a further moral disadvantage in relation to the president, although their increasing interest in submitting themselves for election – even if it means resigning their seat again immediately – shows that they do not wish to be regarded as mere functionaries.

THE CONSTITUTIONAL POSITION OF PARLIAMENT

Since 1962 the National Assembly, the Lower House of Parliament, has had a majority in sympathy with presidential policies. Thus no serious constitutional difficulties have arisen which could provide a precedent for what one may expect to happen if president and Parliament disagree. The Constitution provides no guide for such a contingency, having only made what looked like the policy-making government responsible to Parliament, not the president. Presumably the president can be indirectly called to account through his government, but since both Parliament and president are elected by universal suffrage it is not clear who should give way in case of conflict between the two. Article 16 provides the president with emergency powers 'in case the institutions of the Republic . . . are seriously endangered', leaving it largely to the president to determine when such a situation has arisen. Since it is also the president who nominates the prime minister, it is difficult to see what Parliament could do in the event of such a conflict. The president can govern without the collaboration of Parliament. Parliament cannot govern at all.

THE FOREIGN MINISTER

It may be taken for granted that on the interpretation of the Constitution as outlined above, the president of the Republic will take upon himself the making of policy in areas in which he is particularly interested. In the case of General de Gaulle, this meant especially foreign affairs, and President Pompidou has shown much interest in that area too. As a result, the function of the foreign minister is at best that of an adviser to, and negotiator for, the president. However, in the case of major negotiations, it is likely that the president himself will undertake these too, since in his capacity as president, as so far interpreted, it will be he, and not the prime minister aided by his appropriate colleagues, who receives high-ranking foreign guests for discussions. Equally it is the president who goes on foreign tours in which negotiations often take place with other heads of state or governments. On such occasions the foreign minister is clearly no more than an adviser, with quick access to experts and information from the Quai. In fact, the minister is not even needed to fulfil that function, because a diplomatic counsellor in the president's own Office is in constant touch with the foreign minister's Office at the Quai and can, through that channel, have access to any information that may be needed. In any case, the president sees all important telegrams at all times.

In his advisory capacity, the foreign minister attends the weekly Wednesday meetings of the council of ministers which are chaired by the president. At these meetings the international scene is reviewed, but it is unusual for major foreign policy decisions to be taken at them. Under de Gaulle, it was more likely that such decisions were sprung on the foreign minister and the world at large at a presidential press conference or in some other dramatic manner. The foreign minister is also a member of the Defence Committee which meets at roughly two-monthly intervals at the Elysée Palace, where he helps to coordinate military planning with foreign policy. *Ad hoc* meetings with the president, attended by the prime minister if general political questions are involved, are held as deemed desirable.

In his executive capacity, the foreign minister attends meetings of the government at the prime minister's official residence, and with his colleagues determines the manner in which policy decisions can best be implemented. In matters in which foreign affairs interests are predominant, the foreign minister will seek the cooperation of his colleagues to ensure that in so far as their Ministries are concerned the main lines of foreign policy are properly followed. Since many different Ministries are now involved in activities which bring them into the field of foreign affairs – one need only think of the Ministries of Finance and Agriculture for example in relation to international organisations of a technical character, like the Common Market and the Coal and Steel Community – the foreign minister has to remain in constant contact with all of them to keep them in line with the broad aims of French policy. To that end, he also often meets other ministers for consultation, quite apart from the more general meetings they all have with the president or the prime minister. The basic text which is usually cited to support the foreign minister's duty to preside over all relations with foreign countries is a decree of 25 December 1810. Still in force, the decree orders that all negotiations, at whatever level, must be channelled through the Ministry of Foreign Affairs.[1] Equally, only the Quai can sponsor the ratification of treaties and is responsible for their interpretation, although in the case of those dealing with international conventions of labour the Ministry of Labour has co-responsibility.[2]

It is a moot point whether the concept of policy formation extends to the negotiating of treaties or other conventions, but since this is one of the few realms in which the foreign minister has a certain scope for decision-making it seems reasonable to include it here. The minister in fact controls the purse strings of all French delegates to meetings abroad, irrespective of the Ministries to which they may belong. This means that, theoretically, the foreign minister can control all negotiations abroad. But the order of 1 January 1951 which brought this procedure into effect is not adequate fully to guarantee the foreign minister's control in this area either, because officials from Ministries other than the Quai going on individual missions are not covered by it. Baillou and Pelletier wrily note in this context that even in the cases that are covered by the order, the foreign minister's consent is usually given on grounds unrelated to foreign political considerations. At least since 1957, thought has been given to the best way in which the Quai's control can be tightened up. Perhaps the fact that nothing concrete has so far emerged is due to the overall presidential control which, as has been seen, is a characteristic of the Fifth Republic, and which makes the claims of the Quai of little more than petty parochial interest.

THE SPECIAL POSITION OF THE FOREIGN AFFAIRS COMMISSION OF THE NATIONAL ASSEMBLY

Although the Foreign Affairs Commission as one of the six permanent Commissions of the National Assembly has, under the Constitution of the Fifth Republic as it is applied at present, no more impact on actual policy formation than has the Assembly as a whole, its role as a forum for informed analysis of French foreign policy should not be underestimated. As long as the president of the Republic appears to pay some heed to the wants of his countrymen, and wishes to avoid a direct collision with Parliament, he will not be able systematically to ignore the views of this Commission. In any case, the membership of Parliamentary Commissions is directly representative of the composition of Parliament as a whole, so that at least since 1962 there has been a majority of Gaullists in both, not all of whom have been unconditional supporters of the official Gaullist line of the day. For these reasons the Commission has to be treated with some deference, and it in its turn has played its role as sympathetic examiner of the projects and performances of those who have charge of French foreign policy with a distinct inclination to allow the examinees to pass, preferably with flying colours. In any case, however, where a matter of projected policy is concerned, the text which is finally submitted for the approval of Parliament – and many of course are not thus submitted at all – is that of the government and not the text as the Commission would want to amend it, as used to be the case before 1958.

However, most of the time of the Commission is usually taken up with the examination of the current performance of the government in foreign affairs, not with questions of general policy.[3] It may perform this function in a variety of ways. Any one of its subcommittees – constituted at the beginning of each legislature in terms of the geographical areas likely to be of special interest at the time – or the Commission as a whole may tackle a particular issue, and on their own initiative send a report of their findings to the foreign minister or the prime minister. On the other hand, it is open to the Commission to invite either the foreign minister or the prime minister to appear before it and discuss with it specific questions of interest to it. While there is no obligation on the part of either minister to accept such an invitation, it is rare for it to be declined. But, under the Fifth Republic, instances on which the ministers themselves have asked to be heard by the Commission have been even rarer than they used to be before 1958 when ministers were still far more at the mercy of Parliament and its Commissions than they have been since.

The Commission's relations with Parliament are mainly governed by the fact that it is its job to provide Parliament with reports on foreign policy issues whenever this is desired, either because a particular policy matter has been referred to it or because it sees fit to do so on its own initiative. In this latter role it may act as a kind of ginger group, as for example at the time of the Suez crisis when it used its considerable influence in the direction of intervention.

It may be concluded that, like Parliament as a whole, the Foreign Affairs Commission plays a largely negative part in the formation of policy. The constitutional dice are loaded so heavily against Parliament that it would take a very great issue indeed before the Commission could convince itself and Parliament that it was worth risking a general election rather than try to find some way of accommodating its views to those of the president and his government. And, as has been shown, if it did risk an election it is not in the least clear what the concrete political result might be for the particular issue, even if the majority of the new Parliament agreed with those who had provoked the elections: Article 16 of the Constitution might always be invoked by the president. As regards the Foreign Affairs Commission of the Senate, this shares in addition the ultimate impotence of the Second Chamber as a whole in relation to the National Assembly. According to Article 45 of the Constitution, in case of apparently irresolvable conflict between the two Chambers, it is the Lower House which has the last word.

THE PAST AS A POSSIBLE GUIDE TO THE FUTURE

Until it becomes clear whether a president of the Fifth Republic resigns when he finds himself in conflict on important matters of policy with the National Assembly – particularly once new elections have confirmed the attitude of the old Assembly – there must remain the presumption that there is no material difference between the Fifth Republic and the first decades of the Third Republic (or the period preceding 1870) in the realm of ultimate responsibility for foreign policy decision-making. Admittedly, even on a hostile interpretation of the Constitution of the Fifth Republic the president is no longer irresponsible, as his predecessors had been, because since 1962 he submits himself for election to the whole electorate. On the other hand, he can hardly be expected to provide detailed policy statements for his seven-year term of office before he is elected, so the president has wide discretion to implement such policies as he thinks fit during his years at the Elysée. The Constitution provides for no form of control except that of Parliament, and it has been shown that the effectiveness of this control remains to be tested. The conflict between president and Parliament in 1962 provides no useful precedent, because the electorate resolved it in favour of the president. The problem of what heed the president would pay to the hostile outcome of a general election therefore remains.

That the head of state had supreme political power at a time when, before 1877, there was not even a pretence at parliamentary democracy in France may be taken for granted. And that this supreme power in foreign affairs survived through the first three decades of the Third Republic, until 1902, is partly to be accounted for by the acceptance of the doctrine that the negotiation of treaties is a delicate matter which should not be subjected to the kind of publicity one has progressively come to associate with parliamentary control. Whatever the reasons, however, the early presidents of the Third Republic were just as egomaniac when it came to foreign affairs as their royal predecessors had been. President Grévy was reported to have said that there were two spheres in which he would tolerate no interference: war and foreign policy; as for the rest, 'I am very easy'.[4] Similarly, the resignation of President Casimir Périer was very much accelerated by his conviction that his ministers kept him out of talks with Germany at the time of the Dreyfus affair: 'I was laying myself open to the possibility of being told one day by a foreign ambassador, perhaps in graver circumstances, that what I was telling him did not square with what he had been told by the minister of foreign affairs'.[5]

Thus until the turn of the century the statement in the Constitution of the Third Republic that the president negotiates and ratifies treaties was taken seriously. It was of course taken for granted that he would inform Parliament when he thought it proper to do so. Indeed, treaties did not officially come into force until they had received parliamentary approval. In those days, however, presidents were irresponsible, and on such occasions as Parliament refused to work with them they had the democratic good sense to resign; Grévy and Casimir Périer illustrate this fact. However, the increasing trend towards greater ministerial, and therefore parliamentary, control over foreign affairs led to the position where, in 1912, President Fallières had to ask his government at least to keep him informed of diplomatic developments.[6] The Constitution of the Fourth Republic endorsed this shift of responsibility by omitting the clause giving the president the task of negotiating treaties. Clearly, this marks the point where policy formation may be said to have passed to the government in Parliament. Being entirely at the mercy of the elected representatives of the people, a government's foreign policy, like all other policy, had then to accord with the wishes of a parliamentary majority.

Article 52 of the 1958 Constitution, as has been shown, sought to reverse this evolution towards greater parliamentary control over foreign policy. It reverted to the wording of the 1875 Constitution and stated that the president, among other things, negotiates treaties. It is also clear that President de Gaulle took this as literally as the early presidents of the Third Republic had done, and there is no evidence that President Pompidou sees the position differently. No doubt their election by universal suffrage reinforced their view that they had a right to do so.

If one has to speculate about the future of the president's role in foreign affairs, one might feel it proper to be guided by the historical fact that the French have never for long, since the 1789 revolution, allowed themselves the luxury of sitting back while others govern them. Under the Fifth Republic, in the case of an irresolvable conflict between president and Parliament, the former might well seek to invoke article 16 and govern alone. Certainly, Pompidou has stated that if he had to choose between a presidential and a parliamentary system he would choose the former.[7] In such a situation, if the president possessed the qualities which made General de Gaulle acceptable to the French, he might even get away with it for a while. But once the Gaullist interlude is over and the dust of these uncertain post-1958 years has settled, it is likely that the threat of Article 16 will no longer be able to prevent parliamentary control over governmental policy. It is not consonant with the modern political traditions of France that a single man, whatever the mode of his designation, should be able to rule the country alone for seven years at a time. When this again clearly becomes evident, the role of Parliament – and of its Commissions in particular – in the formation of policy will once more be considerable. Ministers and governments will again have to heed the views of these popularly representative bodies, on pain of dismissal. Written and oral questions in Parliament will again play their part in keeping ministers in line with the temper of those to whom the French people has temporarily delegated its sovereignty.[8]

Bibliography

Titles are arranged in accordance with the subject matter of the various chapters. Articles cited in the text are not mentioned in the Bibliography.

GENERAL

Aron, Raymond, *Immuable et changeante: De la IVᵉ à la Vᵉ République*, Paris, 1959.
Auriol, Vincent, Journal du Septennat, 1947–1954 (vol. 1), Paris, 1970.
De Gaulle, Charles, *Discours et messages* (ed. François Goguel), Paris, 1970.
Duverger, M., *La Vᵉ République*, Paris, 1960; *La VIᵉ République et le régime présidentiel*, Paris, 1961.
Elgey, Georgette, *Histoire de la IVᵉ République*, Paris, 1965.
Fauvet, Jacques, *La IVᵉ République*, Paris, 1959.
Julliard, Jacques, *La IVᵉ République 1947–58*, Paris, 1959.
Passeron, André, *De Gaulle parle 1958–1962*, Paris, 1962; *De Gaulle parle 1962–1966*, Paris, 1966.
Pickles, D., *The Fifth French Republic*, London, 1960.
Wahl, N., *The Fifth Republic*, New York, 1959.
Werth, Alexander, *La France depuis la guerre 1944–1957*, Paris, 1957.

GENERAL: FOREIGN POLICY STUDIES ETC.

Couve de Murville, M., *Une politique étrangère 1958–1969*, Paris, 1971.
De Carmoy, Guy, *Les politiques étrangères de la France 1944–1966*, Paris, 1967 (English edition: *French Foreign Policy 1944–68*, Chicago, 1970).
Documentation Française, *La politique étrangère de la France, textes et documents*, Paris.
Duroselle, J.B. (ed.), *La politique étrangère et ses fondements*, Paris, 1954.

Grosser, A., *La IVe République et sa politique extérieure*, Paris, 1961; *La politique extérieure de la Ve République*, Paris, 1965.

Hamon, Léo (ed.), *L'élaboration de la politique étrangère*, Paris, 1969.

Kulski, W.W., *De Gaulle and the World: The Foreign Policy of the French Fifth Republic*, Syracuse, 1966.

Laloy, Jean, *Entre guerre et paix*, Paris, 1966.

Newhouse, John, *De Gaulle and the Anglo-Saxons*, New York, 1970.

Reynaud, Paul, *La politique étrangère du Gaullisme*, Paris, 1964.

THE NEED FOR ECONOMIC AID AND
FRANCO-AMERICAN RELATIONS

Blum, Léon, *Naissance de la Quatrième République*, Paris, 1958.

Brown, W. Adams, and Opie, Redvers, *American Foreign Assistance*, Washington, 1953.

De Lattre, André, *Les finances extérieures de la France*, Paris, 1959.

Deporte, A.W., *De Gaulle's Foreign Policy 1944–1946*, Harvard, 1968.

Diebold, W., *Trade and Payments in Western Europe: a study in economic cooperation 1947–51*, New York, 1952.

Ellis, Howard S., *The Economics of Freedom: The Progress and Future of Aid to Europe*, New York, 1950.

Jeanneney, J.-M., *Forces et faiblesses de l'économie française 1945–1959* (2nd ed.), Paris, 1959.

Jones, J.M., *The Fifteen Weeks, February 21–June 5 1947*, New York, 1955.

Kissinger, Henry A., *Les malentendus atlantiques*, Paris, 1965.

Reitzel, William *et al.*, *United States Foreign Policy 1945–1955*, Washington, 1956.

Van der Beugel, E., *From Marshall Aid to Atlantic Partnership*, Amsterdam, 1966.

Viorst, Milton, *Hostile Allies*, London, 1965.

FRANCE AND GERMANY

Adenauer, Konrad, *Memoirs 1945–1953*, London, 1966; *Erinnerungen 1953–1963*, Stuttgart, 1966.

De Gaulle, Charles, *Mémoires de guerre: L'Appel* (1940–1942), *L'Unité* (1942–1944), *Le Salut* (1944–1946), Paris, 1954.

Deporte, A.W., *De Gaulle's Foreign Policy 1944-1946*, Harvard, 1968.

Freymond, Jacques, *Le conflict sarrois 1945-1955*, Brussels, 1959.

Girardet, R., *La crise militaire française*, Paris, 1964.

Grosser, A., *L'Allemagne de l'occident 1945-1952*, Paris, 1953; *Germany in our Time*, London, 1971.

Korff, Adalbert, *Le revirement de la politique française à l'égard de l'Allemagne 1945-1950* (thesis), 1965.

Lauret, René, *Notre voisin allemand: deux peuples s'affrontent*, Paris, 1960.

Manfred, Michel, *German Rearmament as a Factor in Anglo-West German Relations* (thesis), 1963.

Moch, Jules, *Histoire du réarmement allemand depuis 1950*, Paris, 1965.

Neumann, William L., *Making the Peace 1941-1945*, Washington, 1950.

Renouvin, Pierre, *Les relations franco-allemandes 1871-1890*, Paris, 1952.

Salomon, Michel, *Faut-il avoir peur de l'Allemagne?*, Paris, 1969.

Snell, J.L., *Dilemma over Germany*, New Orleans, 1959.

Willis, F. Roy, *The French in Germany*, Stanford, 1962; *France, Germany and the New Europe 1945-1967*, Oxford, 1968.

Windsor, Philip, *German Reunification*, London, 1969.

Wullus, Rudiger, J., *Français et allemands, ennemis héréditaires?* Paris, 1965.

EUROPE

Amme, Carl, H., *NATO without France*, Stanford, 1967.

Aron, R. and Lerner, D. (eds), *La querelle de la C.E.D.*, Paris, 1956.

Bjøl, E., *La France devant l'Europe*, Copenhagen, 1966.

Bonnefous, E., *L'idée européenne et sa réalisation*, Paris, 1950.

Boris, George, *Servir la République*, Paris, 1963.

Delorme, Hélène and Tavernier, Yves, *Les paysans français et l'Europe*, Paris, 1969.

Diebold, W., *The Schuman Plan 1950-1959*, New York, 1959.

Elgozy, G., *La France devant le Marché Commun*, Paris, 1958.

Fontaine, André, *L'alliance atlantique à l'heure du dégel*, Paris, 1959.

Gerbet, P., *Le Plan Schuman et les origines de la C.E.C.A.*, Paris, 1962.

Haas, Ernst B., *The Uniting of Europe*, Stanford, 1958.

Hassner, P. and Newhouse, J., *Les diplomaties occidentales*, Paris, 1966.

Imbert, A., *L'union de l'Europe occidentale*, Paris, 1968.

Jouve, Edmond, *Le Général de Gaulle et la construction de l'Europe, 1940–1966*, Paris, 1967.

Kitzinger, Uwe, *The European Common Market and Community*, London, 1970.

Mann, P., *Le R.P.F. et les problèmes européens*, Paris, 1966.

Massip, R., *De Gaulle et l'Europe*, Paris, 1963.

Meynaud, J. and Sidjanski, D., *Les groupes de pression dans la communauté européenne*, Montreal, 1969.

Philip, André, *L'Europe et sa place dans l'économie internationale*, Paris, 1953.

Raux, J., *Les relations extérieures de la communauté économique européenne*, Paris, 1966.

Ritsch, F.F., *The French Left and the European Idea 1941–1949*, New York, 1966.

Schumann, M., *La France et ses alliés*, Paris, 1966.

Serfaty, Simon, *France, De Gaulle and Europe: The Policy of the Fourth and Fifth Republics towards the Continent*, New York, 1968.

Smet, André de, *La communauté européenne de défence: expériences et leçons*, Luxembourg, 1966.

Szokolóczy-Syllaba, Janos, *Les organisations professionelles françaises et le Marché Commun*, Paris, 1965.

FRANCE AND THE SOVIET UNION

Aron, Robert, *Histoire de la libération de la France*, Paris, 1959.

Catroux, Général, *J'ai vu tomber le rideau de fer*, Paris, 1952.

De Grünwald, Constantin, *Les alliances franco-russes*, Paris, 1965.

Duclos, J., *Octobre 17 vu de France*, Paris, 1967.

Fontaine, André, *Histoire de la guerre froide* (2 vols), Paris, 1965.

Hytier, Adrienne, *Two Years of French Foreign Policy, Vichy 1940–2*, Paris and Geneva, 1958.

Mollet, Guy, *Bilan et perspectives socialistes*, Paris, 1958.

Mourin, Maxime, *Les relations franco-soviétiques 1917–1967*, Paris, 1967.

République Polonaise, *Les relations polono-allemandes et polono-soviétiques 1933-1939*, Paris, 1940.

Ribbentrop, Joachim von, *De Londres à Moscou*, Paris, 1954.

Rossi, A., *Deux ans d'alliance germano-soviétique*, Paris, 1949.

Sherwood, R., *Le mémorial de Roosevelt*, Paris, 1950.

Tournoux, J.R., *Secrets d'état*, Paris, 1960.

Wolfe, Thomas W., *Soviet Power and Europe 1945-1970*, Baltimore, 1970.

FRENCH POLICY OUTSIDE THE ATLANTIC AND SOVIET BLOCS

Aron, R., *La tragédie algérienne*, Paris, 1957; *L'Algérie et la République*, Paris, 1958.

Auphan, P., *Histoire de la décolonisation*, Paris, 1967.

Balous, Suzanne, *L'action culturelle de la France dans le monde*, Paris, 1970.

Bar-Zóhar, M., *Suez ultra-secret*, Paris, 1964.

Basdevant, J. (ed.), *Les affaires étrangères*, Paris, 1959.

Bernard, Stéphane, *The Franco-Moroccan Conflict 1943-1956*, New Haven, 1968.

Berque, J., *French North Africa: The Maghreb between Two World Wars*, London, 1967.

Bonnefous, E., *Les millions qui s'envolent: l'aide française aux pays sous-développés*, Paris, 1963.

Bosc, Robert, *Le tiers monde dans la politique internationale*, Paris, 1968.

Bouissou, Michel, *La reconnaissance de la République populaire de Chine devant l'opinion*, Paris, 1967.

Bromberger, M. and S., *Les secrets de l'expédition d'Egypte*, Paris, 1957.

Catroux, Général, *Deux actes du drame indochinois*, Paris, 1959.

Chaffard, G., *Les carnets secrets de la décolonisation*, Paris, 1965.

Chailley, Marcel, *Histoire de l'Afrique occidentale française, 1638-1959*, Paris, 1968.

Cole, Allan B., *Conflict in Indochina and International Repercussions, A Documentary History 1945-1955*, New York, 1956.

Courrière, Yves, *La guerre d'Algérie*, Paris, 1968.

Debeauvais, M., Sourria, J.-C. and Valm, El., *Tiers-Monde: l'assistance technique*, Paris, 1962.

Delavignette, R., *Du bon usage de la décolonisation*, Paris, 1968.

BIBLIOGRAPHY

De Lusignan, Guy, *French-Speaking Africa since Independence*, London, 1969.

Devillers, P., *Histoire du Vietnam 1940–1952*, Paris, 1952.

Dumont, René, *False Start in Africa*, London, 1966.

Durand-Reville, L., *L'assistance de la France aux pays insuffisament développés*, Paris, 1961.

Duquesne, Jacques, *L'Algérie et la guerre des mythes*, Paris, 1958.

Fall, Bernard, *Le Viet-Minh 1945–1960*, Paris, 1960.

Favrod, C.-H., *La révolution algérienne*, Paris, 1959.

Ferrandi, J., *Les officiers française face au Vietminh, 1945–1954*. Paris, 1966.

Direction de la coopération culturelle et technique, Reports.

Gordon, David C., *The Passing of French Algeria*, Oxford, 1966.

Grimal, H., *La décolonisation 1919–1963*, Paris, 1965.

Hammer, E.J., *The Struggle for Indochina 1940–1955*, Stanford, 1966.

Hargreaves, John D. (ed.), *France and West Africa*, London, 1969.

Hayter, Teresa, *French Aid*, London, 1966.

Hoffner, R., *Coopération économique franco-africaine*, Paris, 1968.

Judd, Peter, *African Independence*, New York, 1963.

Lacouture, J. and Devillers, P., *La fin d'une guerre, Indochine 1954*, Paris, 1960.

Lacouture, J., *Cinq hommes et la France*, Paris, 1961.

Laniel, J., *Le drame indochinois*, Paris, 1957.

Lewis, W.H. (ed.), *French-Speaking Africa*, New York, 1965.

Ligot, Maurice, *Les accords de coopération entre la France et les états africains et malgache d'expression française*, Paris, 1964.

Ling, D.L., *Tunisia, From Protectorate to Republic*, Indiana, 1967.

Mabileau, A. and Meynet, J., *Décolonisations et régimes politiques en Afrique*, Paris, 1967.

Merle, M. (ed.), *L'Afrique noire contemporaine*, Paris, 1968.

Mortimer, E., *France and the Africans, 1944–1960*, London, 1969.

Mus, P., *Vietnam: sociologie d'une guerre*, Paris, 1952.

Navarre, Henri, *Agonie de l'Indochine 1953–1954*, Paris, 1958.

Neves, Philip, *French-Speaking Africa*, Oxford, 1962.

O'Ballance, E., *The Algerian Insurrection, 1954–1962*, London, 1967.

Outrey, A., *L'administration française des affaires étrangères*. Paris, 1954.

Pickles, D., *Algeria and France: From Colonisation to Cooperation*, London, 1963.

Rous, J., *Chronique de la décolonisation*, Paris, 1965.

Sauvy, A., *Le tiers monde: sous-développement et développement* (2nd ed.), Paris, 1961.

Savary, Alain, *Nationalisme algérien et grandeur française*, Paris, 1960.

Tainturier, J. (ed.), *De Gaulle au Québec: le dossier des quatre journées*, Montreal, 1967.

Tillion, G., *Les ennemis complémentaires*, Paris, 1960.

Thomas, Hugh, *The Suez Affair*, London, 1967.

Viatte, A., *La francophonie*, Paris, 1969.

Werth, Alexander, *De Gaulle*, London, 1965.

Williams, Ann, *Britain and France in the Middle East*, London, 1968.

THE DIPLOMATIC SERVICE

Baillou, J. and Pelletier, P., *Les affaires étrangères*, Paris, 1962.

Basdevant, J. (ed.), *Les affaires étrangères*, Paris, 1959.

Dumaine, J., *Quai d'Orsay 1945–1951*, Paris, 1955.

Annuaire diplomatique et consulaire.

Outrey, Amédée, *L'administration des affaires étrangères*, Paris, 1954.

Notes

CHAPTER 1

1 Charles de Gaulle, *Mémoires,* vol. 3, Paris, 1959, pp. 5–6.
2 IFOP (Institut Français d'opinion publique), 16 April 1945.
3 *Ibid.,* 1 January 1946.
4 *Ibid.,* 1 February 1946.
5 *Ibid.,* 16 February 1946.
6 De Gaulle, *Mémoires,* vol. 3, p. 463.
7 *Ibid.,* pp. 465–6.
8 See André de Lattre, *Les finances extérieures de la France,* Paris, 1959, pp. 161–3.
9 See Société des amis de Léon Blum, *L'oeuvre de Léon Blum: 1945–1947,* Paris, 1958, pp. 202–3.
10 IFOP, 1 October 1947.
11 William Adams Brown and Redvers Opie, *American Foreign Assistance,* Washington, 1953, p. 186 *et seq.*
12 Guy de Carmoy, *Les politiques étrangères de la France, 1944–1966,* Paris, 1967, p. 84.
13 William Reitzel *et al., United States Foreign Policy, 1945–1955,* Washington, 1956, p. 191.
14 IFOP, 1 September 1947.
15 Quoted in Ernst van der Beugel, *From Marshall Aid to Atlantic Partnership,* Amsterdam, 1966, p. 105.
16 *Ibid.,* p. 104.
17 *Ibid.,* p. 216.
18 See Jean Godard, 'L'aide américaine à la France', in *Revue de Science Financière,* July – September 1956, p. 438 *et seq.*
19 IFOP, 15 February 1949.
20 *Ibid.,* 16 February 1948.
21 *Ibid.,* 1 April 1949.
22 Godard, *loc. cit.,* p. 450.
23 OEEC, *Report on Internal Stability in Member Countries,* August 1950, p. 49.
24 See, for example, Godard, *loc. cit.,* p. 453.
25 *Ibid.,* p. 457.

[26] De Lattre, *op. cit.*, p. 337.

[27] *Ibid.*, p. 346.

[28] *Ibid.*, p. 350.

CHAPTER 2

[1] P. Renouvin, *Les relations franco-allemandes, 1871–1890*, Paris, 1952, *passim*. For a more detailed analysis of the earlier period, see P. Renouvin (ed.), *Histoire des relations internationales*, Paris, 1900, vols. 2–5, *passim*.

[2] See William L. Neumann, *Making the Peace, 1941–1945*, Washington, 1950, *passim*, for accounts of and documents relating to these agreements.

[3] J. L. Snell, *Dilemma over Germany*, New Orleans, 1959, p. 111.

[4] See de Gaulle *Mémoires*, vol. 3, p. 57.

[5] *Ibid.*, for arguments to separate the Ruhr from the rest of Germany. See also *Documents français relatifs à l'Allemagne, 1945–7* (hereafter *Documents*) Paris, 1947, pp. 57–64.

[6] See, for example, an interview with de Gaulle in *The Times* (London), 10 September 1945, in *Discours et Messages* (hereafter *Discours*), ed. F. Goguel, vol. 1, p. 614, *et seq.*

[7] *Documents*, p. 16.

[8] See F. Roy Willis, *The French in Germany*, Stanford, 1962, p. 33.

[9] *Ibid.*, p. 109 *et seq.*

[10] *Ibid.*, p. 167 *et seq.* and p. 244.

[11] *Documents*, pp. 42 – 64.

[12] See the National Assembly debate, in *Journal Officiel*, 12 June 1948, pp. 3491–7.

[13] See *Année Politique*, 1946, p. 409; see also Willis, *op. cit.*, p. 53.

[14] *Journal Officiel*, Assemblée Nationale, 13 February 1948, pp. 741–7.

[15] See US State Department *Germany, 1947–9. The story in documents*, Washington, 1950, p. 75 *et seq.*

[16] *Ibid.*, p. 76 *et seq.*

[17] *Journal Officiel*, Assemblée Nationale, 16 June 1948, p. 3579 *et seq.*

[18] *Journal Officiel*, Assemblée Nationale, 12 June 1948, p. 3491 *et seq.*

[19] For example, Georges Boris, *Servir la République*, Paris, 1963, p. 417.

[20] *Pour l'Europe*, Paris, 1963, *passim*.

[21] See E. Bjol, *La France devant l'Europe*, Copenhagen, 1966.

[22] *Discours*, vol. 2, p. 377.

[23] See *Année Politique*, 1951, pp. 456–77, for text.

[24] See, for example, Jacques Soustelle during the ratification debate, in *Journal Officiel*, Assemblée Nationale, 11 December 1951, p. 9007; but see also the ineffective opposition of the French steel industry in Jean Meynaud, *Nouvelles études sur les groupes de pression en France*, Paris, 1962, pp. 257, 313.

[25] *Discours*, vol. 2, p. 16.

[26] *Ibid.*, pp. 348–50.

[27] See *Journal Officiel*, Assemblée Nationale, 25 July 1949; Schuman underlined this position on the following day: see particularly p. 5312.

[28] Jules Moch, *Histoire du réarmement allemand depuis 1950*, Paris, 1965, p. 28.

[29] Manfred Michel, *German Rearmament as a Factor in Anglo-West German Relations*, Ph. D. thesis, London School of Economics, 1963, pp. 96–101.

[30] Moch, *op. cit.*, p. 63.

[31] *Ibid.*, p. 129 *et seq.* See also R. Aaron and D. Lerner (eds.), *La querelle de la CED*, Paris, 1956, p. 127, *et seq.*

[32] *Journal Officiel*, Assemblée Nationale, 24 October 1950. See also Moch, *op. cit.*, pp. 93, 97, 131, 243–4.

[33] *Journal Officiel*, Assemblée Nationale, 25 October 1950.

[34] *Sondages*, 1951, no. 1, p. 24.

[35] Konrad Adenauer, *Memoirs, 1945–1953*, London, 1966, p. 357.

[36] See *Journal Officiel*, Assemblée Nationale, 19 February 1952; the preoccupations of the Assembly are well brought out in the recommendations it made to the government at the end of the debate.

[37] See *La querelle de la CED*, pp. 32–3.

[38] General de Gaulle set the tone for this kind of objection at a special press conference on 25 February 1953: see *Discours*, vol. 2, pp. 564–730.

[39] *La querelle de la CED*, p. 40 *et seq.*

[40] R. Girardet, *La crise militaire française*, Paris, 1964, pp. 164–8.

[41] Moch, *op. cit.* pp. 315–8.

[42] *Journal Officiel*, Assemblée Nationale, 29 August 1954.

[43] Jean Stoetzel, in *La querelle de la CED*, p. 142.

[44] *Ibid.*, p. 209.

[45] Moch, *op. cit.*, p. 336.

[46] See Bjøl, *op. cit.*, p. 156.

[47] *Ibid.*, p. 141 *et seq.*

[48] For the main points of the London Agreement, see *Année Politique*, 1954, pp. 638–45; and for the Paris Agreements, *ibid.*, pp. 657–77.

[49] Adenauer, *op. cit.* (1953–5), pp. 374–7.

[50] *Ibid.*, p. 376.

[51] See, for example, A. Grosser, *La 4ᵉ République et sa politique extérieure*, Paris, 1961, p. 325.

[52] For the debate, see *Journal Officiel*, Assemblée Nationale, 23 to 30 December 1954.

[53] See Philip Windsor, *German Reunification*, London, 1969, *passim*.

[54] Bjøl, *op. cit.*, p. 115, from his interview with Monnet.

[55] *Ibid.*, p. 108, from his interview with Uri.

[56] *Ibid.*, p. 118.

[57] Adenauer, *op. cit.* (1955–9), p. 23.

[58] *Sondages*, 1955, no. 1. For the attitudes of French business interests, see Janos Szokoloczy-Syllaba, *Les organisations professionnelles françaises et le Marché Commun*, Paris, 1965.

[59] *Journal Officiel*, Assemblée Nationale, 15, 18, 25 January 1957.

[60] *Discours*, vol. 2, p. 350.

[61] Bjøl, *op. cit.*, p. 214.

[62] See *Journal Officiel*, Assemblée Nationale, 15, 18, 25 January 1957, and 10 July 1957, for the final ratification debate.

[63] *Ibid.*, 1957, p. 216.

[64] *Ibid.*, 2 July 1957, p. 3134.

[65] See, for example, Bjøl, *op. cit.*, p. 228.

[66] Adenauer, *op. cit.* (1955–59), p. 415.

[67] *Ibid.*

[68] *Ibid.*, p. 424.

[69] See, for example, de Gaulle's press conference of 16 March 1950, in *Discours*, vol. 2, p. 349.

[70] A. Grosser, *La politique extérieure de la Vᵉ République*, Paris, 1965, p. 85.

[71] *Discours*, vol. 3, pp. 84–5.

[72] See de Gaulle, *Mémoires*, vol. 3, p. 75.

[73] Adenauer, *op. cit.* (1955–9), p. 429.

[74] *Ibid.*, pp. 427–8.

[75] *L'Alliance atlantique à l'heure du dégel*, Paris, 1959, p. 94.

[76] See Adenauer, *op. cit.* (1959–63), p. 71 *et seq.*

[77] *Ibid.*, p. 75.

[78] *Ibid.*, p. 76.

[79] Adenauer's detailed account is to be found at *ibid.*, p. 76 *et seq.*

[80] *Ibid.*

[81] *Ibid.*, pp. 101–2.

[82] *Ibid.*, pp. 200–1.

[83] Grosser, *La politique extérieure de la 5ᵉ République*, p. 88.

[84] *Discours*, vol. 4, p. 13.

[85] *Ibid.*, p. 155.

[86] A comment made at a garden party and quoted in *Année Politique*, 1963, p. 280.

[87] *Discours*, vol. 4, pp. 377–81; and vol. 5, pp. 20–2.

[88] *Ibid.*, vol. 5, pp. 241–5.

[89] *Année Politique* 1967, p. 206 *et seq.*

[90] *Ibid.*, 1966, p. 223.

[91] See *ibid.*, 1969, p. 225.

[92] That is, the Six of EEC (without Luxembourg), the United States, Canada, Great Britain, Sweden, Japan.

[93] *Discours*, vol. 5, p. 244.

[94] *Année Politique*, 1968, p. 216.

[95] *Ibid.*, p. 304.

[96] *Ibid.*, 1969, p. 232.

[97] *Ibid.*, p. 233.

[98] See, for example, *Le Monde*, 26 November 1968.

[99] *Ibid.*, 11 March 1969 (an article by André Fontaine).

[100] 20 November 1969.

[101] See *Le Monde*, 4 August 1970.

[102] See *Le Monde*, 20 November 1969 (article by P. Drouin); also Michel Salomon, *Faut-il avoir peur de l'Allemagne*, Paris, 1969.

[103] See *Le Monde*, 9–10 November 1969 (article by R. Delcour).

[104] See *Le Monde*, 3 July 1970 (article by R. Delcour), and 7 July 1970 by the same author.

[105] See *Le Monde*, 7 July 1970 (report from Bonn).

CHAPTER 3

[1] See J. Duclos, *Octobre 17 vu de France*, Paris, 1967.

[2] 27 January 1923.

[3] Quoted in Mourin, *Les relations Franco-Soviétiques, 1917–1967*, Paris, 1967, p. 167.

[4] Quoted in *ibid.*, p. 202.

[5] See République Polonaise, *Les relations polono-allemandes et polono-soviétiques, 1933–1939*, Paris, 1940.

[6] Ribbentrop's *De Londres à Moscou*, Paris, 1954, makes fascinating reading on this episode; but a more reliable account is in A. Rossi, *Deux ans d'alliance germano-soviétique*, Paris, 1949.

[7] Mourin, *op. cit.*, p. 254 *et seq.*

[8] See Adrienne Hytier, *Two Years of French Foreign Policy, Vichy 1940–2*, Geneva and Paris, 1958, p. 293.

[9] See de Gaulle, *Mémoires*, vol. 1, p. 545.

[10] *Ibid.*, pp. 316–7 and 410.

[11] Mourin, *op. cit.*, p. 262.

[12] De Gaulle, *Mémoires*, vol. 1, p. 197 *et seq.*

[13] Mourin, *op. cit.*, p. 263.

[14] *Ibid.*, p. 264; cf. Churchill, The Second World War, vol. 5, p. 159.

[15] De Gaulle, *Mémoires*, vol. 2, pp. 167–8.

[16] Robert Aron, *Histoire de la libération de la France*, Paris, 1959, p. 636 *et seq.*

[17] De Gaulle's Memoirs contain many references to Stalin's habit of wanting to clear with London and Washington most of his dealings with de Gaulle; see for example vol. 3, p. 75.

[18] Mourin, *op. cit.*, p. 266.

[19] See, for example, R. Sherwood, *Le Mémorial de Roosevelt*, Paris, 1950, vol. 2, p. 313 *et seq.*; de Gaulle, who must have known, made no mention of this in his Memoirs.

[20] De Gaulle, *Mémoires*, vol. 2, pp. 249–50.

[21] *Ibid.*, p. 254 *et seq.*

[22] *Ibid.*, vol. 3, p. 60 *et seq.*

[23] Churchill, *op. cit.*, vol. 6, p. 222; de Gaulle (*Mémoires*, vol. 3, p. 66) states that the initiative came from the Russians.

[24] Churchill, *op. cit.*, vol. 6, p. 223

[25] De Gaulle, *Mémoires*, vol. 3, p. 67; the Consultative Assembly was an *ad hoc* body representing most political interests except Vichy prior to the first postwar elections.

[26] There is a detailed account of these talks and their results in De Gaulle, *Mémoires*, vol. 3, pp. 66–96 and 379–96.

[27] *Ibid.*, p. 101.

[28] See Milton Viorst, *Hostile Allies*, New York, 1965, p. 230 *et seq.*; also Mourin, *op. cit.*, pp. 277–9, and Churchill, *op. cit.*, vol. 6, pp. 308–9, 445.

NOTES

²⁹ See his *J'ai vu tomber le rideau de fer,* Paris, 1952, *passim.*
³⁰ De Gaulle, *Mémoires,* vol. 3, p. 236 *et seq.*
³¹ *Ibid.,* p. 249.
³² *Ibid.,* p. 254; see *Discours,* vol. 1, p. 614 *et seq.*
³³ Mourin, *op. cit.,* p. 286.
³⁴ Catroux, *op. cit.,* pp. 151–2.
³⁵ *Ibid.,* p. 214 *et seq.*
³⁶ See A. Fontaine, *Histoire de la guerre froide,* Paris, 1965, vol. 1, p. 396.
³⁷ See Mourin, *op. cit.,* pp. 294–5.
³⁸ Quoted in Mourin, *op. cit.,* p. 297.
³⁹ Quoted in Georgette Elgey, *La république des illusions,* Paris, 1965, p. 408.
⁴⁰ Quoted in Mourin, *op. cit.,* p. 300.
⁴¹ Keesing's Contemporary Archives, 9924B.
⁴² For the Soviet note, see *Année Politique,* 1950, pp. 375–6, and for the French reply, *ibid.,* pp. 383–4.
⁴³ 20 October 1952.
⁴⁴ *Année Politique,* 1953, p. 344.
⁴⁵ *Ibid.,* p. 384.
⁴⁶ *Ibid.,* pp. 379–82.
⁴⁷ *Ibid.,* 1954, pp. 325–30.
⁴⁸ *Ibid.,* pp. 333–5.
⁴⁹ For the Soviet note, see *ibid.,* pp. 678–80, and for Mendès-France's UN reply, *ibid.,* p. 475.
⁵⁰ *Ibid.,* pp. 488–9.
⁵¹ Radio speech, 18 December 1954; see *ibid.,* p. 489.
⁵² *Journal Officiel,* Assemblée Nationale, 23 December 1954.
⁵³ Text in *Année Politique,* 1954, p. 706.
⁵⁴ Guy Mollet, *Bilan et perspectives socialistes,* Paris, 1958, p. 30 *et seq.*
⁵⁵ See Mourin, *op. cit.,* p. 317.
⁵⁶ See *Documentation française, Articles et Documents,* no. 0361, 26 May 1956.
⁵⁷ *Année Politique,* 1956, p. 302.
⁵⁸ See Mourin, *op. cit.,* pp. 319-20.
⁵⁹ Adenauer, *op. cit.* (1953–5), p. 528.
⁶⁰ *Année Politique,* 1956, p. 304.
⁶¹ *Ibid.,* p. 376.
⁶² *Ibid.,* pp. 525–6.
⁶³ *Ibid.,* p. 526.

[64] *Journal Officiel*, Assemblée Nationale, 18 December 1956.

[65] *Année Politique*, 1957, p. 359.

[66] *Ibid.*, p. 360; for the full French translation of the note, see *Documentation française, Articles et Documents*, no. 0511, 24 May 1957.

[67] *Année Politique*, 1958, pp. 290–1.

[68] Quoted in *ibid.*, p. 288.

[69] *Ibid.*, pp. 289–90.

[70] *Discours*, vol. 3, pp. 82–7.

[71] Quoted in France, *Les Relations Franco-Soviétiques 1958–1966*, Paris, 1966 (Notes et Etudes Documentaires), Documentation Française, p. 9 (hereafter *Relations*).

[72] *Pravda*, 22 September 1958.

[73] *Discours, loc. cit.*; see also J. R. Tournoux, *Secrets d'Etat*, Paris, 1960, p. 418.

[74] *Discours, loc. cit.*

[75] *Ibid.*, p. 130.

[76] *Ibid.*, p. 131.

[77] Quoted in *Relations*, p. 11.

[78] Quoted in *Année Politique*, 1960, p. 425.

[79] *Ibid.*, p. 426.

[80] *Relations*, p. 14.

[81] 30 July 1960.

[82] *Discours*, vol. 3, p. 268.

[83] *Ibid.*, pp. 335–7.

[84] See *Année Politique*, 1961, p. 518; also *Relations*, p. 15.

[85] *Discours*, vol. 3, p. 385.

[86] *Ibid.*

[87] *Relations*, p. 17.

[88] *Ibid.*, pp. 16–17.

[89] *Ibid.*, p. 17.

[90] *Ibid.*, p. 18.

[91] *Discours*, vol. 4, p. 78.

[92] *Relations*, p. 18.

[93] *Ibid.*

[94] *Ibid.*

[95] *Discours*, vol. 4, pp. 122–3.

[96] *Relations*, p. 20.

[97] *Ibid.*, p. 22.

[98] *Ibid.*

[99] *Discours*, vol. 4, p. 315.

[100] *Ibid.*, p. 341.

[101] *Relations*, p. 23.

[102] *Ibid.*, pp. 23–4.

[103] *Ibid.*, p. 26; see *Journal Officiel*, Assemblée Nationale, 13 April 1966.

[104] *Discours*, vol. 5, pp. 211–4.

[105] Report in *Le Monde*, 9 November 1968.

[106] *Ibid.*, 25 October 1968.

[107] See, for example, André Fontaine, in *Le Monde*, 11 March 1969.

[108] *Le Monde*, 30 January 1968.

[109] See *ibid.*, 31 October 1968.

[110] See *ibid.*, 28 May 1969.

[111] See *ibid.*, 3 February 1970.

[112] Michel Tatu, in *ibid.*, 15 October 1969.

[113] Quoted in *ibid.*

[114] See *ibid.*, 6 June 1970.

[115] Quoted in *ibid.*, 3 November 1970.

CHAPTER 4

[1] In J. Basdevant (ed.), *Less Affaires etrangères*, Paris, 1962, p. 59.

[2] Quoted in S. Balous, *L'Action culturelle de la France dans le monde*, Paris, 1970, p. 13.

[3] A. Outrey, *L'Administration française des affaires étrangères*, Paris, 1954, p. 63.

[4] Balous, *op. cit.*, p. 177.

[5] René Dumont, *False Start in Africa*, London, 1966, p. 88 *et seq.*

[6] *Mémoires*, vol. 3, p. 235.

[7] This and the following quotation in Balous, *op. cit.*, p. 35.

[8] See *Le Monde*, 14–5 June 1970.

[9] See *Le Monde*, 10 October 1968.

[10] *Ibid.*, 25–6 May 1969.

[11] *Ibid.*, 30 March 1970.

[12] *Ibid.*, 11 May 1968.

[13] Balous, *op. cit.*, p.180.

[14] Teresa Hayter, *French Aid*, London, 1966, p. 36. I am indebted to this book for most of the statistical information to 1961, which had not been compiled earlier.

[15] e.g., for 1967 *Le Monde*, August 1968, quotes 1.64 per cent and

the *Bulletin mensuel d'information* of the French Embassy in London quotes 1.55 per cent.

[16] See, for example, Hayter, *op. cit.*, p. 47, table 7, for figures to 1964.

[17] 21–2 June 1970.

[18] Hayter, *op. cit.*, p. 102.

[19] OECD, Development Assistance, 1970 Review, p. 201.

[20] Hayter, *op. cit.*, p. 131.

[21] *Journal Officiel*, Assemblée Nationale, 10 June 1964, p. 1785.

[22] Quoted in Dumont, *op.cit.*, p. 37.

[23] Photocopy in British Library of Political and Economic Science, p. 32.

[24] Vol. 3, p. 249.

[25] Photocopy in British Library of Political and Economic Science, p. 32.

[26] Vol. 3, p. 261.

[27] *Ibid.*, p. 260.

[28] Guy de Lusignan, *French-speaking Africa since Independence*, London, 1969, p. 12.

[29] Quoted in Grosser, *La 4ᵉ République et sa politique extérieure*, p. 250.

[30] For example, G. Chaffard, *Les carnets secrets de la décolonisation*, Paris, 1965; J. Rous, *Chronique de la décolonisation*, Paris, 1965; P. Auphan, *Histoire de la décolonisation*, Paris, 1967.

[31] There are many detailed accounts of the Suez war; see, for example, M. Bar-Zóhar, *Suez Ultra-Secret*, Paris, 1964; M. and S. Bromberger, *Les Secrets de l'expédition d'Egypte*, Paris, 1957.

[32] Quoted in Grosser, *La IVᵉ République et sa politique extérieure*, p. 35.

[33] *Discours*, vol. 2, pp. 637–8.

[34] *Mémoires*, vol. 1, p. 21.

[35] *Ibid.*, p. 49.

[36] *Mémoires*, vol. 1, p. 21.

[37] See *Les attitudes des jeunes Africains à l'égard de l'aide extérieure* (Appendix to Jeanneney report).

[38] See Paul Balta, 'La France et le Monde Arabe', in *Revue de Défense Nationale*, May 1970.

[39] See *Le Monde*, 10 October 1970, Annual report of 'Union syndicale des industries aéronautiques et spatiales', and 28 October 1970, front page report on Paris visit by Prince Juan Carlos.

[40] See *Le Monde*, 23 October 1970; it contains a report of carefully worded statements made by the Zambian president after he had seen President Pompidou about arms for Pretoria. It appears that no unambiguous promises were made.

[41] See Michel Bouissou, *La reconnaissance de la République populaire de Chine devant l'opinion*, Paris, 1967.

[42] See A. Werth, *De Gaulle*, London, 1965, p. 337.

[43] *Mémoires*, vol. 3, pp. 234–5.

[44] *Discours*, vol. 3, p. 296.

[45] Sondages, 1958, nos 1 and 2.

[46] *Discours*, vol. 4, p. 337.

[47] See *Le Monde*, 20–1 December 1970, for a report on the work of the French delegation at the United Nations in 1970.

CHAPTER 5

[1] Decree of 21 January 1920.

[2] See Claude Lebel, in J. Basdevant *et al*, *Les Affaires Etrangères*, Paris, 1959, p. 59.

[3] Lebel, *loc. cit.*

[4] J. Baillou and P. Pelletier, *Les affaires étrangères*, Paris, 1962, p. 339.

[5] Amédée Outrey, *L'administration française des affaires étrangères*, Paris, 1954, p. 46.

APPENDIX

[1] Baillou and Pelletier, *op. cit.*, pp. 31–2.

[2] See, for example, the decree of 14 March 1953, Article 1.

[3] See the excellent paper of Maurice Schumann, in Basdevant *et al*, *op. cit.*, p. 22 *et seq.*

[4] *ibid.*, p. 21.

[5] *ibid.*, p. 33.

[6] *ibid.*, p. 38.

[7] See *Le Monde*, 2–3 July 1967: report of a television interview.

[8] The influence of extra-parliamentary pressure groups may be gauged from J. P. Buffelan, *Introduction à la sociologie politique* Paris, 1969.

Index

Addis Ababa, 208

Adenauer, Konrad, 6, 70, 87, 88; and German rearmament, 50–1, 59; and the Saar, 64–5; Franco-German relations under de Gaulle, 75–85, 99, 147; Soviet-German relations, 132–3, 144; resignation, 86, 93, 149

Administrative Conventions and Social Affairs, Directorate for, 223–4

Africa, French colonial empire in, 31; postwar French responsibilities in, 11, 76; cultural aid to, 169, 171, 173; economic and technical aid to, 178, 183; de Gaulle's visit to, 198; and Political Directorate, 218, 219, 230

Agence de coopération culturelle et technique, 173

Ailleret, General Charles, 154

Albania, 148

Algeria, 113, 138, 173; US refusal to finance war in, 23, 25–6; causes financial problems in France, 72, 75; and Franco-German relations, 81, 83; and Franco-Soviet relations, 134, 136, 143; and NATO, 139; reasons for revolt, 192–4; end of war, 85, 145; independence, 146, 178, 200, 207; cultural aid to, 169–70; economic and technical aid to, 175, 180–3; French policy in, 189, 191, 195, 197–9; *see also* Evian agreements

Alphand, Hervé, 119

Alsace, 30, 101

Anglo-American agreement (1962), 84, 85

Anglo-Soviet treaty (1942), 126

Annuaire Diplomatique, 229, 233

Arab League Council, 200

Archives Department, 225, 230

Argentina, 212

Aron, Raymond, 59

Artistic Exchanges, Service for, 223

Atomic Affairs, Department of, 223

Attlee, Clement, 35

Austria, 15, 19, 29, 30, 84, 132

Baden, 38, 101

Bad Kreuznach, 77

Baillou, J., 241

Bandoeng Conference (1955), 8, 195, 196–7, 199

Bank of France, 126

Bar-le-Duc Speech (de Gaulle), 49

Barthou, Jean Louis, 106

Belgian Congo, 143

Belgium, 54, 125, 155, 173

Ben Barka, 205

Beneš, Eduard, 115

Bergery, Gaston, 111, 112

Berlin, 37, 38, 104, 117, 129, 145; blockade, 45, 50, 123–4, 125, 126; Wall, 145

Berlin Congress (1878), 31

Berthelot, Marcellin, 237

Bevin, Ernest, 51

Bidault, Georges, and European Advisory Commission, 36; and the Saar, 42, 119–21; and ERP, 44; and ECSC, 49; and EDC, 55; and Indo-China, 63; Franco-Soviet treaty (1944), 117; Franco-Soviet relations, 122–4, 128, 130; out of office, 45

Billotte, General Pierre, 48

Billoux, François, 121

Bismarck, Otto Edward Leopold von, 2, 29, 30–1, 33

Bjøl, E., 73

Blum, Léon, 13 ,14, 15

Boissy d'Anglas, François Antoine de, 186

Bolshevist, 127

Bonn agreement (1952), 61

Borbón y Borbón, HRH Prince Don Juan Carlos, 206
Boumediène, Colonel Houari, 181
Bourguiba, Habib, 172, 182, 205
Brandt, Willy, 92, 96, 101–4, 162
Brazil, 212
Brazzaville conference (1944), 187–8, 196
Brentano, Heinrich, 86
Bretton Woods conference (1944), 14
Breznev, Leonid Ilyich, 161
Briand, Aristide, 109, 237
British Gold Coast, 195
Brussels, 96, 155, 168
Brussels Pact (1948), 61, 63, 124
Bulganin, Marshal Nikolai, 132–3, 135, 136–7
Bulgaria, 120, 124, 173
Burundi, 173
Byrnes, James, 14, 39

Cachin, Marcel, 125
Cambodia, 20, 150, 169, 171, 182
Cameroun, 171, 173
Canada, 125, 169–70, 172, 173, 183, 219
Caracas, 168
Catroux, General Georges, 118, 119, 123
Caucasus, 113
Ceausescu, Nicolae, 160
Chad, 173, 202
Charlemagne, 50
Chile, 184
China, 7, 134, 209, 230: as superpower, 11; and testban treaty, 148; French recognition of Communist regime in, 149; and Russia, 161; and Third World, 200; and Indo-Chinese war, 210; Franco-Chinese relations, 211
Christian Democratic Party, see Mouvement Républicain Populaire
Churchill, Sir Winston, 128; and allied policy on Germany, 34–7; and German rearmament, 50; London conference (1947), 60; and de Gaulle, 113, 115, 117, 213
Cold War, 122, 124, 127, 128
Colombia, 212

Colonial policy, background, 186–7; policy 1944–58, 187–94; decolonisation, 8, 9, 163, 195–200; see also Algeria, Indo-China, Morocco, Tunisia
Cominform, 123, 133
Common Market, see European Economic Community
Congo crisis, 213
Constantine plan (1958), 180
Consulates, categories of, 228; functions of, 228–9
Control Commission, 37, 39, 41, 123
Costa Rica, 168
Cot, Pierre, 119
Council of Europe, 49, 68, 71, 218
Cour des Comptes, 232
Couve de Murville, Maurice, 76, 115, 138, 140 ,155, 200
Cuba, 174; Cuban missile crisis, 84, 85, 147
Cultural Exchanges, Service for, 222
Cultural, Scientific and Technical Affairs, General Directorate for, 165, 182, 221–3
Czechoslovakia, 50, 104, 108, 115, 124, 156, 157, 159

Dahomey, 173
Daniel, Yuli, 152
Danube River, 124
Danube Shipping Conference (1948), 124
DDR (German Democratic Republic), see Germany
Debré, Michel, 81, 82, 98, 154, 157, 197
Decision-making in French foreign policy, 238 ff
Defferre, Gaston, 195
Delcassé, Théophile, 31
Denmark, 84, 125
Der Spiegel, 85
Dien-Bien-Phu, 191, 193
Die Welt, 93
Diori, Hamani, 172
Directeur du Cabinet du Ministre, 237
Djibouti, 178
Dreyfus, Alfred, 244

Dubček, Alexander, 156
Dulles, John Foster, 56, 59, 69, 79
Dunkirk treaty (1947), 120

Ecole des Sciences Politiques, 236
Ecole Nationale d'Administration (ENA),
  231, 232, 233, 235
*Ecole Nationale des Langues Orientales
  Vivantes*, 231, 232, 233
Economic and Financial Affairs, Direc-
  torate for, 220, 221
Economic and Financial Affairs, Minis-
  try for, 183, 184, 221
Economic Cooperation Administration
  (ECA), 19, 20
Eden, Sir Anthony, 60, 115, 132
Eden Plan, 61, 62, 63
Egypt, 134–5, 174, 194, 204
Eisenhower, Dwight, NATO command-
  er-in-chief, 54, 126; and Suez, 25, 73,
  135, 136; and de Gaulle, 80, 87, 214;
  and east-west relations, 132, 141, 143
Elbe River, 7, 145, 159
Embassies, organisation of, 226–8
Erhard, Dr. Ludwig, 75, 86–8, 90, 93
Estaing, Valéry Giscard d', 149
Ethiopia, 174
Euratom, 69, 70, 73, 74, 218, 227
European Advisory Commission
  (EAC), 35, 36
European Army, 51–4, 59
European Coal and Steel Community
  (ECSC), 74, 96, 240; creation of,
  47–50; forerunner to EDC, 52;
  British rejection of, 54; and Jean
  Monnet, 68–9
European Defence Community (EDC),
  49, 68, 71; creation of, 52–3; and
  German rearmament, 55–6; French
  rejection of, 57–9; London Confer-
  ence (1954), 60–3; and Franco-
  Soviet relations, 65–6, 129–31
European Economic Community
  (EEC), 9, 26, 59, 82, 87, 175, 201,
  206, 209, 210, 218, 221, 227, 240;
  creation of, 68, 70; Britain's refusal
  to join, 71–2; and Euratom, 73–4;
  competitive demands of, 75; applica-

European Economic Community (cont.)
  tion for British membership, 84–5;
  and Franco-German relations, 90–6,
  99, 100, 102; and Franco-Soviet
  relations, 136, 145, 155, 158, 159–60;
  benefits to former colonies of, 10,
  179
European Free Trade Area (EFTA),
  84
European Fund for Overseas Development, 179, 185
European Payments Union, 24, 25
European Recovery Program (ERP), 19,
  20, 42, 44, 45
Evian agreements (1962), 146, 200, 207
Exchange Stabilisation Fund, 24

Fallières, Armand, 244
Faure, Edgar, 132, 192, 196
Faure, Maurice, 72
Ferry, Jules, 33, 187
Fifth Republic, 9, 75, 139, 178, 195,
  238, 241–3
Finland, 111, 120
First National Plan, 21
FLN, *see* Front de la Libération
  Nationale
Fontaine, André, 80
Foreign Affairs Commission, 241–3
Foreign Affairs, Ministry of, 165, 166,
  169, 178, 181, 216, 217, 231, 241;
  see also Political Directorate, Eco-
  nomic and Financial Affairs, Direc-
  torate for; Cultural, Scientific and
  Technical Affairs, Directorate for;
  Administrative Conventions and
  Social Affairs, Directorate for; Per-
  sonnel and General Administration,
  Directorate for
Foreign Aid Act (1947), 16
Foreign Assistance Act (1948), 19
Foreign policy decision making 238 ff.
Fourquet, General Michel, 159
Fourth Republic, 23, 120, 138; and
  Algeria, 75, 136, 194, 197; and
  Franco-German relations, 76; Con-
  stitution of, 175, 176, 244; and Indo-
  China, 190–1

Franco Bahamonde, Generalísimo, 206
Franco-Arab Chamber of Commerce,
    204, 205
Franco-German treaty (1963), 85–7,
    90, 93, 99, 104, 147, 149
Francophonie, 172, 178
Franco-Soviet Chamber of Commerce,
    153
Franco-Soviet treaty (1944), 60, 65–6,
    117, 119, 126, 129, 131, 132
Frankfurt Charter (1948), 43
Frankfurt, Treaty of, 30, 33
Frederick the Great, 31
Free French movement, 106–12, 187,
    see also Gaulle, General Charles de
French Civil Service, 216, 231, 232
French Committee for National Libera-
    tion, 35, 113, 114
French Communist Party, *see* Parti
    Communiste Français
French Community, 178, 195, 199
French Diplomatic Service, 165; Minis-
    try of Foreign Affairs, 216–25; repre-
    sentation abroad, 225–9; organisation,
    229–31; personnel, 231–6
French Economic and Social Council,
    183
French Mediterranean fleet, 88
French Revolution, 164, 186
French Second Quinquennial Plan for
    Cultural Expansion, 166
French Socialist Party, *see* Section
    Française de l'Internationale Ouvrière
Front de la Libération Nationale,
    (FLN) 139, 146

Gabon, 173, 202
Gaillard, Félix, 137, 138
Gambetta, Léon Michel, 33
Gaulle, General Charles de, 4, 7, 11, 48,
    102, 167, 172, 174, 178, 208, 210;
    World War II, 12, 13, 35–8, 112–17,
    187–9; and American aid, 14, 16;
    occupation of Germany, 40, 49, 118;
    German rearmament, 55, 63; and
    Oder-Neisse line, 79; resigns (1946),
    13; united Europe, 72, 73; return
    to power (1958), 9, 27, 75, 138, 195;

Gaulle, General Charles de (cont.)
    Franco-German relations:
        Adenauer administration, 6, 76–86,
        142, 147; Erhard administration,
        86–90, 99, 104
    and NATO, 87, 88, 139, 158, 161; and
    EEC, 90–2, 94, 99; relations with US,
    94–6, 148–9, 211; and RPF, 122–3;
    Franco-Soviet relations:
        Free French movement and Soviet
        Union, 118–9; anti-Soviet phrase
        (1958–63), 140–8; Russian entente,
        (1963–8), 148–56; disillusionment,
        (1968–9), 157
    and Arab-Israeli war, 154–5, 204;
    and South American visit, 184, 211–12;
    and Yugoslavia, 207; and Vietnam,
    210; and Quebec, 169–70; and bid for
    Third World, 201; and Algeria, 146,
    194, 198, 200; colonial policy, 195–7,
    199, 200, 202–3, 205; policy decision-
    making, 238–40; and constitution, 239;
    refusal to devalue franc, 98; dislike
    of UN, 185, 212–13; out of office (1969),
    98, 100, 160
General Agreement on Tariffs and Trade
    (GATT), 14
Geneva agreement (1954), 150
Geneva disarmament conference (1968), 156
Germany, 7, 11, 13; Franco-German
    relations before World War II, 2, 3, 5,
    6, 29–34; plans for postwar occupa-
    tion of, 35–8; Franco-German re-
    lations (1945–9), 39–47; union of
    allied occupation zones, 43, 44, 61;
    creation of German Federal Republic,
    44–5; German rearmament, 51–5,
    58, 60, 61, 64, 129–31; admission to
    NATO, 66; east-west unification, 67,
    104, 127–8, 144;
    Franco-German relations under de
    Gaulle:
        1958–63, 75–86, 144
        1963–8, 86–98
        1968–9, 98–100
    refusal to devalue mark, 97; and
    EEC, 100, 102, economic growth,
    100; Russo-German relations, 107–

Germany (cont.)
11, 132, 154, 160, 162
Deutsche Demokratische Republik
(DDR), 86, 104, 126, 130, 132, 140,
144–5
German War College (Hamburg), 85
Ghana, 195
Giraud, General Henri, 113
Goethe, Johann Wolfgang von, 32
Gomulka, Wladyslaw, 155
Great Britain, 3, 11, 14, 17, 31, 34;
Franco-British entente (1904), 31;
World War II, 36, 38, 111, 117, 189;
postwar occupation of Germany, 41,
44–5, 51; and NATO, 53, 125; German rearmament, 55; EDC, 61; EEC,
71–2, 84, 92–4, 99, 100; attitude to
Soviet Russia, 110; and Suez crisis,
134–5, 194; and UN contributions,
185; and Libya, 204–5; trade with
France, 180; French policy towards,
1, 2, 49, 120
Greece, 206, 218
Grévy, Jules, 244
Gromyko, Andrei, 127, 136, 143, 151–2,
161

Hague Conference (1969), 102, 160
Hague Congress (1948), 49
Haiti, 172
Haute Volta, 173
Heath, Edward, 208
Henri III, 229
Herriot, Edouard, 189, 190
Hesse-Cassel, 38
Hesse-Nassau, 38
Hitler, Adolf, 29, 33, 34, 111, 143;
Third Reich, 3, 106; and Soviet
Union, 109, 112, 122; and Free
French, 114, 115; Munich agreement,
124
Ho-Chi-Minh, 126, 190
Holland, 125
Hungary, 120, 134, 135

Iceland, 125
India, 173–4, 200, 208–10
Indo-China, war in, 52, 128, 189; Amer-

Indo-China (cont.)
ican aid for war, 20, 23–4; end of
war, 25, 56, 63, 130, 133; Soviet recognition of 'rebel' government, 126;
independence, 131, 178, 210; cultural
aid to, 169, 171; colonial policy in,
190–5; decolonisation, 195–6, 208
Inter-Allied Commission for Italy, 115
Institute for Political Studies, 222, 233
International Bank for Reconstruction
and Development, 14, 15, 24
International Monetary Fund (IMF),
14, 15
Israel, 134–5, 153–4, 174, 200, 204,
208–9
Israeli-Arab War (1967), see Six Day War
Italy, 100, 120, 125n, 207; American
aid to, 15, 19; and ECSC, 49; and
German rearmament, 54; Brussels
Treaty, 63; and NATO, 66, 206;
Locarno Treaty (1926), 108; and
Soviet Union, 154, 157
Ivory Coast, 173, 202
Izvestia, 108

Japan, 13, 127, 187
Jaurès, Jean, 33
Jeanneney report (1963), 165, 176, 177
Johnson, Lyndon B., 88, 155
Juin, Marshall Alphonse, 57

Kennedy, John F., 83–5, 88, 92, 144,
147–8
Kiesinger, Kurt Georg, 75, 93, 104, 154
Kirillin, Vladimir, 154
Kirillin-Debré Commission, 158
Korean War, 21–2, 24, 50, 55, 126, 128,
210
Kosygin, Alexei, 150, 153–5, 161
Krushchev, Nikita, 128, 134, 152; reunification of Germany, 67; SovietGerman relations, 132; and Kennedy,
83; state visit to London, 133; and
de Gaulle's anti-Soviet phase, 139–
47; dismissal from power, 150

Labour, Ministry of, 241
Laniel, Joseph, 63

Laos, 20, 150, 169, 171
Laval, Pierre, 33, 112
League of Nations, 31, 33, 106, 111, 230
Lebanon, 169
Lebel, Claude, 165
Légion tricolore, 112
Le Monde, 100, 181
Libya, 113, 204–6, 219
Locarno Treaty (1926), 31, 108
London Conference (1947), 44–5, 60, 62, 64, 67, 123, 131
Lorraine, 30
Louis XIII, 229
Louis XIV, 29, 229
Louvois, François Michel le Tellier, Marquis de, 28, 29, 30, 31, 34
Lusaka Conference (1970), 207, 208
Luxembourg, 49, 54, 125, 173, 211

Macmillan, Harold, 84, 141, 143
Madagascar, 171, 173, 189–90, 198–9, 201–2, 209
Maghreb countries, 169–70, 175, 193, 204
Malenkov, Georgi, 128–9, 132
Mali, 173, 199
Malinowsky, Rodion, 147
Marshall, General George, 15, 18
Marshall Plan, 15, 17, 19, 21, 24–6, 42, 44, 122, 125
Massigli, René, 36
Mauritania, 171
Mayer, René, 68, 69
Mémoires (C. de Gaulle), 12, 188, 196, 197
Mendès-France, Pierre, and American aid, 13; and EDC, 57–60, 131; Eden plan, 61–3; National Assembly rejects Paris agreements, 64–6; and EEC, 70, 72–4; decolonisation, 191, 192, 197
Messina Conference (1955), 68, 69, 72, 74
Messmer, Pierre, 159
Mexico, 168, 211, 212, 219
Mikoyan, Anastas, 119
Military Pacts and Disarmament, Department of, 220

Moch, Jules, 51, 59, 62
Mollet, Guy, 69, 76; prime minister 1956, 70, 132; and Euratom, 73; and *force de frappe,* 88n; Franco-Soviet relations, 133–6; and Algeria, 194, 197
Molotov, Vyacheslav, 111, 119–20, 122, 125, 128, 134, 136
Monaco, 173
Monnet, Jean, 21, 47–9, 68–9
Morgenthau Plan, 35
Morocco, colonial policy in, 189, 191–3; decolonisation, 195–7; relations since 1962, 203, 205, 206; cultural aid to, 169–71; economic and technical aid to, 181–4
Moscow Conference (1947), 41, 42, 120
Moselle, 101
Mouvement Républicain Populaire (MRP), 48, 62–3, 65–6, 71
Multilateral Force (MLF), 88
Munich Conference (1938), 106
Mutual Defense Assistance Act, 20
Mutual Security Act (1951), 22, 24

Napoleon I, 29
Napoleon III, 30, 33
Nassau Agreement (1962), 84, 85
Nasser, President Gamal, 134, 194
Netherlands, *see* Holland
Niamey, 173
Niger, 172–3
Nineteen-Nation Commission, 146
North Atlantic Fleet, 88
North Atlantic Treaty Organisation (NATO), 25, 51, 82, 155, 206, 219, 220; creation of, 20, 22, 124–5; proposals for German participation in, 53–4, 56–8, 60–1, 64; admission of Germany to, 66; and Franco-German relations, 78, 102–3; and de Gaulle, 80–1, 83–4, 87–90, 138–9, 158–9, 214; French withdrawal from, 5, 152–3; and Soviet Union, 127, 130, 136, 140–1, 149
Norway, 84, 125
Novotny, Antonin, 156
Nuclear Test Ban treaty (1963), 148

Oder-Neisse line, 38, 79, 86, 116
OECD, 220, 221
Office Franco-Allemand pour la Jeunesse, 100
Organisation for European Economic Cooperation (OEEC), 19, 21, 22
Organisation of African Unity, 208
Ottawa, 168
Oufkir, General, 205
Outrey, A., 167

Pakistan, 200, 208, 209
Palatinate, 38
Paris-Bonn treaty (1963), *see* Franco-German treaty
Paris Conference (1954), 63, 131
Parti Communiste Français (PCF), 41, 107, 189; and American aid, 18; opposition to German rearmament, 58, 65, 66; and Euratom, 73; and Free French movement, 114; and Soviet Union, 121, 152, 157; and RPF, 122–3; and NATO, 125–7
Pelletier, P., 241
Périer, Casimir, 244
Personnel and General Administration, Directorate for, 224, 225, 230
Peru, 212
Pétain, Marshal Henri Philippe, 111, 112
Petersberg Agreements (1949), 50
Peugeot company, 153
Pflimlin, Pierre, 76
Phelippeaux, Raymond, 229
Philip, André, 45, 46
Pinay, Antoine, 26, 76
Pineau, Christian, 133, 135
Pisani, Edgard, 72
Pleven, René, 51, 52–4
Pleven Plan, 52–4
Podgorny, Nikolai, 149, 153, 161
Poland, 79, 104, 108, 110–11, 115–16, 119, 124, 134, 155
Political Directorate, 218–20, 223, 231
Pompidou, Georges, becomes president, 100; devaluation, 101; and EEC, 102; and Franco-German relations, 104–5; NATO, 152; and

Pompidou, Georges (cont.)
Franco-Soviet relations, 155, 160–2; and Quebec, 170; relations with Mediterranean countries, 203–7; and UNO, 214, 215
Portugal, 84, 125
Potsdam agreement (1945), 38–40, 118, 123, 126, 127, 148
Pravda, 110, 119, 151
Press and Information Service, 220, *see also* Political Directorate
Prussia, 28–31

Quebec, 35, 169–70, 172–3
Queuille, Henri, 21

Racine, Jean, 165
Ramadier, Paul, 120–1
Rapacki, 137, 138, 140
Rapallo conference (1922), 104, 108
Rassemblement du Peuple Français (RPF), 48, 123
Renan, Ernest, 32
Renault company, 153
Renouvin, Professor P., 30
Reparations Commission, 38, 118
Revue de Défense Nationale, 159
Rey, Jean, 96
Reynaud, Paul, 45
Rhine River, 29, 30, 32, 36, 109
Rhineland, 37–8, 42, 44, 119
Ribbentrop, Joachim von, 111
Ribbentrop-Molotov pact (1939), 107, 111
Richelieu, Cardinal Armand, 28
Rome Treaty (1957), 74, 76, 90, *see also* European Economic Community
Roosevelt, Franklin D., 34–7, 116, 117, 213
Royal Air Force, 61
Ruanda, 173
Ruhr, 36–8, 40–2, 44–7, 108, 120
Rumania, 120, 124, 156, 157, 160
Russia, *see* Soviet Union

Saar, 36, 38, 40–2, 64, 65, 120, 121
Sahara Desert, 8, 9, 88n
Sakhiet, 138

Savary, Alain, 73
Schiller, Karl, 102
Schröder, Gerhard, 86
Schuman, Robert, 47–9, 51, 55, 66, 71
Schumann, Maurice, 160, 162
Section Française de l'Internationale Ouvrière (SFIO), 13, 48, 57, 62, 69, 71, 132, 133
Sedan, 30
Selassie, Emperor Haile, 174
Senegal, 172–3, 179, 190, 199, 202
Senghor, Léopold, 172, 190
Service des Oeuvres, 167
Shepilov, Dmitri, 134, 136
Siniavsky, André, 152
Six Day War, 93, 153–5, 203, 207
Soames, Christopher, 158
Soustelle, Jacques, 197
South Africa, 207–9, 214
South America, 167, 183, 184, 211
South Vietnam, 173
Soviet Union, interwar relations with Germany, 107–9; World War II, 34, 37–9, 111–12, 114–16, 127; occupation of Germany, 41–4; and ECSC, 47; opposition to EDC, 60, 129; and German rearmament, 56, 59, 65, 66, 131; German reunification, 67, 78, 103, 144; creation of DDR, 126, 140; opening of diplomatic relations with W Germany, 132; NATO as deterrent to, 83, 125–6; application to join NATO, 130; Bonn-Moscow non-aggression pact (1970), 162; Franco-Soviet relations, 6, 133:
 Cold War, 122–3; post-Stalin thaw, 67, 133; Franco-Russian entente 1963–8, 148–52, 155, 156; relations since 1969, 162; cultural relations, 169; used by France as counterweight to Germany, 5, 6–7, 30, 103; French hostility to, 106–7, 142–6
and Indo-China, 126; and Suez, 134–5; recognition of FLN, 146; and Six Day War, 154–5; and Vietnam, 156; Nuclear Test Ban treaty, 146; involvement in Mediterranean, 160,

Soviet Union (cont.)
 161; Russian Communist Party 20th Congress, 67, 133
 21st Congress, 139
 22nd Congress, 145
Sozialdemokratische Partei Deutschlands (SPD), 87, 94
Spaak, Paul Henri, 69
Spain, 206
Sputnik, 137
Staël, Anne Louise Germaine Necker, Madame de, 32
Stalin, Joseph, 133, 213; and German occupation zones, 35–6; and de Gaulle's Free French movement, 79, 112–19; French mutual assistance treaty, 109–10; Cold War, 127–8
Stalingrad, Battle of, 147
Strasbourg, 29, 150
Sudan, 195, 204
Suez Canal, 8, 24, 75, 154, 200, 243; Nasser announces nationalisation of, 134; Franco-British intervention, 135–6, 194; and Eisenhower, 25–6, 73
Sweden, 84
Switzerland, 84

Talleyrand-Périgord, Charles Maurice de, 230
Tashkent, 153
Tassigny, General de Lattre de, 46
Teheran Conference (1943), 35, 115
Third Reich, 3, 106
Third Republic, 5, 33; and teaching of French abroad, 167; colonial policy of, 175, 187; and French Diplomatic Service, 235; constitution of, 239, 243, 244
Third World, 149, 199, 212; Bandoeng Conference (1955) 8, 197; France as partner to, 9, 11, 200–1; Algeria's place in, 180, 186; Yugoslavia's place in, 207; and arms sales to S Africa, 208, 214; French relations with since 1962, 203–4
Thorez, Maurice, 114, 125
Tito, Marshal (Josip Broz), 133, 134, 207

Togo, 173
Truman, Harry S., 14, 38, 39, 118, 188
Tukhashevsky, Marshal, 110
Tunisia, 31; colonial policy in, 189, 191–3; independence, 8, 195, 197; cultural influence in, 169–70, 172–3, 222; economic and technical aid to, 181–4; relations with France since 1962, 203, 205–6
Turkey, 218

Ukraine, 109
UNESCO, 220
Union Africaine et Malgache, 172
United Arab Republic, 174, 200
United Nations Organisation (UNO), 65, 133, 150, 191; and Cold War, 125–6; and Algeria, 134; and Suez, 135; and Six Day War, 155; and arms to S Africa, 207; China's absence from, 211; Third World attitudes to, 8; French as an official language of, 172; and *groupe francophone*, 173; French attitudes to, 185, 212–14; Political Directorate department for, 209; French representation at, 227
United States of America, 7, 11, 49, 200; World War II, 34, 36–8, 114, 127; occupation of Germany, 41, 42, 44–5, 120; aid to France, 4, 13–16, 18, 20, 22–4, 26; and NATO, 43, 53, 87, 125, 136; and German rearmament, 50–1, 55–6; 126, 129; and EDC, 60–1; and EEC, 95–6, 136;

United States of America (cont.)
European rôle of, 3, 84, 102, 103, 116, 137; investment in France, 100; and Franco-German relations, 81–3, 102; war in Indo-China, 20, 25; war in Algeria, 25; relations with Russia, 141, 143; and Cuban missile crisis, 147; and Soviet military threat in Europe, 17; and Libya, 205; and South America, 212; economic problems of, 4, 94–6; as superpower, 6
Uri, Pierre, 69

Vichy Government, 111–12
Vietnam, 8, 20, 150, 156, 161, 169, 171, 182, 201, 207, 210
Vinogradov, Vladimir, 146, 151
Vishinsky, 125
Volkswagen company, 73
Voltaire, François Marie Arouet de, 32
Voroshilov, Klimenti, 110

Waldeck-Rochet, 152
Warsaw Pact (1955), 66, 132, 136
Western European Union (WEU), 63–4, 66–9, 72, 94
Wilson, Harold, 207
Württemberg, 38

Yalta Conference (1945), 36–8, 117, 126, 144, 148
Yaoundé, 179, 180
Yugoslavia, 200, 207, 218

Zorin, Valerian, 151